THE GRACE COURSE

FROM FREEDOM IN CHRIST MINISTRIES

STEVE GOSS, RICH MILLER & JUDE GRAHAM

A 6-WEEK DISCIPLESHIP COURSE FOR EVERY CHRISTIAN
LET GOD'S GRACE FREE YOU TO **BE REAL AND BEAR MUCH FRUIT**

FOREWORD BY DR. NEIL T. ANDERSON

Published by Monarch Books
an imprint of
Lion Hudson plc
Wilkinson House, Jordan Hill Road,
Oxford OX2 8DR, England
Email: monarch@lionhudson.com
www.lionhudson.com/monarch

ISBN 978 0 85721 324 2
e-ISBN 978 0 85721 267 2

First edition 2012

A catalogue record for this book is available from the British Library

Printed and bound in Malta, September 2012, LH28.

Book Design And Illustrations: Ezekiel Design, Manchester, www.ezekieldesign.co.uk

Presentation CD Design: Vivid Broadcast, Horsham, www.vividbroadcast.co.uk

THE GRACE COURSE

What leaders say about *The Grace Course*

"This empowering material is accessible to those in the very early stages of pursuing life with Christ and yet highly stimulating and challenging for mature believers. I highly recommend it as a key discipleship tool for the whole church. It makes fabulous home group material and is ideal for every discipleship team."

Lynn Chetcuti
Network Vineyard Church, Reading, UK

"So many Christians, including myself in the past, have made the Christian life a performance rather than an intimate love relationship. If true revival is to come to our nations, it will start with this message of grace. Want to be refreshed? Then this course is for you."

Dr. Howard Ostendorff
Ministry leader with Campus Crusade for Christ for 38 years, Little Rock, Arkansas, USA

"*The Grace Course* deepened people's sense of identity in Christ and stirred them up to greater love and faithfulness from a point of grace — not obligation or legalism. It spoke powerfully to people in our church from many ethnic backgrounds and life situations. We recommend it highly."

Revd. Dr. Rodney Woods
City Temple, London, UK

"*The Grace Course* does a marvelous job in introducing the concept of grace in a simple, engaging and, at times, even humorous way. It is short and to the point, taking an incredibly deep theological issue and making it understandable and practical."

Dr. Jeff Stam
Set Free Ministries, Grand Rapids, Michigan, USA

"Several times during *The Grace Course* there was the sheer joy of lights being suddenly switched on, and I myself gained many fresh insights into God's amazing love in Christ. Be prepared for life-changing encounters with God and experience how Bible passages as familiar as the story of the Lost Son can speak in powerful new ways. A truly compelling course."

Revd. Charles McMullen
West Church (Presbyterian), Bangor, Northern Ireland

"Steve Goss and Rich Miller combine wit and wisdom to resource the 21st century church with essential teaching on spiritual maturity grounded in grace. *The Grace Course* will inspire you, encourage you and take you to a deeper understanding of the love of God."

Chris Campbell
Youth specialist and director of Generation Freedom, Bridgeport, West Virginia, USA

"*The Grace Course* has challenged us to look again at our understanding of grace. It has brought about a heart transformation and released a new spiritual freshness into all areas of our discipleship."

Major Jackie Leswell
Viewpoint Community Church (Salvation Army), Parkstone, UK

Thanks!

Creating a resource such as *The Grace Course* is a huge undertaking and could not possibly have been done without the help of many, many people. We particularly want to thank the following:

- The members of Freedom In Christ Ministries' team around the world who regularly give so much to help churches pass on this life-changing message of freedom and grace, particularly our intercessors who have supported us so much during the development process. Without you none of this could have happened.

- Tony Collins, Jenny Ward and the excellent team at Monarch for making *The Grace Course* possible and for giving us so much freedom in the creative process.

- The team who reviewed the content over many months and made so many invaluable suggestions. Thanks especially go to Craig Millward, Tim Baynes Clarke, Mike Benford, Bart Gavigan, Gareth Burgess, Jackie Leswell, Charles McMullen, Steve Prince, Derek Frank and Rod Woods.

- The churches who trusted us to try out the material on them so that it could be tested and refined: the churches of LEAF, the Local Evangelical Alliance in the New Forest, UK; The Evangelical Baptist Church of Geneva, Switzerland; West Church, Bangor, N. Ireland, UK; City Temple, London, UK; Network Vineyard, Reading, UK; Emmanuel Methodist Church, Chennai, India; Viewpoint Salvation Army, Poole, UK; Réunions Évangéliques, Mulhouse, France.

- Those who have worked so hard on the technicalities of the content: Zoë Goss for her help at the filming and work on the content of *The Steps To Experiencing God's Grace*; Rachel Mozley for transcribing the DVDs so that we can provide subtitles for the hearing-impaired; Elaine Jones for doing the technical work on the subtitles; Vic Ford for checking the manuscripts so helpfully and thoroughly.

- The lovely people who shared their stories so helpfully in being filmed for the DVDs.

- London School Of Theology who allowed us to turn their wonderful chapel into a film studio and supported us in many other ways.

- Rory Springthorpe, Stephen Montgomery and the tireless team at Vivid Broadcast who put so much creativity into producing superb quality DVD presentations.

- Jon Smethurst at Ezekiel Design for his wonderful designs and illustrations.

The Grace Course is dedicated to

Dr. Neil T. Anderson and Joanne Anderson, founders of Freedom In Christ Ministries,

in the year that they celebrated both 40 years in Christian ministry and Neil's 70th birthday and in which they handed on the baton of international leadership of Freedom In Christ Ministries to Steve Goss.

Thank you so much for all you have done to spread the message of freedom throughout the world in a spirit of gentle humility, grace and compassion. We appreciate you more than we can say.

"O Lord, you will ordain peace for us, for you have indeed done for us all our works."

Isaiah 26:12

Contents

Foreword

By Dr. Neil T. Anderson

Founder and President Emeritus of Freedom in Christ Ministries

A newly adopted child found himself in a big mansion. His new Father whispered in his ear, "This is yours and you have a right to be here. I have made you a joint heir with my only begotten Son. He paid the price that set you free from your old taskmaster who was cruel and condemning. I purchased it for you, because I love you." The young boy couldn't help but question this incredible gift, "This seems too good to be true. What did I do to deserve this," he wondered. "I have been a slave all my life and I have done nothing to earn such a privilege!"

He was deeply grateful, however, and began to explore all the rooms in the mansion. There were many other people in the mansion who also had been adopted. He began to form new relationships with his adopted brothers and sisters. He especially enjoyed the buffet table from which he freely ate. Then it happened! While turning away from the buffet table he knocked over a stack of glasses and a valuable pitcher that crashed to the floor and broke. Suddenly he began to think, "You clumsy, stupid kid! You will never get away with this. What right do you have to be here? You better hide before someone finds out, because they will surely throw you out."

At first he was caught up with the wonder of living in the mansion with a whole new family and a loving Father, but now he was confused. Old tapes laid down in early childhood began to play again in his mind. He was filled with guilt and shame. The thoughts continued, "Who do you think you are? Some kind of a privileged character? You don't belong here any more, you belong in the basement!" "The old taskmaster was right about me, I don't belong here," thought the newly adopted child. So he descended into the basement of despair.

The cellar was dreary and dark. The only light came from the open door at the top of the long stairs. He heard his Father calling for him, but he was too ashamed to answer. He was surprised to find others in the basement. Upstairs everybody talked to each other and joined in with daily projects that were fun and meaningful. Nobody talked to each other in the basement. They were too ashamed and most felt that the basement was where they really belonged anyway. Those old tapes questioned the love of this new Father, and he began to question whether he was ever adopted in the first place.

He made a few half-hearted attempts to return to the light, but eventually he found a dark corner to lie down in. Then one day a shaft of light penetrated his mind and reason returned. He began to think, "Why not throw myself on the mercy of this person who calls Himself my Father. What do I have to lose? Even if He makes me eat the crumbs that fall from the table, it would be better than this." So he decided to take the risk of climbing those stairs and face his Father with the truth of what he had done. "Lord," he said. "I knocked over some glasses and broke a pitcher." Without saying a word, his Father took him by the hand and led him into the dining room. To his utter amazement his Father had prepared for him a banquet. "Welcome home Son," his Father said. "There is therefore now no condemnation for those who are in Christ Jesus" (Romans 8:1).

Oh the deep, deep love of Jesus, and the matchless grace of God! The door is always open for those who are willing to throw themselves upon the mercy of God. "In love He predestined us to be adopted as His sons through Jesus Christ, in accordance with His pleasure and will — to the praise of His glorious grace, which He has freely given us in the One He loves" (Ephesians 1:5,6). He doesn't want us to live self-condemned lives in the basement of guilt, shame, fear and legalism. He wants us to know that we are adopted, forgiven, and forever alive in Christ and that we can live every day as beloved children.

I urge you to take seriously this course that will help you live a liberated life under the grace of God and go on to bear much fruit, fruit that will last for ever — and equip others to do the same.

Welcome!

Welcome to *The Grace Course*!

We feel humbled, privileged and very excited to share this exciting teaching with you. It has had such an impact on our own lives and ministries.

Our intention is to put a tool into your hands that will enable you to see Christians in your church become more fruitful than they could imagine as they allow God's grace to permeate their lives.

This Leader's Guide is designed to give you everything you need to run a highly effective course. We suggest that you get started as follows:

- register with us for free access to all the additional online info and downloads (see page 10).

- read these few introductory pages — they will help you understand the scope and intention of the course and how to run it well.

- watch the teaching sessions on the accompanying DVD (available separately) or read the session notes in this Leader's Guide thoroughly.

- ensure you have grappled with the concepts in your own life and have been through the ministry component (*The Steps To Experiencing God's Grace*) personally before leading others.

Remember that we at Freedom In Christ Ministries are always ready to respond to questions from church leaders so feel free to get in touch.

May God bless you as you lead others into this amazing grace of His!

Steve Goss, Rich Miller & Jude Graham.

First, please register as a user

It costs nothing and you will receive:
- access to a web area with helpful info for course leaders
- downloads that will make running your course even easier
- details of training events near you and occasional news from Freedom In Christ (if you request to receive these)

To register simply go to www.ficm.org.uk/gracecourse

Or call 0118 321 8084 in the UK or 865-342-4000 in the USA.

We never share your contact information with third parties. We will not bombard you with unwanted e-mails.

Running *The Grace Course*

What is *The Grace Course* about?

Jesus said that people would recognize His disciples by their love (John 13:35). Paul said: "For the love of Christ compels us" (2 Corinthians 5:14 NIV). *The Grace Course* is a tool for churches to help Christians recover their first love for God (see Revelation 2:4) so that they go on to love others and make a great impact on the world. In order for Christians to be motivated purely by love, we have to help them get rid of "false motivators" such as:

Guilt

We know, in theory at least, that salvation is by grace through faith, and that we cannot earn it. But many of us unconsciously fall into the trap of believing in effect that we **maintain** God's acceptance by working hard and "doing the right things". Guilt conditions us to believe that our ongoing acceptance by God is a product of how well we are performing and makes us behave as if our growth in Christ is primarily up to us. We end up stressed out, burned out or fed up.

Shame

How we see ourselves determines how we will live. We give mental assent to the truth that we have become "new creations" in Christ (2 Corinthians 5:17), but in practice shame leads us to allow our identity to be determined by our past rather than by what Christ did for us on the cross. Many of us feel that we are "a let-down" to God and other people, that we are fundamentally flawed. This is compounded when we find ourselves stuck in sins that we can't seem to escape from.

Fear

Some know full well that they are in the grip of fears but have lost hope that they can resolve them. Others don't see themselves as fearful because they have learned to live with their fears, thinking, "That's just how I am". In both cases, fear holds us back from stepping into all that God has for us and from telling others the wonderful news about Jesus and His salvation.

Pride

Pride leads us to turn what should be a living relationship with Jesus into nothing more than dry religion. Religious people are into rules rather than relationship. They put laws above love and they are more concerned about being right than being real. The highest aim of the religious is to know the Word of God rather than to know the God of the Word. Humility is the gateway to true unity amongst God's people, which is what will lead to the world knowing that the Father sent Jesus (see John 17:21).

A true understanding of God's grace provides the antidote to these false motivators. *The Grace Course* is designed to help Christians understand the mind-blowing benefits of what it means to be God's child: that, no matter what's in the past, we are perfectly acceptable to God; that we don't have to try hard to "act like we think Christians should act"; that we can simply live out of the truth of who we now are — free, innocent, unashamed, courageous, humble and ready to bear much fruit!

The Grace Course puts the emphasis on knowing the truth, not just in our heads but in our hearts. It is full of practical exercises for people to engage with and has a gentle, effective ministry component called *The Steps To Experiencing God's Grace.*

If you can encourage Christians to "do business with God" during *The Grace Course*, the end result will be that they will be so bowled over by a new sense of God's grace that they will want to live for Him, not because they feel they have to but because they really love Him. And they'll go on to bear much fruit, fruit that will last (see John 15:16). Imagine how different your church could be! Imagine what an impact that would make on your community.

What is the structure of the course?

There are 6 teaching sessions and a ministry component that comes between Sessions 5 and 6:

Session 1: Free!
We all know that we are saved by grace through faith alone. Yet when it comes to living out our Christian lives, it's easy to slip into thinking that it comes down to obeying a set of rules or living up to certain standards. But God is not looking for slaves who obey because they have to — instead, He wants to free us to rest in His grace so that we serve Him because we really want to.

Session 2: Innocent!
Many of God's people struggle with a low-grade fever of guilt which makes us "act like we think a Christian should act". Understanding that we have been declared not guilty once and for all brings us back to a real relationship with God where we can be ourselves and do what we do purely out of love. In Christ we measure up in full to God's righteous demands!

Session 3: Unashamed!
Past experiences, what others say and our struggles to break free of sin can leave us feeling that there is something fundamentally wrong with us. The truth is that we have become completely new people who can break the cycle of returning time and again to the same old sin issue. In Christ we have become completely new creations at the core of our being!

Session 4: Courageous!
Our God is an awesome God. But His children can come boldly into His presence without being afraid — we are absolutely secure and safe. And if this God is for us, who can be against us? We need fear no one and nothing except God Himself, and the fear of God is not a cringing mistrust but a deep awe of His great majesty and holiness.

Session 5: Humble!
In the Old Testament, God gave His people the Law. When Jesus came, He stated plainly that He had not come to do away with the Law but to fulfil it. If we understand how this works, we will resist the temptation to set ourselves up as nit-picking "guardians of the truth" but will be guided by the Law that is now written on our hearts. We will humble ourselves before God and before each other.

Ministry component: *The Steps To Experiencing God's Grace*
This kind and gentle ministry session will help us deal with the things that get in the way of experiencing God's grace. It is designed to be run on an "away day" retreat between Sessions 5 and 6 or in an individual one-on-one appointment.

Session 6: Fruitful!
When we feel ground down and exhausted, Jesus makes us an astonishing offer: a light yoke and an easy burden. And He really means it! It seems a paradox, but genuinely fruitful ministry that will have value for eternity comes only when we enter into that rest through the gateway of brokenness and learn to depend completely on Him.

How does *The Grace Course* work together with *The Freedom In Christ Discipleship Course*?

The Freedom In Christ Discipleship Course is a best-selling course consisting of 13 sessions plus *The Steps To Freedom In Christ* ministry component — there are further details on page 223 or visit www.ficm.org.uk. The look and feel of *The Grace Course* is modelled on the *Discipleship Course* so will be instantly familiar to previous users.

The Grace Course can stand alone but is also designed to work well with the *Discipleship Course*. They very much complement each other.

The overall theme running through both courses could be characterized as, "know the truth and the truth will set you free". Both courses have similar main emphases: knowing who you are in Christ; and the importance of renewing the mind.

With 13 sessions, the *Discipleship Course* is more comprehensive. In particular, it has more to say on the crucial areas of why we need to forgive others, the battle for our minds, recognizing that all of us are predisposed to a particular worldview and understanding how to bring our goals into line with God's goals for our lives. It tends to draw from the epistles a little more than the gospels. *The Grace Course* on the other hand covers some key areas in a lot more depth than the *Discipleship Course*: guilt; shame; fear; pride; and ministering out of rest. It tends to draw from the gospels a little more than the epistles.

We showed *The Grace Course* to several leaders who are experienced users of the *Discipleship Course*. All said that the two courses work together extremely well. They felt that, having experienced one course, people would definitely want to go on and do the other and it would be highly beneficial for them to do so.

Nearly all said they would want to use both courses, for example by running one course for a period followed in the next period by the other course, giving participants opportunity to do both. They were, however, split on which course they would put participants through first: some said one, some said the other!

So, if you choose to use both courses, our recommendation is that you do not worry too much which order you do them in. We would, however, recommend that, if you do *The Grace Course* first, you consider giving participants an opportunity to go through *The Steps To Freedom In Christ* (the ministry component from the *Discipleship Course*) before they go through *The Steps To Experiencing God's Grace* (the ministry component from *The Grace Course*) or even instead of it if there is only opportunity to do one or the other. It would also be beneficial if possible to show the DVD of Session 9 — "Forgiving From The Heart" — from the *Discipleship Course* during the away day retreat for *The Grace Course* because forgiveness is an integral part of the ministry components for both courses and is covered much more comprehensively in the *Discipleship Course*. There is more information on this on pages 19–20.

In summary then:
- each of the courses stands alone so can run perfectly well without the other
- there are real benefits to participants if they do both courses
- if participants do *The Grace Course* on its own or before the *Discipleship Course*, consider finding a way for them to do *The Steps To Freedom In Christ* and Session 9 — "Forgiving From The Heart" — from the *Discipleship Course*.

See page 19 for more information on *The Steps To Freedom In Christ*.

How can *The Grace Course* be used?

The Grace Course works equally well with those who have just become Christians and those who have been Christians a long time. It has been designed to be flexible enough to use in a variety of church situations:

In Small Groups
This is how most churches use our discipleship resources. If people miss a session, make sure that they have access to the DVD so that they can catch up.

We recommend that, where possible, small groups use the teaching sessions on the DVDs and that you use the "Pause For Thought" (default) option on the DVD so that the sessions pause automatically for group discussion. Each small group session is designed to last 2 hours and you will find a detailed time plan for each session in this Leader's Guide.

Systematic Preaching With Small Group Follow-Up
Each of the Word sections can be delivered as a straight talk (in person or via the DVD). You could, therefore, use them as a main church teaching programme (for example in a Sunday service or US Sunday School program). This could be followed up in small groups during the week if there is no opportunity for group discussion.

Mid-Week Meeting
In a mid-week setting where there are no established small groups, you could bring everyone together and deliver the talk (in person or via the DVD) and then divide people into groups for the group discussion questions. Alternatively, you could deliver the talk in sections, allowing the groups to discuss the Pause For Thought questions as you go.

Alongside An Outreach Course
It is possible to combine the course with an outreach course such as Alpha. You could bring both groups together for a meal before sending the not-yet Christians into the outreach course and new Christians into *The Grace Course*. Even if people have not become Christians on the outreach course, this should not preclude them from going on to *The Grace Course*, which will show them clearly in the first three sessions the differences that take place when someone becomes a Christian.

One-On-One Discipling
It is time-consuming to run the course for just one person but it works very well indeed. It's a great way to disciple a new convert or as a mentoring tool for those who have been Christians for a while.

Which method do you recommend?

Freedom In Christ Ministries has been producing resources for churches around the world since 1988, all designed to help Christians become fruitful disciples. We have found that by far the most effective way for most people to learn in a church environment is in a small group where they are encouraged to discuss what is being taught. In preparing *The Grace Course* our focus has primarily been on creating a small group resource but you will find it will work well in any of the ways outlined above.

What materials are required?

We recommend that everyone leading a group has their own copy of this **Leader's Guide** with presentation CD. You will probably also want the **DVD Set** with video presentations by the authors of the talks and *The Steps To Experiencing God's Grace*. Even if you are planning to present the course yourself rather than use the DVD presentations, watching the DVDs aids preparation enormously.

Each participant will need a copy of the **Participant's Guide** which contains notes for each session, Pause For Thought questions and *The Steps To Experiencing God's Grace*.

We recommend they also have a set of three **Biblical Truths postcards** one of which is handed out after each of the first three sessions. These postcards contain some of the key memorable illustrations from the course and the accompanying biblical truths. They are an excellent aid to help participants remember the key points and provide great encouragement to participants to keep declaring and believing the truths they will learn. The postcards are as follows:

> Welcome Home! (Session 1)
> Innocent! (Session 2)
> My New Name (Session 3)

Customisable **invitations** and **posters** to promote your course are also available from Freedom In Christ Ministries.

The various components are listed below with their Freedom In Christ order code and ISBN number (if applicable):

The Grace Course Leader's Guide	Order code: FC301	ISBN: 9780857213242
The Grace Course DVD Set (PAL format — outside USA)	Order code: FC302	ISBN: 9780857213228
The Grace Course DVD Set (NTSC format — for USA)		ISBN: 9780857214423
The Grace Course Participant's Guide (single)	Order code: FC303	ISBN: 9780857213259
The Grace Course Participant's Guide (five pack)	Order code: FC304	ISBN: 9780857213235
The Grace Course Full Colour Postcards (20 x 3 types)	Order code: FC308	
The Grace Course Customisable Colour Invitations (50)	Order code: FC309	
The Grace Course Customisable A3 Publicity Poster (3)	Order code: FC310	

Items with ISBN numbers can be ordered from Freedom In Christ Ministries or book suppliers. Other items are available only from Freedom In Christ Ministries.

The best way for most people to get started is by ordering *The Grace Course* **Church Starter Pack** which contains all of the main items plus enough material for 20 participants. It is sold at a substantial discount to individual item prices and is available only from Freedom In Christ Ministries.

For further details or to order, go to **www.ficm.org** in the USA, **www.ficm.org.uk** in the UK or any Freedom In Christ office around the world (see page 222 for details of how to find your nearest office).

How do the teaching sessions work?

Each session follows the same format and contains the following elements:

Leader's Notes
An introduction for the leader of the session to help you prepare.

Welcome
For small-group settings — an opening question designed to help group members develop deeper relationships with each other and, usually, to help them to start talking about the theme. During this part of the session, it's more important to encourage group participation and interaction than to do any teaching. The main objective is to build relationships.

Worship
For small-group settings. We have suggested a theme but it is only a suggestion. The main thing is that Jesus is placed at the centre of each session.

Prayer & Declaration

For small-group settings. This leads on from the worship section. It's an opportunity to encourage people to pray together out loud and then to make a declaration. A prayer is said to God whilst a declaration is spoken out to the spiritual world in general. Encourage people to declare it boldly as the children of God they are!

Word

This is the main part of each session. Each talk lasts between 60 and 67 minutes in total (excluding Pause For Thought discussions) but is split into three or four segments of between 2 and 25 minutes separated by "Pause For Thought" discussions. This includes the filmed testimonies on the DVD that help to illustrate the main points.

If you choose to present the material yourself, you will find the talk written out in full in this Leader's Guide together with some useful additional material. We recommend that you stick as closely as possible to the notes (but without reciting them parrot fashion), ideally supplementing them with illustrations from your own experience to replace those of the authors (this is particularly pertinent to Session 6). The CD that accompanies this book (inside the back cover) contains PowerPoint presentations for each talk and *The Steps To Experiencing God's Grace* that you can use via a computer and projector.

The notes show the PowerPoint slides in their correct position and indicate when to move on to the next bullet point or slide.

Pause For Thought Discussions

The Word section contains two or three sets of Pause For Thought questions. In small groups, we suggest that you stop at each Pause For Thought and give time for discussion (the DVD sessions pause automatically by default). Each session builds on the previous one and it's important that people have the opportunity to grasp the main points of each. At the beginning of each session, we have suggested timings for each part of the session including the Pause For Thoughts.

Witness

This question is intended to get small groups thinking about how what has been learned could impact those who are not yet Christians and to encourage them to apply it. In practice it functions like an additional Pause For Thought question and can either be used in addition to the existing questions or as a replacement. The Witness question is not included as a separate element in the time plans.

In The Coming Week

One or two suggested activities for participants to do before the next session. We especially want to encourage people to engage practically with God through this material. Please make sure, however, that participants know that the suggestions are completely optional so that they feel no pressure whatsoever to follow them.

What advice do you have for leading a small group?

A good structure for an evening would be something like this:

Getting Started

Start with coffee and get people to chat and mingle for a while. You could use the Welcome question during this time.

Welcome

The Welcome question functions as an icebreaker and is designed for a bit of fun and to get people interacting at the start of the session. It works well to split people into twos or threes. There is no need to feel that you have to do any teaching at this stage. It can be helpful at this point to invite feedback from the previous session. What struck people particularly from last week? Have they benefited from what they learned during the week in any practical ways?

Worship

For small-group settings — it is recommended that someone other than the person doing the talk leads this short time of worship. Include worship songs — if you have no worship leader, recorded worship songs could be used. Consider reading the Bible verses out loud together.

Prayer & Declaration

Try to get everyone praying and declaring boldly and loudly. Some are not used to this but will grow to enjoy it over time. We are trying through this section to encourage people to realize that they can be active in taking spiritual authority and responsibility in their lives.

Focus Truth and Verse

Introduce the Focus Verse and the Focus Truth for the session. There is no need to say more than is written in the Leader's Guide. Then go straight into the Word section.

Word

Play the DVD or start the talk, pausing for discussion at the Pause For Thought questions as indicated. If you are presenting yourself, keep an eye on time and try to resist the temptation to deviate too much from the notes so that the main points are not lost. The time plans for each session will help with timekeeping. Registered users can download a customisable Excel spreadsheet — just insert your own start time and all the timings for each week will be instantly calculated for you.

Pause For Thought Discussions

If your group is larger than eight, split people down into sub-groups of no more than seven or eight for the discussion and mix the groups up each week. Occasionally it is helpful to split people up by gender. For variety, consider some discussions in smaller groups of three to four to allow quieter ones to talk. As a leader of a discussion group, one of your main roles is to try to get others to talk rather than talk yourself. Don't be afraid of silences.

In addition to the questions given, you could start any Pause For Thought with the following open questions:

- What do you think about what you just heard?

- Was there anything you heard that you didn't understand or that needs further clarification?

- How do you think what you have heard applies to you?

Try not to let the conversation wander too far from the main points and keep an eye on the time (a suggested time for each Pause For Thought section is given at the start of each session). Draw the discussion to a close at the appropriate time by summarizing briefly. The Pause For Thought objectives in this Leader's Guide make a good basis for that summary.

At The End

Discuss the Witness question, point out the In The Coming Week suggestion (but remember that it is completely optional) and give out any notices such as the away day retreat details.

Any other hints and tips?

- Church leaders — send a message that "this is for everyone" by going through the teaching and the ministry component and writing a Stronghold-Buster (see pages 18–19) yourself first.

- Join the Freedom Fellowship, an invaluable source of advice — see page 24.

- Surround your course with prayer — see page 20.

- Emphasize that every participant will need to apply ongoing effort to maintain the freedom gained and continue to grow as a disciple.

- Take it slowly — our courses are not generally something that a church does just once but tend to become a regular part of church life. As such it is worth taking the time and effort at the outset to make sure that the courses run as well as they possibly can.

- Look out for the enemy's attack — often through the least expected people.

- Decide early on how you are going to approach running *The Steps To Experiencing God's Grace* (there are more details in *The Steps To Experiencing God's Grace* Session). If you decide on the away day retreat approach, ensure that you book a suitable venue in good time and give everyone the date as early as you can. Make sure that participants understand that this is an integral part of the course and not to be missed!

- Keep emphasizing that this is discipleship for everyone — not just for "hard cases" or any particular section of the church.

- "Transformed lives transform lives" — be prepared for the course to make a positive difference throughout your church and beyond as people come to a fresh understanding of God's grace. Think about how it could impact your community as Christians discover afresh for themselves that Jesus really is the answer to the issues out there.

- Remember that Freedom In Christ Ministries exists to equip leaders. Don't hesitate to get in touch if you have a question or need any advice.

Renewing the mind — "Stronghold-Busting"

Throughout the course, we want to encourage people that, as new creations in Christ, they have the ability and responsibility to be active in their Christian life. That is why, for example, we have included a declaration at the start of each session — we want participants to get used to wielding the power and authority they have in Christ. In short we want to see them transformed in their Christian walk. In the New Testament, the word "transformed" is a strong word. Its literal meaning is "metamorphosis", the change a caterpillar undergoes in order to become a butterfly. In Romans 12:2, Paul tells us what it is that will cause this transformation in us: "be transformed by the renewal of your mind".

Most people will come to *The Grace Course* expecting to "receive". Of course, we expect them to receive some really helpful teaching but it's unlikely that they will be transformed if all they do is "receive". In order to be transformed, they have to work on the renewal of their mind, throwing out old ways of thinking based on lies they have come to believe and replacing those ways of thinking with what God tells us is really true in His Word.

All of us have been conditioned by past experiences to believe things that do not line up completely with God's Word. Given that God's Word is the truth, we can legitimately call these false beliefs "lies". When a lie becomes deeply ingrained it becomes a "stronghold", a habitual way of thinking that is inconsistent with what God says in His Word (or, if you prefer, any wrong belief or action that has a "strong hold" on you). It's like having a solid wall in your mind that prevents you from going the way God wants you to.

In Sessions 3 and 4 and during *The Steps To Experiencing God's Grace* session, we introduce a strategy called "Stronghold-Busting". It is a 40-day process of replacing lies with truth — see pages 139–141. Why 40 days? Psychologists tell us that it takes around six weeks to form or break a habit. Once you have dealt with any footholds of the enemy, a mental stronghold is simply a habitual way of thinking. We cannot emphasize enough how significant Stronghold-Busting is to participants who actively engage with it. They really are transformed at a deep, core level. The challenge is to help people believe that genuine transformation really will take place so that they will follow through on the process.

In order to help participants become aware of faulty thinking, we pause at the end of each session and invite them to allow the Holy Spirit to bring to their mind any lies they are believing. We suggest some possible lies but there may well be others. We then encourage them to write those lies down in the *Lies*

List at the back of their Participant's Guide. For some, those two pages will not be enough and they may need to use separate sheets of paper or a separate notebook. Make sure you set aside enough time at the end of each session for people to complete the exercise.

Once participants have identified faulty thinking, they will need to be encouraged to go and find what is actually true from God's Word. This can be quite difficult because by definition the lie feels absolutely true to the person who believes it. Be prepared to spend some time helping people find appropriate verses and talking it through with them. Then participants will need strong encouragement to sit down and write their Stronghold-Buster and, particularly, to persevere with it for 40 days.

In our experience the best way for people to be encouraged to do that is testimony of transformation in others. That is why there are testimonies on the DVD about Stronghold-Busting. Even if you are not using the DVD for the teaching, it would be well worth using it to show these particular testimonies in Sessions 3 and 4. Even better would be for those leading to have their own testimonies. So one of our key recommendations for leaders is that you develop a Stronghold-Buster of your own and go through it before running the course for others. Then you can share your own experiences.

The Steps To Freedom In Christ

The Steps to Freedom In Christ is a structured process of prayer and repentance written by Dr. Neil T. Anderson (founder of Freedom In Christ Ministries) which has been used by millions of people around the world. It has been published in many languages and formats and is the ministry component of *The Freedom In Christ Discipleship Course* (see page 223).

The person going through the Steps (whom we will call "the freedom seeker") takes responsibility for their life and growth by asking the Holy Spirit to show them any area in their life where an issue needs to be resolved. They then choose to repent of everything He shows them thus removing any grounds the enemy may have had in their life. It is a very straightforward approach that is kind and gentle — but amazingly effective.

Each Step starts with a biblically-based prayer of repentance which the freedom seeker prays as a general preliminary, asking the Holy Spirit to bring to mind the specific areas that apply to them. Then there are particular instances listed and a short written prayer of renunciation which the freedom seeker will use to deal with specific areas they want to renounce. Some sections also include doctrinal affirmations which are declarations of the freedom seeker's choice and acceptance of primary scriptural truth set out in a very straightforward way.

It has seven Steps which cover: Cult and occult involvement, idols; Deception including self-deception and ingrained defence mechanisms; Forgiveness as a choice of the will, not dependent on feelings; Rebellion, for example against family, church leaders, work and God Himself; Pride; Habitual sins and attitudes including sexual sins and deeply-rooted issues; Generational sin.

It is a process that every Christian will benefit from (not just "hard cases") and we recommend that people go through it as a regular spiritual check-up on an annual basis. It is possible for people to go through the process either in the context of a group "away day" retreat or in an individual "freedom appointment" in the context of their local church.

The Steps To Freedom In Christ and *The Grace Course*

The ministry component of *The Grace Course* (*The Steps To Experiencing God's Grace*) is based on the same principles of the believer taking responsibility for their life and choosing to submit to God and resist the devil (James 4:7). The format will be very familiar to those who have been through *The Steps To Freedom In Christ* but it focuses on different areas (apart from an overlap on the key area of forgiveness).

We recommend where possible that participants on *The Grace Course* go through *The Steps To Freedom In Christ* before *The Steps To Experiencing God's Grace*. Many will already have been through them as part of *The Freedom In Christ Discipleship Course* but, if you have a group that has not done that course, you could choose to do *The Steps To Freedom In Christ* instead of *The Steps To Experiencing God's Grace* between Sessions 5 and 6 and then come back to *The Steps To Experiencing God's Grace* at a later date. In order to do that, you would need to purchase *The Steps To Freedom In Christ* book for participants and possibly *The Steps To Freedom In Christ DVD* which guides a group through the process. We recognize that this involves a small amount of additional cost but if you want to make these principles a "way of life" in your church, it would be well worth it.

It is not, however, essential to do this and you can run *The Grace Course* just as it is and expect great results! Feel free to contact us (see page 222) if you want to discuss the best approach for your church.

Prayer for *The Grace Course*

Prayer is a vital part of preparation for your course and should not stop once the course gets underway. If you can assemble a group of people to pray for your course, you will really notice the difference. Here is a prayer they might like to use to get started.

Dear Heavenly Father,

Thank You for *The Grace Course*.

We ask You to use it to give Your people a new revelation of who You are and how much You love them so that they see how good it is in Your house, come to their senses and return to You again from their "distant land". In You ALL the treasures of wisdom and ALL the riches of wisdom are stored up (Colossians 2:3). We ask that Your people will go deep into You to know You as You really are.

Lord, please set Your sons and daughters free from dark dungeons and bring them into the light to be conformed more and more to the image of Jesus Christ!

Please cleanse Your Church now of our filthy rags, those works done in independence of You (Isaiah 64:6) and any striving to live up to certain standards and reliance on external actions which only bring more distance between us and You.

We choose Your light and easy yoke, Lord Jesus. We throw off any other yokes that would seek to make us slaves again (Galatians 5:1). We particularly renounce guilt, shame, fear and pride, and declare that they are not part of the inheritance of the sons and daughters of God. We ask You, Father, to break the hold they have on Your people and bring release of abundance of fruit that glorifies You.

Father, we ask for Your Spirit of wisdom and revelation to come to those who are leading the course so that they would know release from heavy burdens of striving and perfectionism and in turn release others.

We refuse any spiritual intimidation and instead ask that You please fill us with the Spirit of Truth, who brings light and freedom as we journey through *The Grace Course*. We declare that the schemes of the enemy against the course will not succeed (Isaiah 54:17).

God of all Grace, we give You glory for what You are going to do through *The Grace Course*. May all praise and honour and thanks return to You, the Worthy One.

In the precious name of Jesus Christ our Lord,

Amen.

Technical Matters

How does the slide presentation CD work?

In the inside back cover of this Leader's Guide, you will find a CD containing PowerPoint presentations to accompany each session. These are for use if you decide to do the presentations yourself rather than use the video presentations on DVD (available separately).

Insert the CD into a computer and it should load automatically. If it does not, navigate to the CD and double click on the file "menu.pps" or "play.bat". You may need to confirm that you do want to run PowerPoint Viewer, the program that runs the slide presentations (PPTVIEW.EXE).

You do not need a copy of PowerPoint to run the presentations on a single screen but will need to accept the terms and conditions of the free PowerPoint viewer software that comes with the presentations if you have not used it before. To use them on a dual-screen set-up, open them in a full version of PowerPoint (when doing that, PowerPoint will ask you for a password because the presentations are password-protected. Simply select "Read Only").

Then follow the menus.

The presentations assume you are going to use the optional Pause For Thought questions and a slide with the questions will come up at the appropriate point. However, if you prefer not to use these, the title screen of each presentation has an option bottom right that you can click to run it without the Pause For Thought slides.

The presentations work with standard PowerPoint keys:

- To move the presentation on: click the mouse or press **Enter**, **space bar**, **down arrow** or **pg dn**
- To go back: press **up arrow** or **pg up**
- To go back to the beginning: press **Home**
- To blank the screen: press **B**

Note that the presentations are password-protected to prevent them being edited (because we want to protect the integrity of the presentations).

If the text on the presentations is not displaying correctly, it is probably because the common font "Arial" is not installed on your computer.

How do you run the video sessions on DVD?

You can run the video presentations on DVD (available separately) on a standard television with DVD player or on a computer and project it onto a large screen.

Simply select the session you require from the menu. Note that the sessions will automatically stop at the Pause For Thought questions unless you select the option to run them without Pause For Thought.

There is also an option to select subtitles if you have participants with impaired hearing or who want to see the foreign language subtitles available.

Any tips for presenting from the notes in the Leader's Guide?

The notes in the Leader's Guide are self-explanatory. There is also space for you to write your own notes. The Leader's Guide has a super-strong spine so you can make the pages lie flat without fear of breaking it.

Representations of slides from the slide presentation are shown. In the text, whenever you see this symbol ▶ it's an indication that the slide presentation should be moved on to the next bullet point or slide.

The black boxes contain additional notes and points of explanation that you may find helpful.

Additional notes to speakers in the notes are contained in [square brackets].

What help is there for those with sight and hearing impairment?

The DVD sessions contain optional subtitles for those with hearing impairment.

For people with sight loss, accessible copies of this Leader's Guide and the Participant's Guide in braille and 24 point giant print can be obtained for the same price as the print copy from:

The Torch Trust,
Torch House, Torch Way
MARKET HARBOROUGH
LE16 9NT
United Kingdom.

Email: info@torchtrust.org

Tel: 01858 438260 from within the UK or +44 1858 438260 from outside the UK.

Training & Other Resources

Equipping available in the USA:

Has the Lord set you free? Are you excited about seeing others discover their freedom in Christ? Have you ever wondered if God might be calling you to start a ministry of freedom in your church? If so, then our online training institute, CFM University, just might be the next step to getting started! Check us out at **cfmuniversity.org** and get trained in the comforts of home. Maybe it's time for you to go back to school!

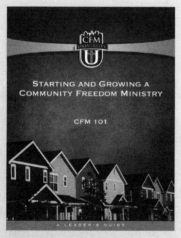

Is the Lord calling you to start a Community Freedom Ministry (CFM)? A CFM is a "freedom presence" in a church where an environment of grace and truth is developed to teach the message of our identity and freedom in Christ, and God's people are helped to become growing, fruitful disciples of Christ. Learn how to build a strong, Spirit-led prayer ministry; understand better how to work alongside church leaders; discover a teaching, training template that you can use anywhere; and more! Go to **freedominchrist.com** to learn more and get started!

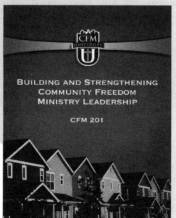

Any ministry stands or falls on the shoulders of its leaders. In this renewing and refreshing course, you'll learn how to guard your heart as well as the hearts of those serving with you in ministry. You'll discover the keys to waging and winning the spiritual battles that come against you, and you'll become more effective at protecting your Community Freedom Ministry. You'll also learn how to stay focused on your "freedom calling" and not get sidetracked. And much more! Go to **freedominchrist.com** for more information.

For more information about FICM-USA: www.ficm.org

Equipping available in the UK:

Training events near you

There are three core events held regularly around the country that will be of particular interest to anyone involved in leading *The Grace Course*. Ideally they should be attended in the order listed below.

Making Fruitful Disciples

Do you want to help your people grow into fruitful disciples? Aimed at church leaders and youth leaders, this event gives an overview of the biblical principles of discipleship and then shows practically how to implement them using the *Freedom in Christ Discipleship Course*, *The Grace Course* and *Freedom In Christ For Young People*. (See also the *Making Fruitful Disciples* DVD training course below).

Helping Others Find Freedom In Christ

This event focuses on *The Steps To Freedom In Christ* and its objective is to help participants feel confident about using it and similar processes such as *The Steps To Experiencing God's Grace*. It is ideal for churches who are using the *Freedom In Christ Discipleship Course*, *The Grace Course* or *Freedom In Christ For Young People*. It will equip you to lead the Steps in individual appointments or on an away day retreat. (For the corresponding DVD course see below.)

Helping Others With Deeper Issues

Freedom In Christ's discipleship courses are for every Christian but the principles in them can be applied highly effectively to those struggling with deeper issues such as past abuse, addictions and dissociative disorders. God does not change our past but He promises to set us free from it completely. This workshop is for those who are already familiar with the basic Freedom In Christ approach and is ideal for church teams.

DVD training resources

As it is not always possible for everyone to attend a "live" event, the content of our two main events are available on DVD (presented by Steve Goss and others) so that it's easy to train a team in your church.

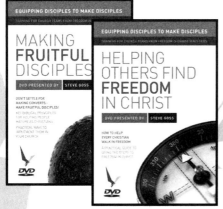

Making Fruitful Disciples

Don't settle for making converts — make fruitful disciples! An outline of the key biblical principles for helping people mature as Christians and practical ways to implement them in your church using *The Freedom In Christ Discipleship Course* and *Freedom In Christ For Young People*.

Helping Others Find Freedom In Christ

How to help every Christian walk in freedom. This DVD is a practical guide to using *The Steps To Freedom In Christ* to lead both individual appointments and away days.

Join the Freedom Fellowship

If you are involved in leading others through *The Steps To Freedom In Christ* in your church, you will benefit from joining the Freedom Fellowship. It's the primary way that Freedom In Christ keeps in touch with people using its approach. You'll get access to a members-only section of our website with:

- guidelines on setting up and running your "freedom ministry"
- suggested ways of working
- sample documents such as the "Confidential Personal Inventory" and "Statement of Understanding"
- guidance on best practice.

More information at ficm.org.uk

Resources to recommend to participants:

The more you can encourage participants to engage with the biblical principles of grace and freedom, the more effective your course will be for them. Freedom In Christ Ministries has a large number of resources that will benefit participants as they go through *The Grace Course*.

Why not order a quantity from Freedom In Christ Ministries to have available at the start of your course? We are usually happy to supply on a sale or return basis and offer quantity discounts too.

We have listed below the resources that we think participants will find particularly helpful but there are many more on our websites.

General reading

Victory Over The Darkness & The Bondage Breaker by Neil T. Anderson

These two classic books by Neil Anderson, founder of Freedom In Christ Ministries, were first published in 1994 and have sold millions of copies worldwide. They will help participants get hold of our main messages in greater depth.

The first looks particularly at the question of our new identity in Christ whilst the second deals with the question of how to win the spiritual battle for the mind that every Christian is in whether they like it or not.

Discipleship Series **by Steve Goss**

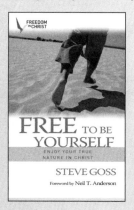 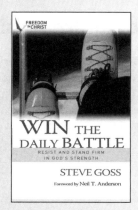  

These short, straightforward books are easy to read yet communicate the key messages powerfully.
Free To Be Yourself: Stop trying to "act like you think a Christian should act" and enjoy your true nature in Christ.
Win The Daily Battle: Understand the world, the flesh and the devil and how to resist and stand firm in God's strength.
Break Free, Stay Free: Don't let "stuff" from the past hold you back but learn how to resolve it in Christ.
The You God Planned: Don't let anything or anyone hold you back as you gradually become more and more like Jesus.

For Session 3

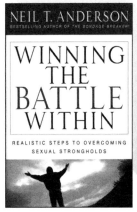

Winning The Battle Within by Neil T. Anderson
For too many, God's wonderful creation of sex has become a source of spiritual slavery rather than blessing. This book shows how to overcome the guilt, anger and fear in sexual struggles and embrace a pure, godly view of this gift.

Overcoming Addictive Behavior by Neil T. Anderson
Gives a message of hope and a plan of action! Helps you identify the root cause of your problem and then take it to God so that your mind and spirit can be renewed to enable you to find your freedom in Christ.

For Session 4

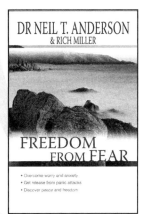

Freedom From Fear **by Neil T. Anderson & Rich Miller**
Anxiety disorders are the main mental health problem in the western world. God's Word speaks directly to these concerns. This book identifies how mental strongholds of fear and anxiety develop, then reveals powerful biblical strategies for defeating them in Christ and finding hope.

For *The Steps To Experiencing God's Grace* session

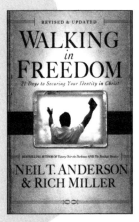

Walking In Freedom **by Neil T. Anderson & Rich Miller**
A superb 21 day devotional specifically designed for those who have been through *The Steps To Freedom In Christ* but of just as much value to those who have gone through *The Steps To Experiencing God's Grace*. We recommend you have a stock available for course members to buy immediately after they go through *The Steps To Experiencing God's Grace*.

For further details of our resources see **www.ficm.org** (USA) or **www.ficm.org.uk** (UK) or any of our other sites around the world.

Session 1:
FREE!

Session 1: Free!

FOCUS VERSE:

1 Samuel 16:7b: "For the Lord sees not as man sees: man looks on the outward appearance, but the Lord looks on the heart."

OBJECTIVE:

To understand that what really matters to God is not only **what** we do but **why** we do it.

FOCUS TRUTH:

In Christ we are perfectly loved and accepted for who we are, not what we do. From that position of security, we can make a free choice to serve God because we love Him, and get rid of any other false motivation.

Leader's Notes

The theme running through this first session could be defined as "sonship versus slavery".

We will focus on the story Jesus told that is generally known as the Parable of the Prodigal Son. We prefer to call it the Parable Of The Two Sons because the context makes clear that the focus of the story is not so much the younger son who went astray but rather the elder brother who appeared outwardly to be doing everything right yet inwardly was far away from his father.

The story appears in a string of parables in Luke 15 dealing with things that are lost: the Parable of the Lost Sheep, the Parable of the Lost Coin, and then this one which could easily be entitled the Parable of the Lost Son. The question is, which of the sons was lost, the younger, the elder or both? By the end of the story it's clear that the younger son, though once lost, has now been found, but the elder son is still lost.

Although the elder son is free to enjoy right now everything his father owns, he is deceived into thinking he has to "slave away" to earn it as a future reward. This attitude keeps him from intimacy with the father and makes him behave in ways that are more in keeping with a hired hand who "slaves away" rather than the son he is.

The key point we want to help participants understand is that they are not just in the position the younger son was in immediately upon his return, that of a "forgiven sinner", someone who has been forgiven but is still essentially the same no good person they always were. We want them to know that, even though they don't deserve it, they have become "sons" with all the authority, responsibility and privilege that implies. From their position as sons, they are free to choose whether to live for the father or not. But when you understand just what this father is like and what he has done, why on earth wouldn't you want to serve him?

We finish the session with something of a paradox. Having said that we don't need to "slave away" for God, we note that the New Testament actually often gives a positive slant to the word "slave" (*doulos* in the Greek), with Paul, for example, calling himself a "slave of Christ" (Romans 1:1). Even though we are free not to serve Him, when we understand how good He is and how loving He is, of our own free will we can commit ourselves to becoming His bondslaves.

The Danger Of Antinomianism

Antinomianism is an old heresy that has afflicted the Church through the ages. The term means "anti-law" and was coined by Martin Luther to refer to the practice of pushing the doctrine of justification by faith alone too far and saying, in effect, that since Christians are saved by faith alone, it does not matter at all how they behave.

The teaching in this session may sound to some as if it is heading in that direction but that is categorically not the case. Encourage any who express concern to bear with it and reassure them that, as the course develops, they will see the whole picture.

D. Martyn Lloyd-Jones, the great proponent of evangelical theology and minister of Westminster Chapel in London, who was prominent in the middle of the 20th Century, said:

> "There is no better test as to whether a man is really preaching the New Testament gospel than this, that some people might misunderstand it and misinterpret it that it really amounts to this: that because you are saved by grace alone, it does not really matter at all WHAT you do, you can go on sinning all you like..."[1]

Note how he says that interpreting Gospel preaching as meaning that it doesn't matter how you behave is to misunderstand it. His point is that, if you don't find some people misinterpreting your teaching in this way, then you are not actually preaching the true Gospel of grace. He goes on to say even more directly (and in capital letters!):

> "I would say to all preachers: IF YOUR PREACHING OF SALVATION HAS NOT BEEN MISUNDERSTOOD IN THAT WAY, THEN YOU HAD BETTER EXAMINE YOUR SERMONS AGAIN, and you had better make sure that you really ARE preaching the salvation that is proclaimed in the New Testament."[1]

Our objective in this course is to help people receive a revelation of God's grace. Most people find that revelation profoundly shocking when it comes. On the face of it, it may seem that we can behave however we like, but anyone who persists in that way of thinking has not had a genuine revelation of grace. Those who truly understand it, go in the opposite direction: they fall more in love with God and want to serve Him with all that they are and have.

1. D. Martyn Lloyd-Jones, *Romans, An Exposition of Chapter 6, The New Man*, (Grand Rapids: Zondervan, 1973), pages 9–10.

Small Group Timings

The following plan is designed to help those leading the course in small groups. It assumes a meeting of around 2 hours in length, and suggests how long each part of the session should last, with an indication of cumulative elapsed time. You will find a time plan in each session.

Welcome	9 minutes	0:09
Worship, prayer & declaration	5 minutes	0:14
Word part 1	22 minutes	0:36
Pause For Thought 1	18 minutes	0:54
Word part 2	19 minutes	1:13
Pause For Thought 2	12 minutes	1:25
Word part 3	18 minutes	1:43
Pause For Thought 3	12 minutes	1:55
Word part 4	5 minutes	2:00

The time allocated for the Word sections is based on the length of the corresponding section of the accompanying DVDs. The Witness section is not included in the time plan as it tends to be used in place of a Pause For Thought section. You will need to add on 5 to 10 minutes if you want to include it separately.

Registered users of the course (see page 10) can download an Excel spreadsheet with these timings. Simply enter your own start time, adjust the length of the various components if desired and you will have a timed plan of your session.

WELCOME

One definition of grace is "getting what you don't deserve". Tell about a time you got what you didn't deserve. What did you deserve? What did you actually get?

WORSHIP

Suggested theme: You belong! See 1 John 3:1.

You could ask people to reflect quietly on God's wonderful love for us in making us His sons and daughters. Then ask each person in the group who is willing to thank God for one, or more, of the many privileges of belonging to God's family by His grace.

PRAYER & DECLARATION

In every session, we want to encourage people to pray out loud and to make a declaration out loud together. A prayer is addressed to God while a declaration is spoken out to the spiritual world in general. Encourage people to make their declaration boldly!

Dear Father God, thank You for adopting us as Your children through Jesus Christ, and for giving us the privilege of calling You "Abba, Father"! Please open the eyes of our hearts so that we may really understand what this means for us. Amen.

I have been bought out of slavery by the blood of Jesus. I choose to submit myself to God and I resist anything that would drag me back into slavery.

 **WORD**

Introduction

Welcome to *The Grace Course*!

What's your favourite hymn? Different people like different ones. If you were a dentist you might perhaps go for "Crown Him With Many Crowns". If you were a paramedic, you might be whistling "Revive Us Again". I guess if you were a baker it would be "When The Roll Is Called Up Yonder"!

For many people, their favourite hymn is "Amazing Grace": "Amazing grace (how sweet the sound) that saved a wretch like me." Apparently John Newton's 250-year-old hymn is sung around 10 million times a year. I've been a Christian a long time and I think I have probably sung it nearly as many times myself!

This course is all about grace. Paul tells us in Romans 5:2 that we have obtained by faith "our introduction… into this grace in which we stand" (NASB). When I first became a Christian, I understood grace as being primarily about God's love when He sent Jesus to die for me. Peter tells us that God wants us to "grow in the grace and knowledge of our Lord and Saviour Jesus Christ" (2 Peter 3:18). The grace that God wants us to experience is for every moment of every day, and that's what this course is about.

And, although John Newton's great hymn starts by talking about the grace that saved us the moment we first turned to Christ, it goes on to say:

> Through many dangers, toils and snares
> I have already come;
> 'Tis Grace that brought me safe thus far
> And Grace will lead me home.

The objective of the course is to help you know what it means to experience God's grace every day so that you can be fruitful to the fullest possible extent. And that's an exciting prospect.

[Do you have a story of God's grace and what it has meant in your life that you could share at this point?]

Grace is so needed in the Church. In preparation for writing a book on legalism and grace with Dr. Neil Anderson and Paul Travis, we contracted the George Barna Research Group to do a scientific survey of American Christianity. We asked followers of Christ to respond to six statements. One of them was: "The Christian life is well-summed up as trying hard to obey God's commands." To our astonishment, we discovered that 82% of those surveyed agreed with that statement; 57% strongly agreed! Well, there's nothing wrong with that statement aside from the fact that it's totally wrong! There's nothing in there about grace... about faith... about love... about relationship. There's nothing in there about Jesus! Our conclusion was — and remains — that law-based living rather than grace-based living is endemic in the Church.

Understanding grace

▶To get us started, I want to ask you to consider a question. Jesus said, "If you love me, you will obey my commands" (John 14:15 NCV). Imagine Him saying that personally just to you. How do you hear Him saying it? What expression is on His face? ▶This?... ▶Or this?... What expression is in His voice? Before we finish this session, we'll do our best to resolve that question.

The story of the two brothers (Luke 15:11–32 NIV)

Let's look now at a story that Jesus told that will really help us come to grips with God's grace.

The younger brother

> And he said, "There was a man who had two sons. The younger of them said to his father, ▶'Father, give me my share of the estate.'" (Luke 15:11–12a)

Do you realize that he might as well have said, "I wish you were dead"? A father's inheritance was to come to his sons after his death. But this son just couldn't wait.

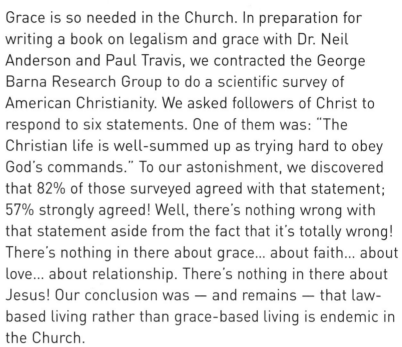

"If you love me, you will obey my commands."

John 14:15 NCV

▶So he divided his property between them. Not long after that, the younger son got together all he had, set off for a distant country and ▶there squandered his wealth in wild living. ▶After he had spent everything, there was a severe famine in that whole country, and he began to be in need. So he went and hired himself out to a citizen of that country, who sent him to his fields to feed pigs. ▶He longed to fill his stomach with the pods that the pigs were eating, but no one gave him anything.

When he came to his senses, he said, "How many of my father's hired servants have food to spare, and here I am starving to death! ▶I will set out and go back to my father and say to him: Father, I have sinned against heaven and against you. I am no longer worthy to be called your son; make me like one of your hired servants." So he got up and went to his father (Luke 15:12b–20a).

The younger boy had turned his back completely on his father and the way of life he had been brought up in.

What Jesus is doing here is painting a picture of someone whose behaviour was the worst imaginable in his culture. He showed no respect whatsoever for his father. He engaged in adultery, spending money on prostitutes. Then, when he had no money left, he even stooped so low as to take a job looking after the animal that to Jews represented the height of uncleanness — pigs. It's difficult to imagine that he could have behaved any worse, or any

less deservingly of his title as son. He himself knew that he had blown it completely and decided to return to his father, not expecting to be received any more as a son but hoping simply for a job as a hired hand, one who would have to earn anything that might come from the father.

▶ But while he was still a long way off, his father saw him and was filled with compassion for him; he ran to his son, threw his arms around him, and kissed him (Luke 15:20b).

Note that the father ran — in that culture, wealthy men never did that. Love for his son overcame all the social norms.

And the son said to him, "Father, I have sinned against heaven and against you. I am no longer worthy to be called your son" (Luke 15:21).

Was that true, that his sin made him no longer worthy to be called a son? Yes, undoubtedly, though of course nothing could change the fact that he was a son, and always would be. But watch how the father reacts: It's almost as if he was not even listening to the words of his son's well-rehearsed confession. The father knew the son's heart and that he was sorry and had come back. And that's all that mattered!

But the father said to his servants, "Quick! Bring the best robe and put it on him. Put a ring on his finger and sandals on his feet. ▶ Bring the fattened calf and kill it. [This is the only character in the story for whom the whole thing is really bad news!] Let's have a feast and celebrate. For this son of mine was dead and is alive again; he was lost and is found." So they began to celebrate (Luke 15:22–24).

▶ The son expected to be disowned or at best to be severely punished — and that would have been what he deserved. Yet the father immediately embraces this smelly, dirty, broken individual, puts the best clothes on him and throws a party to end all parties!

He also gives him three things that had great significance:

▶ First, the **robe** wasn't any old robe but was the best robe in the house, perhaps the father's own robe. It symbolized that the son had once again been given the right to enjoy the place of "right standing" with the father. He had always been loved, but now he was completely restored.

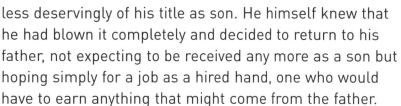

▶Second, the **ring** would have been a signet-type ring that would make a mark on official documents and could be instantly recognizable as the father's mark. Without that mark or seal there would be no authority behind the instructions in the document. The ring symbolized power and authority to carry out the father's business.

This boy, who had squandered his father's wealth in wild living, is being re-commissioned and honoured with the trust of his father to go about his father's business once again, telling people what they need to do. And they will have to do it, because he wears the ring on his finger.

The third thing he tells the servants to bring is ▶**sandals**. In a Jewish household, the only people allowed to wear footwear in the house were the father and his sons. The father was declaring in no uncertain terms that the boy, despite everything he had done, was still his son, entitled to the rights of a son.

This is *The Grace Course*, but what is grace? Let's pause for a minute and take in that scene. A son who has behaved in the worst way imaginable returns. His father, however, restores him simply because he loves him and wants a relationship with him. This is grace: A child utterly bereft of anything throwing himself on the mercy of his father who picks him up, dusts him down and restores him.

This son who has completely and utterly blown it, who has no right whatsoever to expect anything from his father except what he might be allowed to earn, who doesn't deserve any favour whatsoever, stands there in his rich robe, with his ring of authority and the sandals that mark him out as one of the family. This is grace.

Those of us who have been Christians a while know this story well and we tend to relate it to the time that we first came to God, gave our lives to Him and accepted His free gift of grace. But what about now? Does this part of the story have anything to say to us as we live our Christian lives today, or does it just reflect a one-off moment in the past?

[Do you have an incident from your own experience like the one below from Rich Miller that illustrates such grace?]

When I was a kid, I wanted just about every kind of animal that I saw on TV, but what I wanted most was a horse. I didn't know how much a horse cost, but I knew it was more than I had. So I concocted a plot. One Thursday evening I discovered my Mom's purse with a roll of $20 bills in it. My Dad had just been paid. I figured they wouldn't miss one of them, so I took a $20.

The next day I grabbed an envelope and the $20 and went to the woods where I often played. I put the $20 into the envelope and rubbed it in the dirt to make it look like it had been there a while. Then an hour or so later I rushed home and yelled to my Mom, "Hey look! I found $20 in the woods!" My Mom said, "Great, you can use that toward your horse." I thought I had committed the crime of the century. But I didn't count on one other factor... my conscience. The next day I was playing baseball and my Dad was watching from a low hill nearby. When I finished playing I started walking toward him and the closer I came, the worse I felt. Finally when I got to him I sort of blubbered, "Dad, I didn't find that money. I stole it!" My Dad said, "Son, your Mother and I knew that you stole the money. We were just waiting for you to come and tell us." And with that he hugged me and I was bawling.

Even though my Dad wasn't a follower of Christ at that time, I still remember that moment as a place of grace where my Dad was like my Father. And things are the same with us and God. He knows all that we've done yet still loves us. He's just waiting for us to come and talk to Him about it.

▶What is the worst thing you have ever done? Have you got it in your head? OK, write it down on a piece of paper and hand it to the person sitting next to you... . Just kidding! But what if you went out of here and did it again or did something even worse... and then sincerely came back to God, what reception would you get? The logic of this story is that you would be treated in exactly the same way as this boy.

This is grace. And it genuinely is amazing.

Does the thought that you as a Christian could behave in the worst way imaginable and then come back to God with the relationship still secure not sit quite right with you?

The context of the story

Let's step back and look at why Jesus told this story in the first place. The context is that He was clearly setting Himself up as a religious teacher but He sure didn't act like one. He was always mixing with the "wrong" crowd, tax collectors and so-called "sinners", and the religious people complained, saying "This man welcomes sinners and even sits down to eat with them." In response Jesus told a series of stories, of which this is the third. So He told it in response to the accusation that His behaviour was wrong — that it was displeasing to God. The whole point of the story is that it is not our behaviour that puts us into a right relationship with God — it's His grace.

But behaviour does matter

As we will see, it's not that the son's behaviour did not matter. It did. Sin has consequences. But the ending of his relationship with his father was NOT one of those consequences. That's what it means ▶ to be a child of God. You will always be a child of God. ▶ Even if you fall flat on your face and make a complete mess. God gives you freedom to fail. He is rooting for you and has given you everything you need so that you do not have to fail. But if you do, ▶ His loving arms are there to welcome you back and pick you up no matter how badly you have messed up. This is genuinely shocking, don't you find? But that's exactly what the Bible says in 1 John 2:1 NIV:

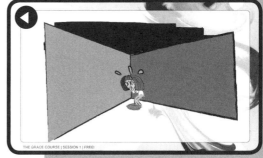

> My dear children, I write this to you so that you will not sin. But if anybody does sin, we have one who speaks to the Father in our defence — Jesus Christ the Righteous One.

There's an old heresy — nearly as old as the Gospel itself — called antinomianism which pushes biblical truth too far and says that, since we are saved by God's grace through faith, there is no need for a moral law, so our behaviour doesn't matter. If it's starting to sound a little like that's where we're going, let me reassure you that it isn't. If you bear with us, you'll get the full picture.

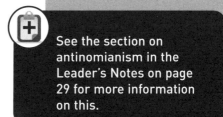

See the section on antinomianism in the Leader's Notes on page 29 for more information on this.

PAUSE FOR THOUGHT 1

OBJECTIVE:

TO HELP PEOPLE START TO GET TO GRIPS WITH THE SHOCKING CONCEPTS OF GOD'S GRACE AND PARTICULARLY THEIR NEW POSITION AS CHILDREN OF GOD.

▶QUESTIONS (ON PAGE 11 OF THE PARTICIPANT'S GUIDE):

WHAT DOES "GRACE" MEAN TO YOU?

THE FATHER GIVES THE YOUNGER SON THREE GIFTS WHICH SYMBOLIZE THINGS THAT GOD HAS GIVEN TO YOU. WHICH GIFT IS MOST MEANINGFUL TO YOU? WHY?

IF YOU KNEW FOR SURE THAT GOD'S ACCEPTANCE OF YOU AND LOVE FOR YOU DID NOT DEPEND ON HOW WELL YOU BEHAVED, HOW MIGHT THAT CHANGE THE WAY YOU LIVE?

The elder brother — slaving rather than serving

▶Maybe you think that it's your behaviour that makes you acceptable to God — as the religious people clearly did. If so, you will struggle to make sense of what we just said. But you're not alone, as the story goes on to show.

Meanwhile, the older son was in the field. When he came near the house, he heard music and dancing. So he called one of the servants and asked him what was going on. "Your brother has come," he replied, "and your father has killed the fattened calf because he has him back safe and sound."

▶The older brother became angry and refused to go in. So his father went out and pleaded with him. But he answered his father, "Look! All these years I've been slaving for you and never disobeyed your orders. Yet you never gave me even a ▶young goat so I could celebrate with my friends. [Somewhere on the farm a goat looks up with a worried expression!] But when this son of yours [notice how the older brother has rejected his relationship with the younger brother] who has squandered your property with prostitutes comes home, you kill the fattened calf for him!"

▶ "My son," the father said, "you are always with me, and everything I have is yours. But we had to celebrate and be glad, because this brother of yours was dead and is alive again; he was lost and is found" (Luke 15:25–32).

There is this other character in the story who is often overlooked, but in many ways he is the one that Jesus was specifically addressing: The elder brother who did not throw everything back in his father's face. He stayed and worked hard. He always toed the line and did what was expected of him. He clearly represents the religious people of the day, the ones who thought they could please God by doing the right things, by behaving the right way.

He was completely unable to get his head around the concept of grace. To him, it's quite straightforward: You earn the father's favour by what you do. When his brother returned after all that he had done and, instead of being turned away or at the very least severely disciplined, he had a party thrown for him, this elder brother was incandescent with rage. You can almost hear him spluttering, "But, but, but... All these years I have done everything right. I've played by the rules. And you never threw a party for me. It's totally unfair!"

▶ He didn't understand that the father's love and acceptance was as little to do with his good outward behaviour as it was with the other son's bad outward behaviour. ▶ It is nothing to do with behaviour. It's all about grace.

This elder brother had an eye on the inheritance that he would one day receive in return for "slaving away" day after day as he put it. ▶ We imagine fathers taking their sons around the estate and saying, "One day son, all this will be yours." That's what this son was thinking. But this father says, "Everything I have is yours". "Look around you. It's already yours. Everything I have is yours."

He could have been enjoying everything the father had for years... ▶ but instead he slaved away thinking that he would have to earn the father's approval and his inheritance. In fact, the father just loved him anyway and the inheritance was there all along for him to enjoy. What a tragedy to go through life slaving away for something that in fact you've already got.

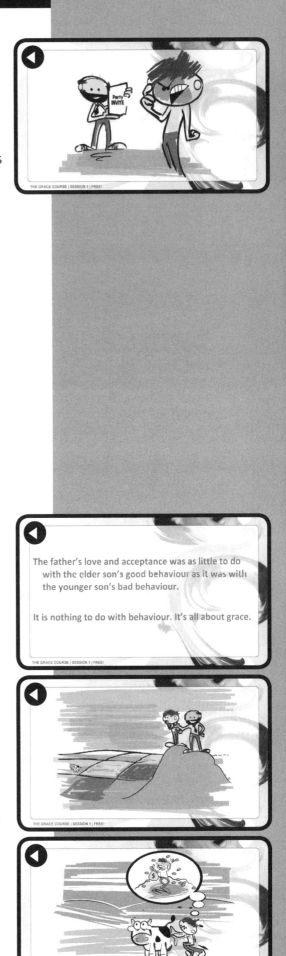

The father's love and acceptance was as little to do with the elder son's good behaviour as it was with the younger son's bad behaviour.

It is nothing to do with behaviour. It's all about grace.

Most Christians I know are like the elder brother. We do not know what we already have — or who we already are. Although theologically we know that the Christian life is about grace and not about obeying rules, we live in practice as if it's about how we behave. We know we are saved by grace but, although we would never put it like this, we end up thinking we have to maintain that salvation by what we do. We may not say it but in practice we show that what we believe is that what determines our right standing with God is how we behave.

The staggering point of the story that Jesus is telling is that your acceptance by God has nothing to do with how you behave. It's entirely down to His grace.

I am well aware that left to my own devices I would be very like the elder brother. Thinking back to when I was a teenager who had just become a Christian, when I went wrong and sinned — usually it was something like lustful thoughts — I didn't realize I could come straight back to God like the younger brother, but I somehow felt I had to earn my way back into God's favour. Yet I didn't dare approach Him because I felt I had let Him down, so I would spin off into the rough for weeks. When I finally did crawl back, I didn't feel worthy until I had had three really good quiet times in a row. That is not how God wants us to be.

The story of the labourers in the vineyard (Matthew 20:1-16)

▶There is a story you may not be familiar with, that Jesus told about some labourers in a vineyard (Matthew 20:1–16). The owner hired some workers in the marketplace early in the morning and offered them the standard payment of 1 denarius for a day's work. The owner went out a little later and hired more workers promising to pay them "whatever is right". He went out three more times and hired even more workers, the final time being "the 11th hour" when there was only an hour left to work.

▶When it came to paying them, they all received the same wage of one denarius no matter how long they had been working. The workers hired initially — even though they received exactly what they had been promised — were outraged. The owner's response was, "Am I not allowed to do what I choose with what belongs to me? Or do you begrudge my generosity?" (Matthew 20:15)

Again, the point is that, what you receive from God is determined by His generosity, not by our hard work. This is grace.

Are we "slaving" for God?

▶The younger son traded in the place of grace and privilege that he had been born into, and chose to walk away from relationship with his father. The elder brother didn't do that. Or did he? Actually he did.

It wasn't just the younger son who was having an identity crisis, and who had removed himself from his position of intimacy and joy of being at home with the father. In reality, neither of them stayed in relationship with him.

The younger brother found himself "in a far country" with the pigs. Although the elder brother never left home physically, in his heart he was a long way away too. ▶In the story, Jesus places him not with the father inside the home, enjoying fellowship as you might expect. Instead he is out in the fields with the hired servants, working hard or as he himself describes it, "slaving away".

This was a dishonourable place for the elder son to be. Instead of taking his place at the father's side, and enjoying the favour and blessings of being in the father's company that were his by right, he had, in effect, taken the identity of a hired servant, the identity that the younger son was also heading towards, thinking it was the best he could get in the circumstances.

The father's presence alone wasn't enough for the elder son. Rather he preferred to strive for what the father could give him, and was trying to make his father bless him by seeking to do everything right externally. But internally his heart was far away.

The younger brother walked away from his identity as son, but joyfully received it back through grace because he chose to turn back to the father. The older brother — who represented the religious people — walked away from it too but did not turn back. The father's grace was available to him just as it had been to his brother — but he didn't experience it because he chose not to turn away from his wrong thinking and turn back to his father.

Jesus was showing the religious people that if they thought that outward behaviour was what it took to earn God's favour, they were terribly deceived.

But what we do is still important

We want to make it clear that what we actually do in this life is very important. Paul tells us that, at the end of the age, there will be a day when what we have done… our works… will be tested. He uses the image of a building and says that Christ is the foundation and that we have a choice of how we build on that foundation:

▶ Now if anyone builds on the foundation with gold, silver, precious stones, wood, hay, straw — each one's work will become manifest, for the Day will disclose it, because it will be revealed by fire, and the fire will test what sort of work each one has done. If the work that anyone has built on the foundation survives, he will receive a reward. If anyone's work is burned up, he will suffer loss, though he himself will be saved, but only as through fire. (1 Corinthians 3:12–15)

▶ So there is a foundation of Christ laid by God's grace — and we have a choice as to how we build on it. When

these works are tested, fire will come and the works that are of no value… those done in our own strength, created by our own minds, designed to make us look good… the Bible calls them "wood, hay, straw" will be burned. While works that are of value… those God wants done and are done in His strength, for His honour — "gold, silver, precious stones" — will remain.

But what we do is still important

Now if anyone builds on the foundation with gold, silver, precious stones, wood, hay, straw — each one's work will become manifest, for the Day will disclose it, because it will be revealed by fire, and the fire will test what sort of work each one has done. If the work that anyone has built on the foundation survives, he will receive a reward. If anyone's work is burned up, he will suffer loss, though he himself will be saved, but only as through fire.

1 Corinthians 3:12-15

THE GRACE COURSE | SESSION 1 | FREE!

THE GRACE COURSE | SESSION 1 | FREE!

I don't know about you, but I'm not interested in one day watching much of my life go up in smoke.

▶ Now, Romans 8:1 assures us that there is no **condemnation** for those who are in Christ Jesus. It is clear that, even if your work is burned up, this is not a salvation issue. You are still saved but "only as through fire", turning up before God with nothing but a pair of singed eyebrows! But the big question is, ▶ will there be any **commendation**? Will the things we do in this life actually be of any value for eternity? The religious people thought that their religious works were good in themselves, but Jesus told them that since they were doing things just to impress other people they had already received their reward... men's approval. But there would be no reward from God.

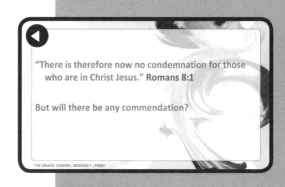

"There is therefore now no condemnation for those who are in Christ Jesus." **Romans 8:1**

But will there be any commendation?

So it's crucial that we understand how to build with gold, silver and precious stones.

Do you think you can look at what someone is doing and tell whether it is pleasing to God or not? Sometimes you can, but by no means always. Jesus tells us that some will come to Him and say, "Lord, Lord, did we not prophesy in your name, and cast out demons in your name, and do many mighty works in your name?" And then I will declare to them, "I never knew you; depart from me, you workers of lawlessness". (Matthew 7:22–23).

Two people can be doing exactly the same thing — feeding the poor perhaps, or spending an hour a day reading His word and praying. One will be delighting God, the other not. What's the difference?

It's not what, but why

When God chose David to be King of Israel, his family couldn't believe it because he was the youngest and smallest. His oldest brother thought he was a pest. But Samuel said, ▶ "The Lord sees not as man sees: man looks on the outward appearance, but the Lord looks on the heart" (1 Samuel 16:7b). Towards the end of the Old Testament, God makes a promise that He will write His laws not on tablets of stone but on our hearts (Jeremiah 31:33).

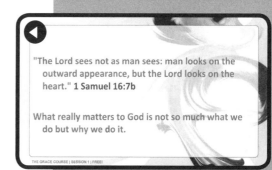

"The Lord sees not as man sees: man looks on the outward appearance, but the Lord looks on the heart." **1 Samuel 16:7b**

What really matters to God is not so much what we do but why we do it.

▶What is important to God is not so much **what** we do but **why** we do it. God has never taken pleasure from people just obeying a set of rules outwardly if they are not doing it from the heart.

▶That's the whole point of 1 Corinthians 13, the great "love chapter".

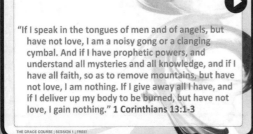

If I speak in the tongues of men and of angels, but have not love, I am a noisy gong or a clanging cymbal. And if I have prophetic powers, and understand all mysteries and all knowledge, and if I have all faith, so as to remove mountains, but have not love, I am nothing. If I give away all I have, and if I deliver up my body to be burned, but have not love, I gain nothing. (1 Corinthians 13:1–3)

The difference is what's happening inside. God judges the thoughts and attitudes of our hearts. It is not to do with our behaviour per se. It's all about our motivation. And if that motivation is not love, then what we do, no matter how good it looks, is worth precisely nothing. It's wood, hay or straw.

▶In 2 Corinthians 5:14 NIV, Paul says, "For Christ's love compels us". God wants our motivation to be love and nothing but love. But we can easily end up motivated by other things:

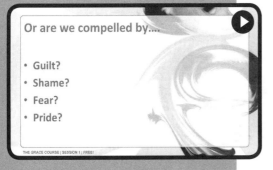

▶Guilt — I don't want God to be upset with me so I try my best to avoid going wrong. But I do what's wrong anyway, and end up feeling even more guilty and in a joyless cycle of self-condemnation.

▶Shame — this is where I know I am a disappointment to God and to others, but feel that if I can just be a better person maybe He'll think I'm worthy of His love.

▶Fear — I'm scared that God might be angry with me. I've heard the promises but they don't really seem to apply to me. Maybe I'm not a Christian at all. Maybe I've committed the unforgivable sin.

▶Pride — pride is like bad breath. Everyone knows you've got it except you! It can go something like this... I know I don't measure up to God's standards but there again who does? I feel much better if I compare myself with other people. I've really studied doctrine and theology and made sure that mine is absolutely right. I measure what others say against it.

In future sessions we will look at each of these issues and we'll have the opportunity to root out these false motivators, and ensure that it's love for Christ that compels us and nothing else.

PAUSE FOR THOUGHT 2

OBJECTIVE:

TO EXPLORE THE CONCEPT THAT WHAT MATTERS TO GOD IS NOT SO MUCH WHAT WE DO BUT WHY WE DO IT AND TO UNCOVER SOME WRONG MOTIVATIONS.

▶QUESTIONS (ON PAGE 15 OF THE PARTICIPANT'S GUIDE):

AT THE END OF JESUS' STORY, THE YOUNGER BROTHER HAS BEEN RECEIVED BACK AS A SON BUT THE ELDER BROTHER CONTINUES TO ACT LIKE A SLAVE. HOW MIGHT THEIR ATTITUDES DIFFER TOWARDS THE WORK THEY DO FOR THEIR FATHER?

GOD WANTS WHAT WE DO FOR HIM TO BE MOTIVATED PURELY BY LOVE. WHAT OTHER THINGS CAN MOTIVATE US INSTEAD? IF YOU ARE ABLE, SHARE HOW YOU HAVE BEEN MOTIVATED BY THESE THINGS.

IF WE REALIZE THAT WE HAVE BEEN MOTIVATED BY THINGS OTHER THAN LOVE, HOW CAN WE CHANGE?

What we do comes from who we are

▶Let's understand a key concept: What we do comes from who we are. Can I invite you to pause with me and consider two pictures:

▶The first picture, with the younger son at the point that he collapses into his father's arms and casts himself on his mercy. He can scarcely believe his father's grace as he realizes that, even though he richly deserves it, he will not

What we do comes from who we are

THE GRACE COURSE | SESSION 1 | FREE!

THE GRACE COURSE | SESSION 1 | FREE!

be punished. He knows that he is forgiven and accepted but he also knows that he is dirty, smelly and broken. He is acutely aware of his failure and deeply ashamed of what he has become. This is how many Christians see themselves: Forgiven but believing they are still essentially the same no-good, rotten people they always were.

It's as if our understanding of the Gospel stopped with Good Friday: Jesus died for my sins and I'm going to go to Heaven when I die. But nothing much changes right now.

But the father does not leave the son there.

▶Here's the second picture. The same son just a matter of minutes later is dressed in the finest robe, with the ring on his finger and the sandals on his feet, feasting on the finest food. He is still aware of his past failures, yet it is dawning on him that he has been not just forgiven but completely restored to his position as son, with free access to everything his father owns, along with great power and authority. He knows he doesn't deserve it at all. He realizes he is totally dependent on the father. It's almost unbelievable but it is actually happening.

Which picture most accurately represents how you see yourself in relation to God? In my experience most Christians get stuck on the first picture, knowing they're forgiven but still feeling like miserable sinners, constantly letting God down.

May we encourage you to move onto the second? We need to make it past Good Friday and through to Easter Sunday. I know you celebrate Easter Sunday, but what do you celebrate? That Jesus rose from the dead. He did, of course, but the whole point is that we rose from the dead with Him and became someone completely new; we need to know that we are now holy ones, saints, that we share God's very nature (2 Peter 1:4). And that's not all. We have also ascended with Christ to the right hand of the Father, the ultimate seat of power and authority in the whole universe. Like the younger son, we have been completely restored to the place of authority and honour.

In order to be free to be motivated by love, we have to know that we are more than just forgiven. We need to know that we are completely restored and deep down inside absolutely acceptable, and indeed a delight to God. And we can stay in that place of utter amazement at the Father's goodness and grace, and retain the healthy awareness that without Him we can't do a single thing of any eternal significance.

This concept that our acceptance by God and our new identity has nothing to do with our behaviour goes against the way you think it should work, doesn't it? It's not what many of us have learned as we've grown up as Christians. We have tended to be like the elder brother, acting as if what we do is the primary thing:

"What must I do to be accepted by God?"

"If you're a Christian, you're already accepted by God!"

"Yes, but what should I DO?"

Most churches have been happy to come up with a list of things to do: Read your Bible every day; come to church every week. Are those good things? Of course! But the problem is that discipleship often ends up becoming a load of rules. And we struggle to obey those rules because we've got things backwards. We think that God is "into" rules, when He's most concerned about relationship.

As part of the research done by the Barna Research Group, we asked people to respond to the statement: "Rigid rules and strict standards are an important part of the life and teaching of our church." We even used words that typically people would recoil at: "Rigid" and "strict". Still, do you care to know what percentage said they agreed with that statement? 66%! Two thirds! Now, I realize that some churches preach grace, but sadly people take it through their own clogged filters and still hear "law". In reality too many churches teach that you've got to work hard and "toe the line" for God to smile at you.

But the way it's supposed to work is that what we do comes from who we are, not vice versa. First we need to know who we are in Christ... God's loved, accepted and secure children.

Read many of Paul's letters to the churches and see how far you get before he gives an instruction on what to do or how to behave. You'll get halfway through at least. The first half is all about what has already been done, what

"If you love me, you will obey my commands."

John 14:15 NCV

you already have, who you already are in Christ. Paul knows that if you grasp that, the rest will flow naturally. ▶"If you love me, you will obey my commands" (John 14:15 NCV).

▶Come back to that picture of the younger brother standing there with the full rights and privileges of a son, yet knowing that he doesn't deserve it one bit. How do you think he will act from that point on? Won't he just want to do his very best for his father? Will it feel like "slaving away"? No! He will be grateful just to be in such an honoured position, and to have a father who loves him that much.

God's love and acceptance of you has nothing — nothing! — to do with your behaviour. But here's the rest of the story: When you stop trying to "act like you think a Christian should act" and just simply live from the truth of who you are now... guess what? You'll find you want to do what's right and you will! You will naturally... or rather SUPERnaturally... obey God!

Steve Goss says: I have spoken many times on the phone to a guy who had been diagnosed as paranoid schizophrenic, but found his freedom simply listening to our teaching and taking himself through *The Steps To Freedom In Christ*. He went from someone who was in

and out of mental institutions and on lots of medication, to someone who keeps leading people to the Lord. He has apparently lost 7.5 stone — that's over 100 pounds. I've never met him so I hope he didn't start at 9 stone.... He called me most recently because he had got into sexual sin with a girl. He had already resolved that God still loved him and dealt with the condemning voices. He had also broken off the relationship to ensure the sin did not repeat and then said, "I used to think God was a guy with a big stick. But now I know that He loves me. The reason I want to stop sinning is because I don't want to keep hurting Someone who loves me so much."

Paradoxically, understanding this concept is the key to behaving in a way that really honours God.

Bondslaves

You may need to explain what *The Steps To Freedom In Christ* process is. See page 19. Also recommend that participants make it a regular practice perhaps on an annual basis like a regular service for a car.

▶The word that the elder son uses for "slaving away" carries the meaning that you would expect from the translation, that of a slave with no rights whatsoever who is forced to obey his master. The New Testament term for a slave with no rights was "bondslave". Despite the fact that he was a son, the elder brother acted like a bondslave.

ndslaves

• Owned by someone else
• No rights whatsoever
• Had to do whatever their master commanded

• Yet former slaves who had been set free sometimes chose of their own free will to stay and serve

THE GRACE COURSE | SESSION 1 | FREE!

Interestingly this word "slave" seemed to take on a positive light in the early Church. Paul describes himself as a "slave of Christ" (Romans 1:1); in Mark 10:44 the disciples are called upon to be the "slave of all". How can slaving be good?

In New Testament times, it was very common for Roman masters to free their slaves. Perhaps they had completed their required service, or their masters were simply being generous. The slaves then became fully-fledged Roman citizens and many went on to do very well for themselves.

▶They were absolutely free to leave — but sometimes of their own free will they decided to stay and continue to serve in the household simply because of love for their master. From the outside what they did day-by-day probably didn't look very different, but there is in fact a world of difference between doing what you do because you are forced to and doing it simply out of love because you make a free choice.

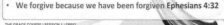

▶ We love because He first loved us (1 John 4:19).

We give freely because we have received freely (Matthew 10:8b).

We are merciful because He has been merciful to us (Luke 6:36).

We forgive because we have been forgiven (Ephesians 4:32).

In Christ you have been set free. But when you know His love as it really is, you are likely to decide of your own free will to make yourself His bondslave. We cannot do this if we have not yet understood what His grace means for us.

God the Father — looking for relationship

▶ So, Jesus said, "If you love me, you will obey my commands." (John 14:15 NCV) ▶ How do you hear Him saying that now? What expression do you imagine on His face? I hope you can see that He is simply stating a fact: "If you love me, you will obey my commands". He's not making a threat, "IF YOU LOVE ME, YOU'LL DO WHAT I SAY!" ▶ I'm certain He's smiling gently at you as He says it. It all starts by really getting to know the One who is love. Everything flows from that intimate relationship.

At the start of our experience of Jesus, we know we're the younger son. We know we need Him.

At that point we're meant to go on a journey of becoming like the Father, but most of us in fact end up becoming like the elder brother instead... slaving away for God.

Yes, we are bondslaves with a master. But consider this master. Is He a good master? Absolutely! He's a GREAT master! He has some significant works that He has prepared in advance for you to do, but He doesn't force you in any way to do them. He will love you whatever you do.

However, as you make a choice to serve Him just because you love Him, you'll find it becomes a real pleasure to do the work He gives you to do! But it all starts with knowing and growing in your understanding of the God of grace.

PAUSE FOR THOUGHT 3

OBJECTIVE:

TO UNDERSTAND THAT WE CAN MAKE A DECISION TO BECOME BONDSLAVES OF GOD BECAUSE HE IS THE PERFECT KIND, LOVING MASTER.

▶QUESTIONS (ON PAGE 19 OF THE PARTICIPANT'S GUIDE):

WHY MIGHT A BONDSLAVE WHO HAS BEEN GIVEN HIS FREEDOM CHOOSE TO REMAIN IN HIS FORMER POSITION, WITH HIS MASTER HAVING COMPLETE OWNERSHIP OF HIM AND CONTROL OVER HIM?

DO YOU FEEL READY TO MAKE A COMMITMENT TO GOD TO BE HIS BONDSLAVE, TO SERVE HIM NOT BECAUSE YOU ARE IN ANY WAY COMPELLED TO BUT SIMPLY BECAUSE YOU LOVE HIM?

Uncovering faulty thinking

▶Jesus said that it is knowing the truth that will set us free (John 8:32). If that is true, then it is believing lies that keeps us trapped. When the Spirit of God touches our lives, He often first exposes to our minds any faulty thinking we have picked up.

At the end of each session, we're going to pause and allow the Holy Spirit to reveal to us any areas where our belief system is not in line with what God tells us in His word is actually true. At the back of your Participant's Guide, there is a section entitled *Lies List.* This is a place where you can keep a running journal of what the Lord shows you during each of these sessions, and when we get to *The Steps To Experiencing God's Grace*, between Sessions 5 and 6, you will have the opportunity to deal with them and formulate a longer-term strategy for renewing your mind.

Let's pray: Lord, we have considered that amazing illustration You gave of the two brothers and their loving father. Would You draw our attention now to areas where we are struggling to believe what is actually true about You and our relationship with You. We ask that in the name of Jesus, the One who made our return to You possible. Amen.

As God draws your attention to a possible lie you have believed, write it down in the left-hand column of the *Lies List* on the last two pages of your Participant's Guide.

Maybe this session has highlighted lies such as:

* what I have done is too bad for God to forgive me or to accept me back

* God loves other people but He can't really love me

* I have to live up to a certain set of standards for God to be pleased with me

* God loves me more when I work hard for Him.

Before the next session, try to fill in the right column of the *Lies List* too by finding one or more verses from the Bible that state the direct opposite to the lie.

Imagine how different your life would be and how different your relationship with God would be if you didn't believe those things, but you were able to take hold of what God says is true in your heart — not just your head. As we go through this course, our prayer is that that is exactly what you will see taking place!

 # WITNESS

People who don't yet know God as their Father are like spiritual orphans. What do orphans need? How can I help meet that need?

 # IN THE COMING WEEK

The story of the two sons turns on the character of the father who, of course, represents God. He is not an inspecting sergeant-major figure looking for us to put a foot wrong. Jesus portrays a father who longs to fellowship with his sons. He runs to meet the younger son. He goes out to plead with the older son.

Sometimes our earthly fathers have not been all they might have been. Maybe we never knew our father. This makes it difficult to know God as the perfect Father He is because we tend to project our experiences onto Him. Use the My Father God statements overleaf every day this week (and for as long as it takes after that) to renounce lies that you may believe and joyfully affirm what is really true about Him.

 This would be a good point to hand out the "Welcome Home" Biblical Truth postcard (see page 15) and encourage people to use it to remind themselves of the truths learned in this session.

 The "In The Coming Week" sections are designed to help people bed down some of the truths they have learned. Encourage people to do them (but try to resist making it sound like compulsory "homework"!). Some people will derive significant benefit from this week's exercise.

My Father God

I RENOUNCE THE LIE THAT MY FATHER GOD IS:	I JOYFULLY ACCEPT THE TRUTH THAT MY FATHER GOD IS:
distant and uninterested in me.	intimate and involved (see Psalm 139:1–18).
insensitive and uncaring.	kind and compassionate (see Psalm 103:8–14).
stern and demanding.	accepting and filled with joy and love (see Romans 15:7; Zephaniah 3:17).
passive and cold.	warm and affectionate (see Isaiah 40:11; Hosea 11:3, 4).
absent or too busy for me.	always with me and eager to be with me (see Hebrews 13:5; Jeremiah 31:20; Ezekiel 34:11–16).
impatient, angry or never satisfied with what I do.	patient and slow to anger and delights in those who put their hope in His unfailing love (see Exodus 34:6; 2 Peter 3:9, Psalm 147:11).
mean, cruel or abusive.	loving and gentle and protective (see Jeremiah 31:3; Isaiah 42:3; Psalm 18:2).
trying to take all the fun out of life.	trustworthy and wants to give me a full life; His will is good, perfect and acceptable for me (see Lamentations 3:22, 23; John 10:10; Romans 12:1–2).
controlling or manipulative.	full of grace and mercy, and gives me freedom to fail (see Hebrews 4:15–16; Luke 15:11–16).
condemning or unforgiving.	tender-hearted and forgiving; His heart and arms are always open to me (see Psalm 130:1–4; Luke 15:17–24).
nit-picking or a demanding perfectionist.	committed to my growth and proud of me as His growing child (see Romans 8:28, 29; Hebrews 12:5–11; 2 Corinthians 7:14).

I am the Apple of His Eye!

Session 2:
INNOCENT!

Session 2: Innocent!

FOCUS VERSE:

Colossians 2:13–14 NASB: "When you were dead in your transgressions and the uncircumcision of your flesh, He made you alive together with Him, having forgiven us all our transgressions, having cancelled out the certificate of debt consisting of decrees against us, which was hostile to us; and He has taken it out of the way, having nailed it to the cross."

OBJECTIVE:

To understand that our true guilt before God was completely dealt with at the cross and that any guilt feelings that remain are not based on reality.

FOCUS TRUTH:

No matter what we have done (even as Christians) and no matter how guilty we may feel, the truth is that our guilt has been completely and utterly paid for by Christ's death on the cross so that we can stand confidently before God, who is pure and holy.

Leader's Notes

You may be surprised how few understand that the sin of one man, Adam, made the many guilty. It comes as a new concept to some that they had true guilt even before they sinned. And many struggle to take hold of the truth that the one Man, Jesus, brought grace and forgiveness. This is a good place in the course to make sure that people are certain of their salvation and invite any who are not yet Christians to consider taking that step.

For some people, this session will raise the question of what happens to unborn babies that die. Our advice is not to raise this topic yourself because it can lead to long fruitless discussions but, if it is raised, you can say that the Bible makes no definitive statement on this subject and Christians have come to different views. Most — but not all — end up concluding that, through some mechanism that we don't understand, God is able to save those who are unborn through the sacrifice of Jesus. At the end of the day, however, we do not know the answer. What we do know is that God is love and that He is a God of perfect justice. He will not do anything unjust or unloving. Advise those for whom this is a pertinent issue to focus on God's love and perfect justice and to come to a place where they are able to trust Him to do the right thing.

This session is about a fundamental truth of the Gospel that many Christians may feel they already know well enough. But no matter how well they know the theology, in practice most Christians struggle with some level of guilt feelings. We want participants to leave the session having put that struggle to rest once and for all.

SMALL GROUP TIMINGS:

Welcome	5 minutes	0:05
Worship, prayer & declaration	8 minutes	0:13
Word part 1	18 minutes	0:31
Pause For Thought 1	20 minutes	0:51
Word part 2	25 minutes	1:16
Pause For Thought 2	15 minutes	1:31
Word part 3	19 minutes	1:50
Pause For Thought 3	8 minutes	1:58
Word part 4	2 minutes	2:00

 WELCOME

Which road sign would best describe where you are on your journey with God right now? (eg, stop, steep gradient, diversion/detour, crossroads)

 WORSHIP

Suggested theme: Thank You for the cross! See John 14:6.

Take a few minutes to pause before another "sign" — the cross of Jesus Christ, an event that is THE turning point not only in history but particularly in our own life story. The cross was God re-opening the way to Himself.

As people are reminded of the enormity of what God did, invite them to worship Him.

PRAYER & DECLARATION

Father, by Your Spirit, please show us life-changing truths that will set us free to experience Your gift of life in all its fullness. Amen.

In Christ, I am forgiven and declared innocent of all the charges that were stacked against me. So by the authority of the Lord Jesus Christ I command any accusing and condemning thoughts in my mind to go now.

 Again, encourage people to say the declaration boldly and loudly. Remind them that in Christ, they have power and authority because they are seated with Him at the right hand of the Father far above all power and authority (see Ephesians 1:18-21, 2:6).

 **WORD**

Introduction

I love reading what is written on gravestones. These examples are absolutely true.

On the grave of a coal miner: "Gone Underground For Good". On a dentist's grave in Scotland: "Stranger tread this ground with gravity. Dentist Brown is filling his last cavity." On an Auctioneer's grave: "Going! Going!! Gone!!!" On a waiter's grave: "Here lies the body of Detlof Swenson. Waiter. God finally caught his eye."

My all-time favourite is on the grave of the comedian, Spike Milligan: "I told you I was ill."

A pastor had a dream. ▶In it he saw what he thought was his gravestone with the inscription, "He failed to live up to expectations." It made him realize how conditioned he was to try and live up to expectations rather than to give and serve out of God's grace and love. He said it was a struggle to come out of that way of thinking but when he did, in his words, "Liberation was sweet!"

"He failed to live up to expectations". Many of us walk around with the sense that we are failing miserably as sons and daughters of God. We try really hard to live up to the standards that we believe we should, but often fall short. So we end up in a near-permanent state of beating ourselves up. We find it impossible to feel good unless we perform perfectly... which of course we never do.

God's way of living is just totally opposite to how we normally think. So if all this grace stuff sounds strange to you, don't worry. You'll get used to it and find it's actually a great way to live!

[The following story is from Rich Miller. You could share one of your own to illustrate the same point.]

On my first visit to the UK, it took some getting used to the fact that the driver sits in the front right seat and cars drive on the left side of the road. Early on, I remember seeing a car coming toward me with a big dog sitting up in the left front seat. "My gosh!" I yelled out, "The Brits have got their dogs driving!" Driving was really scary. I remember everything being counter-intuitive. I was sitting in the right front seat instead of the left. I was shifting gears with my left hand instead of my right. I was driving on the wrong side of the road… okay the left side of the road… instead of the right. And turning corners was the exact opposite of what I was used to! And I had six clueless kids counting on me to get them around safely. I was a stressed-out wreck! I had to talk myself through everything I did. But eventually it became second nature.

If you feel a bit that way about grace you are not alone. Many people have a really hard time getting their minds around God's unconditional love and acceptance. Grace-living can seem so strange, the exact opposite of what we are used to, while living with guilt can actually feel… in a weird way… normal.

In the study we referred to last time, almost 60% of Christians surveyed admitted that they believe they do not live up to God's expectations of them. In other words, they have come to simply live with a "low grade fever" of guilt in their lives.

The problem with a life filled with guilt is that you can become like either the younger or the elder brother. Either you end up with an increasingly wasted life or you try harder to work off the guilt. The motivation for your efforts to avoid sin and do good is a futile effort to somehow gain or maintain God's love, rather than first resting in the unconditional love of God and then being motivated by love to serve.

In his letter to the Galatians, the apostle Paul cried out to God's people, "What has happened to all your joy?" (Galatians 4:15 NIV) Maybe you are asking yourself the same question.

[Do you have a story of your own to use instead of this one from Rich Miller?]

I remember a time some time after becoming a Christian when I felt really guilty. It was my 19th birthday. Even though I knew it was wrong, I was getting drunk anyway. My buddies didn't care. But all of a sudden, one of my friends burst into the dormitory where we were drinking. "Your brother is coming!" Oh no! It was like the apostle Paul had just shown up. When he came in, he saw immediately what was going on and got this really disappointed look on his face. I felt about this small. Then he handed me my present. I knew I was in trouble. It was a book, *The Master Plan of Evangelism* by Robert Coleman. I wanted to crawl into a hole.

Steve Goss says: "I **always** used to feel guilty! When I first became a Christian, it felt like I was a worm crawling into God's presence. There was very little joy."

▶ What is guilt?

▶ We tend to think of guilt as primarily a feeling (as in "I feel really guilty for saying that"), when in fact true guilt has nothing to do with feelings. It's about hard facts.

▶ Guilt is a legal term, used in a court room where a judge or jury, after hearing the facts of the case, comes to a decision that the charge against the defendant is true and pronounces him guilty.

Guilt is defined in relation to the legal authority which has laid down the laws. If we break the laws of that legal authority we are guilty. If we do not, we are innocent. Remember the two robbers, one crucified on either side of the Lord Jesus?

> ▶ One of the criminals who were hanged railed at him (Christ), saying, "Are you not the Christ? Save yourself and us!" But the other rebuked him, saying, "Do you not fear God, since you are under the same sentence of condemnation? And we indeed justly, for we are receiving the due reward of our deeds, but this man has done nothing wrong" (Luke 23:39–41).

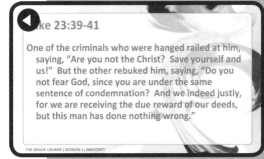

The second robber knew that both he and the first robber were guilty before the law of the land and that the law demanded physical death by crucifixion for the crimes they had committed. They were getting what they deserved.

But that wasn't the end of the matter. There is a higher legal authority, God Himself, to whom all of us must eventually give account. We know that, at the very least, the two robbers had broken one of the Ten Commandments, "You shall not steal", so they were guilty before God as well.

Now, a defendant may not feel guilty; his family may not feel he is guilty; even the public may not feel he is guilty. But if he committed the crime, he is guilty.

▶So there is true guilt and there are guilt feelings and the two are not the same thing. True guilt is not a question of feelings but of facts. Our guilt feelings (or lack of them) are not a reliable guide to our true guilt.

Are you guilty?

▶What about you and me? Are we guilty? Do we have TRUE guilt? We may be law-abiding citizens, innocent before the laws of the land. But where do we stand before the heavenly Judge?

▶Before we can answer that, we need to remind ourselves of just who God is. You can't really appreciate God's grace without somehow grasping at some level God's holiness.

God's holiness

God is holy. The Old Testament often refers to Him as "Holy, holy, holy", the word repeated three times to emphasize the mind-boggling extent of His holiness. I hope you like the nice PowerPoint illustrations we have for this course. At this point, the illustrator was asked to come up with one to illustrate God's holiness. He couldn't do it so we have a blank screen! The trouble is, we simply can't get our minds fully around God's holiness. This is what A.W. Tozer says:

True guilt and guilt feelings are not the same thing.

THE GRACE COURSE | SESSION 2 | INNOCENT!

Are you guilty?

THE GRACE COURSE | SESSION 2 | INNOCENT!

Understanding God's holiness

"We cannot grasp the true meaning of the divine holiness by thinking of someone or something very pure and then raising the concept to the highest degree we are capable of. God's holiness is not simply the best we know infinitely bettered. We know nothing like the divine holiness. It stands apart, unique, unapproachable, incomprehensible and unattainable."

(A.W. Tozer, *The Knowledge of the Holy*)

THE GRACE COURSE | SESSION 2 | INNOCENT!

▶"We cannot grasp the true meaning of the divine holiness by thinking of someone or something very pure and then raising the concept to the highest degree we are capable of. God's holiness is not simply the best we know infinitely bettered. We know nothing like the divine holiness. It stands apart, unique, unapproachable, incomprehensible and unattainable." (A.W. Tozer; *The Knowledge of the Holy*)

One thing we do know about God's holiness. It is such that it would be impossible for Him to tolerate sin, to sweep it under the rug, to say it didn't matter. He wouldn't be God if He did.

When He created the universe, this earth and human beings, the big question was this: ▶Would He make us as robots that had to obey, where He in effect held a remote control in His hand so that it would be impossible for us to do wrong, ▶or would He give us the ability to make genuine choices, despite the risk that that would lead to sin and we would therefore not be able to stay in His presence?

God's choice was to give us free will. So our ancestor, Adam, was created perfect and innocent yet with the capacity to choose good or evil. God didn't burden him with a whole load of rules, but told him he could do whatever he wanted, except one thing that God knew would harm him and others: he was not to eat from a certain tree.

The consequence of sin

Deceived by God's enemy, Satan, Eve ate from the tree, and her husband, Adam, chose to disobey God. That disobedience is the essence of what the Bible calls sin. ▶Paul tells us the consequences of that disobedience: "The wages of sin is death" (Romans 6:23). Adam incurred true guilt before God because He had broken God's law. There were enormous consequences: he was cut off from relationship with God and cast out of His presence; he lost the spiritual life he had been given.

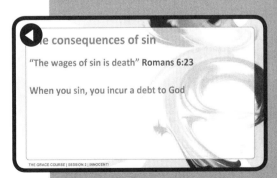

▶In many languages the words "sin" and "debt" are the same. They are in Greek. That's why some people say the Lord's Prayer as "Forgive us our sins", and others prefer "Forgive us our debts". Either way, it's helpful to understand that when you sin, you incur a debt to God.

If you are found guilty before a human court, you incur a debt too. Payment for breaking the law is usually demanded either in the form of a financial penalty (a fine) or time that you have to serve in prison. Once that debt is paid... either as a fine or jail time... you are declared free.

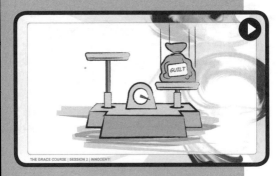

The consequences of sin

"The wages of sin is death" **Romans 6:23**

When you sin, you incur a debt to God

"By the one man's disobedience the many were made sinners" **Romans 5:19**

▶Scales are often used to symbolize justice. In the heavenly courts of justice, sin weighs down one side and so payment needs to be made on the other until they are both level again.

Adam, however, had no resources to pay the debt he had incurred to God, so it was passed down to the next generation, who also couldn't pay. And it has now come all the way down to us. Talking about Adam, ▶Paul says, "by the one man's disobedience the many were made sinners" (Romans 5:19). In other words, when Adam sinned, one of the consequences is that you and I and all the rest of Adam's descendants were made guilty before God too.

That takes some getting your mind around. By way of illustration, think about the National Debt of your country. On the day that it was announced that the National Debt of the UK had exceeded one trillion dollars for the first time, the British media worked out that every British citizen owed the equivalent of £16,400, over $26,000. Imagine a baby born that day. Through no fault of its own, but just by being born British and the overspending of earlier generations, it immediately had a debt of £16,400.

PAUSE FOR THOUGHT 1

OBJECTIVE:

TO CONSOLIDATE THE TEACHING ON THE CONSEQUENCES OF ADAM'S SIN AND HELP PEOPLE START TO DISTINGUISH BETWEEN TRUE GUILT AND GUILT FEELINGS.

▶QUESTIONS (ON PAGE 26 OF THE PARTICIPANT'S GUIDE):

SHARE WITH THE GROUP WHAT THE WORD "DEBT" BRINGS TO MIND. HAVE YOU EVER HAD A DEBT YOU COULDN'T PAY?

WHAT HAPPENED THAT CAUSED US TO BEGIN OUR LIVES OWING GOD A HUGE DEBT WE COULDN'T PAY? HOW DO YOU FEEL ABOUT THAT?

CAN YOU THINK OF AN EXAMPLE OF A TIME WHEN YOU OR SOMEONE ELSE DID SOMETHING WRONG, BUT DID NOT FEEL GUILTY, OR CONVERSELY FELT GUILTY FOR SOMETHING THAT WASN'T ACTUALLY WRONG?

Have you ever noticed that you need to train a child to share but you don't need to train him to be selfish?

▶We came across a great example of this, it's called the Property Laws of a Toddler:

1. If I like it, it's mine.

2. If it's in my hand, it's mine.

3. If I can take it from you, it's mine.

4. If I had it a little while ago, it's mine.

5. If it's mine, it must never appear to be yours in any way.

6. If it looks like mine, it is mine.

7. If I saw it first, it's mine.

8. If you are playing with something and you put it down, it's mine.

9. If it's broken... it's yours!

There are actually three avenues by which the human race apart from Christ has guilt. The first is what we have been talking about... our natural bent toward doing evil: It is the twistedness of the human heart that has been passed down through Adam and shows up in different ways in different families. The second way is through our out-and-out rebellion... intentionally doing what is wrong, shaking our fist at God and His law, so to speak. The third area is when you miss the mark. This means that even when we seek to do that which is right and make our best effort, we still fall short. These three things comprise the true state of guilt for everyone apart from Christ.

Whichever way our independence from God manifests itself in our lives, there is no system by which we can... by ourselves... rid ourselves of our guilt. That is where grace comes in.

Getting rid of guilt

▶In Roman times, if someone was found guilty of breaking the law and sent to prison, an itemized list was made of everything they had done wrong and the corresponding time they had to serve in order to pay the debt. It was in fact called a "Certificate of Debt" and was nailed to the cell door.

Every single person who came after Adam was born with a Certificate of Debt to God. Of course, we are not aware of it. But we do gradually become aware of a sense of guilt, a sense of not measuring up. We don't like that feeling so we want to get rid of it, to feel that we are OK. We tend to try one of three strategies to get rid of the negative feelings.

We may not phrase it like this but in effect we are trying to be declared not guilty or, to use the legal term, to be "justified".

Strategies to get rid of guilt that don't work

Justification by good works

▶Probably the most popular strategy is trying to make yourself right with God by good works; where we try to feel good about ourselves by what we do. We are, in effect, trying to prove our innocence before God by doing good things, perhaps keeping the commandments; reading the Bible; attending church regularly; giving money to the church or to the poor; feeding the hungry; and so on.

Now, all these good works (often referred to in the Bible as "works of the Law") are... well... good. They are not evil. But does loading one side of the measuring scale of our lives with good works overcome the weight of the sins that pile up on the other side? Many of us used to think perhaps that God has a big scale and on one side He would put our sin and on the other our good deeds. If at the end of our life, our good deeds outweighed our bad deeds, we would go to Heaven. ▶Paul, in his letter to the Galatians, says clearly that "a person is not justified by the works of the law" and again, "because by the works of the law no one will be justified." (Galatians 2:16)

That's pretty clear! Good works don't remove our guilt. Not one bit. But you knew that already didn't you? Or did you.... ?

Well, try answering these questions:

- Are you filled with a sense of God's eagerness to bless you, confident of His love for you only when you feel you are doing well as a Christian?

- What happens when you fail to do the things on your spiritual "To Do" list or mess up and do something on your spiritual "To Don't" list? Do those feelings change?

- Are you plagued by a vague, nagging, gnawing sense that God is distant and somehow disapproving of you?

- Do you tend to make a vow to yourself or to God that "I'll do better tomorrow!", and determine to work twice as hard the next day to please Him?

I know that you know that you are not saved by good works — but when it comes to our day-to-day lives, it's easy to think that God changes the rules. We can subtly end up thinking that to remain in God's good graces... to be sure of His love for us... we have to perform well spiritually.

It's almost like we have confused Jesus with Santa Claus! You know, "You'd better watch out, you'd better not cry, you'd better not pout — I'm telling you why... Jesus Christ

Justification by good works

... yet we know that a person is not justified by works of the law but through faith in Jesus Christ, so we also have believed in Christ Jesus, in order to be justified by faith in Christ and not by works of the law, because by works of the law no one will be justified. **Galatians 2:16**

THE GRACE COURSE | SESSION 2 | INNOCENT!

is coming to town. He's making a list, checking it twice, gonna find out who's naughty and nice..." So we try really hard to do right and make God happy, afraid that if we don't perform well, He will ignore us or reject us or even bring some horrible tragedy into our lives.

Justification by religious background

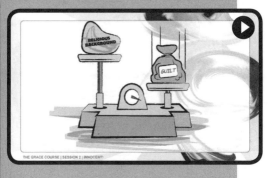

▶Another strategy that doesn't work is trying to make yourself right with God by your religious background, thinking that God will accept you because of your religious upbringing, or religious acts that you do.

The Jewish leaders tried to play this card with John the Baptist and with Jesus, falling back on being "children of Abraham." In other words, they were declaring a form of diplomatic immunity to being guilty because they were part of the chosen people, the Jewish nation. John told them that God could turn rocks into children of Abraham if He wanted to! (Matthew 3:9)

The apostle Paul admitted that he too once put his trust in his religious background:

▶If anyone else thinks he has reason for confidence in the flesh, I have more: circumcised on the eighth day, of the people of Israel, of the tribe of Benjamin, a Hebrew of Hebrews; as to the law, a Pharisee; as to zeal, a persecutor of the church; as to righteousness under the law, blameless. (Philippians 3:4–6 NASB)

Maybe you've been a good Baptist, Methodist or whatever, all your life. You have lived up to the standards required. You are a "pillar of the church", holding it all together perhaps.

But our religious backgrounds mean nothing to God, apart from Christ, and they have no power to remove our guilt. Paul himself came to realize, ▶"But whatever things were gain to me, those things I have counted as loss for the sake of Christ" (Philippians 3:7 NASB). He goes on to use a word usually translated "rubbish" to describe all that he used to trust in for justification, that is, his religious background.

Translators of our English Bibles have tended to chicken out of translating the Greek word for "rubbish" literally, because most people would regard it as unacceptably coarse. Suffice to say that it's something nasty you can step in if you're not taking care when out walking in the streets! That's how worthless all our religious activity is when it comes to removing our guilt.

Justification by comparison

▶ Here's a third way you can try to justify yourself: trying to make yourself right with God by comparing yourself to other people. This shows up in thoughts like, "Well, at least I don't do_____ like so and so." And we fill in the blank with some kind of sin that we deem worse than anything we have ever done, and feel better about ourselves. In Luke 18:10–14, Jesus told a parable:

> ▶ "Two men went up into the temple to pray, one a Pharisee and the other a tax collector. The Pharisee, standing by himself, prayed thus: "God, I thank you that I am not like other men, extortioners, unjust, adulterers, or even like this tax collector. I fast twice a week; I give tithes of all that I get." But the tax collector, standing far off, would not even lift up his eyes to heaven, but beat his breast, saying, "God, be merciful to me, a sinner!" I tell you, this man went down to his house justified, rather than the other. For everyone who exalts himself will be humbled, but the one who humbles himself will be exalted."

So, if all our good works don't remove our guilt; and if all our religious activity doesn't remove our guilt; and if God isn't impressed with how much better a person we are than someone else, how in the world can we be free from this deadly guilt?

God's remedy for guilt

And just as all people were made sinners as the result of the disobedience of one man, in the same way they will be put right with God as the result of the obedience of the one man.

Romans 5:17 GNT

THE GRACE COURSE | SESSION 2 | INNOCENT!

Colossians 2:13-14 NASB

When you were dead in your transgressions and the uncircumcision of your flesh, He made you alive together with Him, having forgiven us all our transgressions, having cancelled out the certificate of debt consisting of decrees against us, which was hostile to us; and He has taken it out of the way, having nailed it to the cross.

THE GRACE COURSE | SESSION 2 | INNOCENT!

"...having forgiven us all our transgressions, having cancelled out the certificate of debt..."

THE GRACE COURSE | SESSION 2 | INNOCENT!

God's remedy for guilt

▶You may be struggling with the concept that one man could represent us all and make us all guilty, but thankfully it worked both ways:

> ▶And just as all people were made sinners as the result of the disobedience of one man [Adam], in the same way they will be put right with God as the result of the obedience of the one man [Jesus]. (Romans 5:17 GNT — words in square brackets added by us for clarification)

▶We were all born with a Certificate of Debt. But Colossians 2:13–14 (NASB) says:

> When you were dead in your transgressions and the uncircumcision of your flesh, He made you alive together with Him, having forgiven us all our transgressions, having cancelled out the certificate of debt consisting of decrees against us, which was hostile to us; and He has taken it out of the way, having nailed it to the cross.

▶How can Jesus' death on the cross cancel out our Certificate of Debt and resolve our guilt? Normally a guilty Roman criminal had to pay for their own debts by spending the allotted time in prison. However, it was technically possible to find someone else who would take their place in the cell and serve out the required time on their behalf as their substitute.

▶That is what Jesus has done, potentially for every person who has ever lived or ever will. His sacrifice is enough to balance the scales for every sin, because He is that unimaginably holy God. When He created us and chose to give us free will, He knew that it would inevitably lead to the point where God Himself would choose to lay down His life out of pure grace.

The thing about God's grace is that He doesn't force us to accept this free offer. Every person has the choice whether or not to receive this gift, but if you do, that's it. It is finished. Absolutely. Completely. Forever.

▶When the Roman prisoner had served out the full time allotted, when he had paid his debt to society, he was released. A judge would take the yellowed, tattered Certificate of Debt and write "PAID IN FULL" across it and he once again became "not guilty" of those crimes. We, on the other hand, could never pay off our sin debt to God, so Jesus took our penalty of sin Himself and paid it.

Just before Jesus died on the cross, He let out a loud, victorious shout (Matthew 27:50) which is usually translated "It is finished" (John 19:30). The word that Jesus used is the exact same word that the Roman judge wrote across the released criminal's Certificate of Debt: "PAID IN FULL!"

▶ So, how many of our sins have been forgiven according to this passage in Colossians? **All!** So, how much guilt do we still have for our sins? None! Absolutely none!

The sacrifice of God's Son is the only thing big enough to outweigh the guilt from our sin.

Go back to that picture of the gravestone, "Failed to live up to expectations." That verdict can never be applied to you. In Christ all God's expectations of you have been met in full.

The best a human court can do is to declare you "not guilty". God's grace goes further than that and declares you "innocent". To all intents and purposes, as far as God is concerned it's as if what you did never took place. This declaration of "innocent" is not just for when we first came to Christ. God's grace is for every moment of every day. For those in Christ Jesus, no sin we commit can ever take away one bit from the full and complete sacrifice Jesus paid for us. Despite our sin, we are still forgiven. Our guilt is still gone. Forever.

God does not have a list and He is not checking it twice to see who is naughty and nice. The "sin list" doesn't exist. The Certificate of Debt has been nailed to the cross — completely dealt with. What does exist is the Lamb's Book of Life in which our names are written.

Last time I jokingly asked you to write down the worst thing you had done and then asked what welcome you would get if you went out and did it again — and then sincerely came back to God. One lady said she looked around and knew that everyone else in the room could be forgiven, but looking at herself, she said she couldn't quite believe her sins would be forgiven.

▶ When you look in the mirror and remember all the terrible things you have done or that have been done to you, perhaps you believe deep down in your heart that you

are different. Too dirty to be loved; too bad to be forgiven. Maybe you have a hard time believing that this really applies to you because you don't live up to God's expectations.

None of us live up to God's expectations. But Jesus has lived up to them on our behalf as our substitute. The writer to the Hebrews tell us that "There is no longer any sacrifice for sin" (Hebrews 10:17–18). Your guilt is gone!

Simon and the sinful woman (Luke 7:36–50)

▶In Luke 7:36–50 we find a story that may help us grasp this. Let's set the stage.

A Pharisee (strict religious Jew) by the name of Simon, invited Jesus over for supper and things were going along pretty well. But then a Pharisee's worst nightmare happened. A prostitute, who was clearly not part of the evening's entertainment, walked in. But she didn't just stand there and drool over the food or check out potential new clients. She did something almost unbelievable. She stood behind Jesus and went to pieces, her tears showering Jesus' feet. She bent down and tried to dry His feet with her hair, kissing His feet in the process. And if that weren't enough, she dumped an expensive bottle of perfume, which she had no doubt purchased from her "earnings", all over Jesus' feet so that the whole house was filled with the aroma.

Simon and the prostitute form quite a contrast. Simon was confident in his religious background and all the good things he did. He saw himself as a fine, upstanding member of society. He didn't realize his guilt before God. He certainly didn't feel guilty.

The woman, on the other hand, knew that she was guilty. She made a living by selling her body. She knew her life was a mess. She knew her guilt. Jesus didn't ignore or "sugar coat" her sins — He spoke of her "many sins" (verse 47) — but He graciously received her acts of remorse and repentance.

He wasn't repulsed by her touch, and He didn't tell her to go away and clean up her life.

At supper, Jesus reminded the guests of the sinful woman's loving actions and contrasted them with Simon's failure to provide Jesus with what would have been customary kindnesses, such as greeting guests with a kiss and washing the dust off their feet as they arrived. Then He blew everyone away when He said:

> "Therefore I tell you, her sins, which are many, are forgiven — for she loved much. But he who is forgiven little, loves little." And he said to her, "Your sins are forgiven." Then those who were at table with him began to say among themselves, "Who is this, who even forgives sins?" And he said to the woman, "Your faith has saved you; go in peace." (Luke 7:47–50)

So how is it that a law-abiding man of good standing remains guilty before God, while a lady who had been up to that point engaged in what many would see as the ultimate sinful life is declared innocent? Jesus told her that her faith had saved her.

Can you see what makes the difference between the two? It's not the amount of sin that each had committed. It's not even the seriousness of the sin that each had committed. It's quite simply that one responded to Jesus in faith. And the other didn't.

It's the same with the two robbers who were crucified with Jesus. Both were guilty before God. Yet one of them responded to Jesus in faith and was immediately pronounced "not guilty". Jesus promised that he would be with Him in paradise later that very day.

If appropriate to your group, you could perhaps at this point invite people to make a decision to turn to Christ for the first time.

▶The apostle Paul explains, "For by grace you have been saved through faith. And this is not your own doing; it is the gift of God" (Ephesians 2:8).

Being declared innocent is a pure grace gift from God. It is activated by faith. What does that look like? Simply turning to Him in sheer desperation and asking Him for salvation. The woman didn't deserve forgiveness, just like we don't. But she desperately needed it, just like we do. And Jesus freely gave it to her in response to her faith and sent her away in peace.

By faith in Jesus Christ we stand in grace... forgiven, justified, at peace with God. The war is over. ▶There is therefore now no condemnation for those who are in Christ Jesus (Romans 8:1). What does "now" mean? **Now!** What does "no" mean? **No!**

You too can go from here today in peace, knowing that your true guilt is gone forever, that you meet God's righteous expectations in Christ. Jesus says to you too who have trusted in Him alone to cleanse you, "Your sins are forgiven... Your faith has saved you; go in peace."

PAUSE FOR THOUGHT 2

OBJECTIVE:
TO HELP PEOPLE DEAL WITH FALSE EXPECTATIONS AND TO INTRODUCE THEM TO THE CONCEPT OF ASKING THE HOLY SPIRIT TO REVEAL ISSUES AND THEN RENOUNCING THOSE ISSUES THAT WE WILL USE IN *THE STEPS TO EXPERIENCING GOD'S GRACE.*

▶**EXERCISE (ON PAGE 31 OF THE PARTICIPANT'S GUIDE):**

WE'RE GOING TO ASK GOD TO REVEAL TO US ALL OF THE FALSE EXPECTATIONS AND STANDARDS THAT WE HAVE FELT WE HAVE TO LIVE UP TO AND WHICH HAVE BECOME A BURDEN TO US OR MADE US FEEL LIKE FAILURES. PRAY TOGETHER:

LOVING FATHER, I THANK YOU THAT IN CHRIST ALL OF YOUR EXPECTATIONS OF ME HAVE BEEN FULLY MET, (ROMANS 8:4) AND THAT YOU HAVE FORGIVEN ME ALL MY TRANSGRESSIONS AND CANCELLED OUT MY CERTIFICATE OF DEBT BY NAILING IT TO THE CROSS (COLOSSIANS 2:13-14). I CONFESS THAT I HAVE BELIEVED THE LIE THAT I HAVE NEEDED SOMETHING MORE THAN CHRIST IN ORDER TO GAIN OR MAINTAIN ACCEPTANCE WITH YOU AND OTHERS. PLEASE WOULD YOU REVEAL TO ME NOW ALL THE EXPECTATIONS, STANDARDS AND DEMANDS THAT I HAVE BEEN LIVING UNDER, BY WHICH I HAVE SOUGHT TO BECOME MORE ACCEPTABLE AND FEEL LESS GUILTY, SO THAT I CAN RETURN IN SIMPLE FAITH TO RELYING JUST ON CHRIST'S WORK ON MY BEHALF. I ASK THIS IN THE NAME OF JESUS CHRIST, WHO DIED FOR ME. AMEN.

▶THEN SPEND TIME JUST BETWEEN YOU AND GOD WRITING DOWN THE FALSE EXPECTATIONS HE SHOWS YOU ON A SEPARATE SHEET. CONSIDER THE FOLLOWING:

* EXPECTATIONS YOU WRONGLY BELIEVED WERE FROM GOD
* EXPECTATIONS FROM PARENTS AND FAMILY
* EXPECTATIONS FROM TEACHERS
* EXPECTATIONS FROM CHURCHES AND CHURCH LEADERS
* EXPECTATIONS FROM EMPLOYERS
* OTHER FALSE EXPECTATIONS

THEN FOR EACH FALSE EXPECTATION THAT YOU HAVE LISTED, SAY THE FOLLOWING:

I RENOUNCE THE LIE THAT I HAVE TO LIVE UP TO THE EXPECTATION OF: _____ IN ORDER TO FEEL GOOD ENOUGH, VALUED OR ACCEPTED. THANK YOU, LORD JESUS, THAT IN YOU I MEET ALL OF GOD'S EXPECTATIONS AND THAT NOTHING I COULD DO COULD MAKE YOU LOVE ME MORE OR LOVE ME LESS. AMEN.

FINALLY, TEAR UP THE LIST YOU MADE AND MOVE ON!

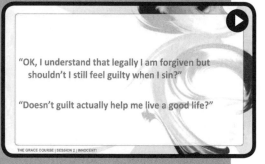

"OK, I understand that legally I am forgiven but shouldn't I still feel guilty when I sin?"

"Doesn't guilt actually help me live a good life?"

Aren't guilt feelings helpful?

▶We've made a distinction in this session between what you might call "true guilt" before God, which refers to our legal position before Him, and "guilt feelings". Maybe you are thinking, "OK, I understand that legally I am forgiven, but shouldn't I still feel guilty when I sin? Doesn't guilt actually help me live a good life?"

Maybe in school you were given an English assignment in which you were given the first part of a story and then had to come up with an ending. If you had been given the story of the two brothers from Luke 15, how would you have finished the story?

Maybe you would have painted the picture of the father very differently from the way Jesus did.

▶Maybe you think he should have been at least a little bit angry, maybe even turning his back and looking the other way as his son approached? Maybe you think that the way the father so quickly forgave his son and restored him to the family was a bit foolish... a little premature in fact... that the father would have been wiser to make the son prove the sincerity of his repentance for a while before having a party thrown for him. ▶Maybe a better strategy on the part of the father would have been to make his son feel really guilty about what he did... at least for a while. After all, he really blew it. Isn't guilt perhaps a very effective deterrent to sin?

Paul saw some significant sin in the Corinthian church. Unlike the younger brother, they clearly did not realize the problem and were certainly not yet "coming back home" in repentance. He felt he had to write a very tough letter to the Corinthian church to help them become aware of their sin, and he clearly agonized over it before he sent it. But in a subsequent letter he was able to rejoice at the positive effect the first letter had had on them.

▶I ... rejoice, not that you were made sorrowful, but that you were made sorrowful to the point of repentance; .... For the sorrow that is according to the will of God produces a repentance without regret, leading to salvation, but the sorrow of the world produces death. (2 Corinthians 7:9–10 NASB)

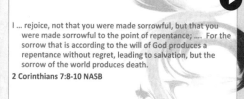

I ... rejoice, not that you were made sorrowful, but that you were made sorrowful to the point of repentance; .... For the sorrow that is according to the will of God produces a repentance without regret, leading to salvation, but the sorrow of the world produces death.
2 Corinthians 7:8-10 NASB

Paul's letter helped them to see their sin and they started to feel something like what the younger son felt about his sin. But just as the father refused to pile guilt onto the younger son, it's clear that Paul did not want the Corinthians to feel guilt either. What he wanted them to feel was godly sorrow which, he says, produces a "repentance without regret".

In my experience, guilt feelings tend to make me want to run away from God rather than come to Him in repentance without regret. In fact, guilt feelings sound to me rather more like what Paul calls "the sorrow of the world" which produces death.

When Judas had betrayed Jesus, he experienced worldly sorrow. He found himself with no hope and, instead of trusting in the One who would go on to hang on the cross for him, he turned away from Him and hanged himself.

To understand godly sorrow on the other hand, look at someone who let Jesus down at the same time, the apostle Peter. He had betrayed his best friend at His greatest hour of need by denying Him three times. He felt terrible about it. Jesus caught up with Peter after His resurrection. Clearly He could have raised the issue in front of the other disciples to make him feel even guiltier than he already did... just to make sure he never did it again. But He didn't. ▶In John 21, we see Jesus cooking breakfast for Peter and the rest of the disciples. After their meal, Jesus asks Peter if he loves Him. Peter affirms his love. But Jesus asks him again. Then He asks him a third time, one time for each of his previous denials. Then, rather than demoting him to "last place" in the disciples' leadership ranks, Jesus restores him to ministry and honours him in front of the others. "Tend My lambs." "Shepherd My sheep." "Tend My sheep." He could have used guilt to motivate Peter, but He didn't. He used grace.

So, although sometimes we need as gently as possible to make others aware of sin, once they are aware of it, the Bible is very clear that ▶grace, not guilt, is the most powerful motivator to keep us from sinning. Why? Because guilt drives us away from God, where we find we are more drawn to sin. Grace on the other hand draws us close to Him — and that's where the only real protection from sin can be found.

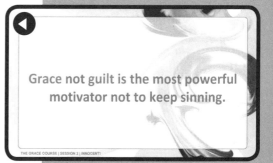

Grace not guilt is the most powerful motivator not to keep sinning.

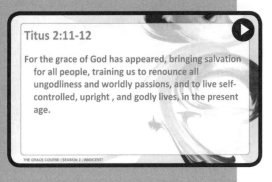

Titus 2:11-12

For the grace of God has appeared, bringing salvation for all people, training us to renounce all ungodliness and worldly passions, and to live self-controlled, upright , and godly lives, in the present age.

THE GRACE COURSE | SESSION 2 | INNOCENT!

THE GRACE COURSE | SESSION 2 | INNOCENT!

▶For the grace of God has appeared, bringing salvation for all people, training us to renounce all ungodliness and worldly passions, and to live self-controlled, upright, and godly lives, in the present age. (Titus 2:11–12)

Counter-intuitively, it's grace that leads us to live a righteous and godly life, not guilt.

When you sin

▶When you sin, God wants your sense of sorrow not to drive you away from Him, but to drive you into His arms where you will find the same welcome the younger son received. When you are there, like the younger son, you will confess your sins. Confession means that we agree with God that we have sinned. But we also need to agree with Him that we are forgiven in Christ. And we also agree that our sin is wrong, so we repent — that is change our mind about our sin — turning away from it, seeking His strength to walk with God in truth again.

And what happens as a result? A restoration of intimacy with Christ: A cleansing of our spirit, soul and body from sin's corruption through the blood of Jesus... with no regret.

"But, what if I still feel guilty after doing all that?"

Then your feelings are lying to you. Either they are the result of a conscience that has yet to fully grasp the wonder of Christ's forgiveness and guilt removal. Or you are listening to the whispers of your enemy, Satan, who wants you to stay stuck in your false guilt feelings.

In either case, the answer is to decide to focus on the truth that you are forgiven, declared innocent and made clean in Christ. Realize that your true guilt has been completely dealt with and that your guilt feelings are not based on truth.

Three helpful pictures

A great deal of our spiritual struggles would be over if we truly understood the greatness and completeness of God's forgiveness of our guilt in Christ. Fortunately, the Bible has painted some beautiful pictures of God's forgiveness. Let's look at them briefly:

▶Isaiah says:

"Come now, let us reason together," says the Lord. "Though your sins are like scarlet, they shall be as white as snow; though they are red like crimson, they shall become like wool." (Isaiah 1:18)

▶When snow falls quietly in a city, it brings everything to a standstill. People stay home; the roads become deserted; the dullness, greyness and hardness of an urban winter are covered by a soft, white blanket. The snow muffles sound and there is a serenity that brings peace to the soul. Streetlights reflect off the snow, turning night into light. A hush falls over the world.

Take a moment to remember a time when you experienced a fresh fall of snow. Think about how it covered everything and made it beautiful. God has forgiven your sins and changed you into the purity, brightness and beauty of new-fallen snow. The neon-light red stain of your sins is gone... turned to soft, pure white by the precious blood of Jesus.

And whereas snow normally melts away, revealing the ugly stuff underneath, in our case, if it ever melted, the stuff underneath has been transformed into beauty, holiness and purity.

Here are two more pictures from Micah 7:19 NIV:

▶You will again have compassion on us; you will tread our sins underfoot and hurl all our iniquities into the depths of the sea.

▶First, God takes our sinful deeds and squashes them, crushing them like a heavy boot crushes a worn out cigarette butt. It's like He does this about a million times, so that there is nothing left of the sin for anybody to see or recognize.

▶Second, He hurls our twisted wickedness (iniquities) into the deepest part of the sea. Do you have any idea what the deepest part of the sea is? Well, it's the Mariana Trench in the Pacific Ocean. Care to guess how deep the Mariana Trench is? It's almost 7 miles under the surface of the sea. That is deeper in the ocean than Mount Everest is higher than sea level!

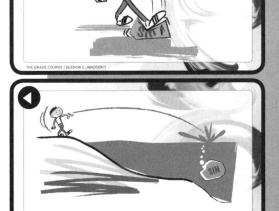

Nobody goes to the bottom of the Mariana Trench to fish and neither should you! God has placed your sins there and there they will stay.

Just prior to these beautiful pictures of God dealing a death blow to our sins, Micah wrote:

▶ Who is a God like you, who pardons sin and forgives the transgression of the remnant of his inheritance? You do not stay angry forever but delight to show mercy. (Micah 7:18 NIV)

Isn't that amazing? God delights to show mercy! When we come to faith in Jesus Christ and God forgives all our guilt, God gets excited. He throws a party in heaven and there is incredible rejoicing there (Luke 15:7). God doesn't want you to feel guilty for your sins when you are not guilty! He wants you to rejoice. He wants to restore your joy.

A truth to remember

This can all sound just too good to be true. Well, it is good. And it is true! For those in Christ Jesus, God loves you before you sin. God loves you after you sin. God even loves you in the midst of your sinning, though He never loves our sinning. But for those who belong to Christ, God never turns His hatred of sin into hatred of us. Never! He loves us and always will.

▶ There is therefore now **no** condemnation for those who are in Christ Jesus (Romans 8:1).

That is not just religious talk or wishful thinking; it is truth.

Micah 7:18 NIV

Who is a God like you, who pardons sin and forgives the transgression of the remnant of his inheritance? You do not stay angry forever but delight to show mercy.

THE GRACE COURSE | SESSION 2 | INNOCENT!

There is therefore now no condemnation for those who are in Christ Jesus.
Romans 8:1

THE GRACE COURSE | SESSION 2 | INNOCENT!

PAUSE FOR THOUGHT 3

OBJECTIVE:

TO HELP PEOPLE GRASP THE FULL EXTENT OF THEIR FORGIVENESS.

▶QUESTIONS (ON PAGE 34 OF THE PARTICIPANT'S GUIDE):

WHICH OF THE PICTURES OF HOW GOD HAS DEALT WITH OUR SIN MEANS MOST TO YOU? WHY?

▶Turn to the *Lies List* on the last two pages of your Participant's Guide. What has God been showing you during this session? What lies has He surfaced or exposed? Let's ask the Holy Spirit to guide us:

Lord, we pray that You will lead us into all truth because it's knowing the truth that will set us free. Please reveal to us now areas where our past thinking has been faulty. Thank You Father. Amen.

This session has addressed the issue of guilt. Perhaps you may realize that you have been living life under the bondage of lies such as:

- I am only forgiven if I confess my sins really hard and cry tears over them.

- Feeling guilty for my sins is the best safeguard against doing them again.

- My sins are too big to be forgiven.

- Guilt is a good way to motivate others to do right.

 Remember to hand out the "Innocent!" Biblical Truth postcard (see page 15) and encourage people to use it to remind themselves of the truths learned in this session.

Write down any lie that God is showing you in the left-hand column of the list, and before the next session, see how many Bible verses you can find that say what is really true, and put those in the right-hand column.

Hopefully you are beginning to get the idea of this exercise and it's already proving to be helpful for you. Ask God to continue working in your heart... opening your eyes to the lies you have believed.

Remember what Jesus says to you: "Your sins are forgiven... Your faith has saved you; go in peace."

 WITNESS

How would you explain to someone with no Christian background why we all need to be declared "Innocent!" by God?

 IN THE COMING WEEK

Choose one of the verses that speak about the full extent of God's unconditional love and forgiveness, and commit to declare it out loud with faith for the next 40 days.

> "Come now, let us reason together," says the Lord. "Though your sins are like scarlet, they shall be as white as snow; though they are red like crimson, they shall become like wool." (Isaiah 1:18)
>
> You will again have compassion on us; you will tread our sins underfoot and hurl all our iniquities into the depths of the sea. (Micah 7:19 NIV)
>
> Who is a God like you, who pardons sin and forgives the transgression of the remnant of his inheritance? You do not stay angry forever but delight to show mercy. (Micah 7:18 NIV)

Session 3:
UNASHAMED!

Planned Clean
Loved Unashamed
Treasured Protected

Session 3: Unashamed!

FOCUS VERSE:
2 Corinthians 5:21: For our sake he made him to be sin who knew no sin, so that in him we might become the righteousness of God.

OBJECTIVE:
To understand that our very identity at the core of our being has been comprehensively transformed.

FOCUS TRUTH:
We have not just been covered with the righteousness of Christ. We have actually **become** the righteousness of God.

Leader's Notes

In our experience, many Christians understand that their sins are forgiven and that they are going to go to Heaven when they die, but they still see themselves as essentially the same no good person that they always were, just "covered" by the blood of Jesus. They have only got as far as Good Friday in their thinking.

The point of this session is to help them progress to Easter Sunday and understand that it is not just Jesus who rose again to new life, but they rose with Him. They have become completely new creations. In fact, as our focus verse makes clear, they have actually **become** the righteousness of God. An exchange has taken place. Christ became sin for me so that I could become the righteousness of God!

Knowing that we are now fundamentally acceptable to God in our very identity is key to living a righteous life. As Neil Anderson loves to point out, no one can consistently live in a manner that is inconsistent with how they see themselves.

Shame strikes at the heart of our identity and tells us that we are not acceptable. It makes us want to cover up and hide away. As people come out of shame, they are free to be themselves without the need to project an image or hide away. It's a wonderful thing to see people take hold of the truth of their new identity in Christ.

One of the key parts of this session is the list called "My New Name". It can be a very powerful aid in helping participants to understand their true identity in Christ. We recommend that you order the postcards that contain the list (see page 15) and hand them out to participants to encourage them to go through the list every day.

SMALL GROUP TIMINGS:

Welcome	8 minutes	0:08
Worship, prayer & declaration	7 minutes	0:15
Word part 1	25 minutes	0:40
Pause For Thought 1	15 minutes	0:55
Word part 2	19 minutes	1:14
Pause For Thought 2	10 minutes	1:24
Word part 3	17 minutes	1:41
Pause For Thought 3	14 minutes	1:55
Word part 4	5 minutes	2:00

 WELCOME

Tell the group about an embarrassing moment you have experienced.

 WORSHIP

Suggested theme: We are welcome in God's presence. (Hebrews 4:16, Hebrews 10:19–22)

You could say something like this: Imagine you are approaching the throne room of God Himself, where God reigns in glory and majesty. Looking up ahead you see the outline of someone standing in the doorway. Coming closer you recognize it is Jesus. When you get to His side, He takes you by the hand and leads you through the open door into the presence of God the King. Approaching the throne you overhear Jesus say to His Father, "This one's with me!"

Suggest that people divide into pairs and take it in turns to read Hebrews 10:19–22 out loud to each other, inserting the other person's name:
"Therefore _____ (their name) since you have confidence to enter the Most Holy Place by the blood of Jesus.... etc."

Allow a short time for those who want to respond in prayer to God.

 PRAYER & DECLARATION

Dear Father, You are holy, pure and without fault, and I confess that there are times when I feel dirty and not good enough to be in Your presence. But I choose to believe the truth that You have made me completely clean and brand new. Please heal any wounds in my heart that would keep me distant from You. Thank You. In the Holy name of Jesus. Amen.

I declare the truth that I am now a new creation in Christ; the old has gone and the new has come! I have been cleansed from sin and no longer have to hide behind masks. I command every enemy of the Lord Jesus to leave my presence.

 **WORD**

Introduction

Have you ever had an embarrassing moment?

I love the true story of a woman in America who got back to her car with her shopping and saw that three men were just about to get into it. Being in America, she reached into her handbag and whipped out a handgun, aimed it at the men and shouted "Get away from the car!" Naturally they scattered very quickly and ran away. After getting her pulse back to near normal again, she got into the driver's seat of the car and tried to start it. Having failed three times even to get the key into the ignition it slowly dawned on her that she was in fact in the wrong car. Because she felt so bad, she went to the police station to tell them what had happened. In the police station, she came across the three men in the process of reporting a carjacking!

How do moments like that make you feel? You want the ground to swallow you up. You feel vulnerable, stupid, extremely embarrassed. Embarrassment is a mild form of shame. But through His grace, God has provided the remedy for the shame we all experience.

The origin of shame

Shame has been around since the Garden of Eden. The story of Adam and Eve is fascinating. They did something stunningly and spectacularly wrong. You'd expect them to feel guilty but it's not obvious that they did.

Before Adam sinned, Genesis tells us, "The man and his wife were both naked and they felt no shame" (Genesis 2:25 NIV). ▶After the fall, "The eyes of both were opened, and they knew that they were naked. And they sewed fig leaves together and made themselves loincloths." (Genesis 3:7). What they immediately felt was somehow deeper than guilt, more fundamental. It was not so much guilt as shame.

The English word "shame" originally meant "covering up". And this strange feeling of shame that they had never experienced before made them want to do just that. But even with the fig leaves, Adam and Eve still felt exposed and tried to hide from God. When God asked them why, Adam's excuse was, "I was afraid, because I was naked" (Genesis 3:10) even though by then they were wearing the fig leaves.

▶In this session we want to explore the subject of shame, something which makes us feel so vulnerable that we want to cover up and hide away from God and other people. We will look at what shame is, where it comes from, how we typically try to deal with it, and finally how God's grace can bring us out of disgrace into freedom.

By God's grace, we can come out of hiding and stand unashamed before God and other people. ▶We can be like the younger son who stood there before his father... accepted, loved and secure... in spite of all he had done. In fact, if you can't quite identify with this picture of the younger son yet but instead feel more like wanting to cover up or hide from God, shame may well be the reason.

So what is shame? Guilt and shame are two sides of the same coin... in that they both drive us away from God... but they are very different.

What is shame?

▶Guilt says, "I **did** something wrong. I made a mistake."

As we saw in our last session, guilt is a legal condition of having broken the law of God and standing... well... guilty before the heavenly Judge. Guilt is about what we have done.

Guilt is a product of what we do:
  "I did something wrong. I made a mistake."

Shame is about who we are:
  "There's something wrong with me. I am the mistake."

THE GRACE COURSE | SESSION 3 | UNASHAMED!

▶Shame says, "There's something wrong with me. I **am** the mistake." It is the painful emotional experience that comes from believing that there is something very wrong, not so much with what we have **done**, but with who we **are** at the core of our being.

In Mark 1:40 we find someone who is in that condition of believing there is something very wrong with them at the core of their being:

▶And a leper came to him, imploring him, and kneeling said to him, "If you will, you can make me clean."

THE GRACE COURSE | SESSION 3 | UNASHAMED!

This man would have been a mass of ulcerating skin all over his body. Hope you haven't just eaten! He would have looked repulsive, smelt terribly, and been on a relentless course toward a slow and agonizing death once the disease had begun to ravage his mind. To make his situation even worse, this is what the Bible itself said about him:

> The leprous person who has the disease shall wear torn clothes and let the hair of his head hang loose, and he shall cover his upper lip and cry out, "Unclean, unclean." He shall remain unclean as long as he has the disease. He is unclean. He shall live alone. His dwelling shall be outside the camp. (Leviticus 13:45–46)

There were some very good reasons for these regulations, of course, having to do with protecting others from this hideous, contagious disease. But can you imagine reading this about yourself — and in God's Word — "He is unclean. He shall live alone"?

We may not suffer from this particular disease, but we can feel that we are somehow different from others. That if people knew what we were really like, they would not accept us. That we are somehow inherently unlovable. Dirty. Alone. Contaminated. Messed up. Unclean.

That is shame. No wonder it makes us want to cover up and hide away.

But this leper... in violation of all common decency and propriety... approached Jesus and asked him a question. The obvious question to ask would be that Jesus would heal him. But actually he didn't ask that. He asked something more fundamental. He begged to be made clean. How did Jesus respond?

▶ Moved with pity, he stretched out his hand and touched him and said to him, "I will; be clean." (Mark 1:41)

Jesus touched him and made him clean. He didn't need to touch him to heal him of leprosy. But I believe He needed to touch him to heal him of the years of pain from being alone and rejected. You wonder how long it had been since that man had felt the kind touch of another human being. That's exactly what Jesus wants to do for you today. Reach out to you, touch you and remove your shame.

▶ Where does shame come from?

Being brought up in a shame-based culture

First, shame can come from being brought up in a shame-based culture.

Where does shame come from?

From being brought up in a shame-based culture

All societies try to find ways of discouraging us from doing things that are not acceptable. Western societies tend to use guilt for this. We are pressured to conform by the threat of punishment, such as disapproving words and looks, the law courts, or teaching that God will punish us.

Other societies, particularly Eastern ones, use shame rather than guilt. Control is maintained by creating a culture where, if you do not conform to social norms, you yourself are not acceptable. Making sure you do what is socially acceptable becomes the main cultural value. The fear of being rejected and ostracized is a powerful motivator.

There was a missionary in an Eastern culture who was puzzled by something he observed. Every morning the friend of a divorced Muslim lady would come round to her house and feel her hair to see if it was damp. He was told that the reason for this was so that she could tell if her friend had committed adultery. The religious belief in that society was that having sex makes you unclean, and that you must bathe and wash your hair in order to be clean again. But what puzzled the missionary is why, if the woman was going to be disobedient enough to commit adultery, her friend thought she would be obedient enough to take a bath.

It was explained to him that it was inconceivable that she would neglect to wash, because her uncleanness would make even the ground she walked on cursed. In other words, being in a state of ritual uncleanness was more unthinkable than committing adultery!

In a shame-based culture what matters most is being clean, being acceptable, particularly in the eyes of other people. It's not so much a question of whether you have done something wrong or right but whether you have done what others expect. If you feel that you don't hit the mark, you experience shame.

Some families and religious institutions — even Christian ones — can create mini shame-based cultures. A church leader or parent may overuse the words "ought to" and "should", to make you feel that you have to behave in a certain way to be an accepted part of the church or family, or to be a "good Christian". They may say things like: You should be ashamed of yourself!; You're a disgrace to the family or church!; Why can't you be more like your brother or sister?; You'll never amount to anything!; I wish you'd never been born!

Things we have done

▶Secondly, we experience shame because of things we have done.

Addictions and any sin that degrades our bodies or causes others to look down on us are a source of shame. Jesus encountered a woman at a well who was caught in sexual sin. Her shame caused her to come to the well at the hottest part of the day because she knew no one else would be there. In order to know freedom from shame, we need to find freedom from these repeated patterns of sins, and we'll look a little later at how every Christian can take hold of that freedom.

Things others have done to us

▶The third way we experience shame is from things others have done to us.

I have lived a fairly sheltered life, but over the years I have had opportunity to sit with people as they go through *The Steps To Freedom In Christ*. I have heard the tragic stories of the sick things people have done to fellow human beings, very often when they were children. Some of it is sexual, some just plain cruel. Some of it is occult in nature.

Too often those victimized by child molesters feel it was their own fault or that they somehow deserved it. That is a terrible deception. Children are not to blame for the shameful acts of perpetrators. But too often the victim is the one that experiences the shame, not the one truly responsible.

If that is where you are today, we are very, very sorry that you have suffered so much. And so is Jesus, the One who came specifically to bind up broken hearts and set you free.

Steve Goss says: "I remember one lady, who had been terribly abused during her childhood for a decade or more, looking for the first time at the awful things that had been done to her, square in the eye rather than hiding them away in the depths of her consciousness, and saying, "They did those things to me Steve". I was able to say gently, "Yes, they did. So what?" We had been talking about who she now is in Christ — pure, holy. She said, "Yes, you're right. Why should I let it bother me? I'm a child of God!" She now runs a really fruitful ministry helping others who have been abused in the same way."

Shame hits at your very identity. Knowing your new identity is the key to escaping from it. Remember what the younger son said when he returned to his father: "I am no longer worthy to be called your son." He didn't just feel guilt. He was experiencing shame that struck at his very identity. "Make me as one of your hired servants." He was ready to exchange his son-identity for that of a servant who would be accepted only on the basis of performance... slaving away.

Rich Miller says: "I remember listening to a man, who was a counsellor in his 50s, sobbing with the recollection of the terrible shame he felt when, as a young boy, his dad had raped him, saying "I'm going to fix you so that no one will ever want you again." Forty years of shame just poured from this man's heart."

Believing wrong messages

▶A fourth way that shame envelopes a life is through believing wrong messages.

(Do you have a story of how shame entered your life through what others said? The following story is from Rich Miller)

I grew up as a pretty normal kid until I was about 11 years old. Then puberty hit! I thought it was a terminal disease. In one year I grew from 5 ft. 6 and 120 pounds to 6 ft. 2 and... 120 pounds! I wasn't skinny, I was skeletal. People would say things to me like, "Hey Rich, turn sideways so you'll disappear!" "Hey bean pole!" I had acne problems... "Hey, here comes Rich, let's play connect the dots!" I had braces on my teeth, walked awkwardly and was extremely shy. Just about every product advertised on TV, I could use! At the age of 17, I was too ashamed of myself and afraid of ridicule to accept an award that would have required me to walk up on stage in front of the whole student body. I just walked around the halls during that ceremony. I was too ashamed of myself, so I just hid. My best friend was my dog, because he would not make fun of me. I would often come home from school and just bury my face in his fur and cry. I spent many hours alone in my room, seething with rage, smothered in shame, contemplating taking my life. My motto came from the old Simon and Garfunkel song, "I Am a Rock." I agreed with the song that friendship is not a blessing but a source of pain. Later on, I had to renounce the lie that I'm a rock. Jesus is the Rock. And I'm not an island either. I may be a peninsula, but I'm not an island; I need other people.

If we believe the world's lies that we have to be beautiful or slim or whatever to fit in, we can feel tremendous shame if we think we don't measure up.

[Steve Goss says:] Even those who excel athletically, academically or in their chosen field can live a shame-based life, if all they ever get is applause and approval when they do well. And I performed well academically. You might think that's great but actually the message that can come across loud and clear is: You are not worth anything in and of yourself. You are only valuable and worthy of approval if you perform well. And that left me with a sense that I always had to hit standards to feel good about myself. And no one can hit them all the time. When you don't do so well, the words of encouragement stop; the pats on the back are gone; you are met with disapproval and disappointment because your performance wasn't so good. This is a crushing message and can set you up for a life-time of battling shame.

▶Shame drives us to cover up and hide.

Ways we try to cover up and hide

There is a wide spectrum of shame. It runs from embarrassment (which is a mild form of shame), to utter humiliation, ridicule and being ostracized at the other gut-wrenching extreme.

Wherever we may be on that spectrum, we all have developed strategies to try to alleviate shame and to cover up and hide. Some of the more common include:

▶ Lying about your accomplishments or things in your past you're ashamed of

▶ Pretending that everything is okay and that you are doing great when you know you're not

▶ Blame-shifting by making everyone else appear to be the problem rather than you

▶ Compromising moral or biblical values to fit in, so as to avoid the shame of rejection

▶ Compensating for shameful deficiencies in one area by seeking to excel in others

▶ Moralizing by preaching hard against ways you yourself have behaved and are ashamed of

▶ Criticizing others harshly in order to make them appear inferior to you [slide not depicted]

▶ Self-medicating in order to blunt the sting and numb the pain of your own shame [slide not depicted]

▶ Striving for perfection in your behaviour or your looks to compensate for the painful belief that you fall far short of who you believe you should be [slide not depicted]

But like Adam and Eve's fig leaves, these defence mechanisms don't work. They may provide temporary relief, even convincing us for a time that we are safe. But in the end, like all strategies of the flesh, they fail. God's way to remove disgrace is grace.

PAUSE FOR THOUGHT 1

OBJECTIVE:

TO HELP PEOPLE REALIZE HOW SHAME MAKES US COVER UP AND HIDE AND TO START THINKING ABOUT THE FUNDAMENTAL ISSUE OF OUR IDENTITY.

▶QUESTIONS (ON PAGE 42 OF THE PARTICIPANT'S GUIDE):

ADAM AND EVE USED FIG LEAVES TO TRY TO COVER THEIR SENSE OF SHAME. WHAT SORT OF THINGS DO PEOPLE USE NOWADAYS? ARE YOU AWARE OF A TENDENCY TO USE ANY OF THESE THINGS?

IF SOMEONE ASKED YOU, "WHO ARE YOU?", HOW WOULD YOU DEFINE YOURSELF?

IS YOUR DEFINITION BASED MORE ON WHAT YOU DO OR WHO YOU ACTUALLY ARE?

God's remedy for shame

What is God's remedy for shame?

▶Shame says that we are what is wrong, and puts us into what we call "the less mess". We believe that we are "less" than others. We feel helpless, worthless, meaningless, powerless, and hopeless. It strikes at our belief about who we are, our identity.

How can we genuinely alleviate that sense that we are worth less than others, that there is something at the core of our being that makes us... even as Christians... somehow flawed or contaminated? By understanding the truth about our identity, about who we now are in Christ.

The "less mess"

Shame makes us feel:
- Help*less*
- Worth*less*
- Meaning*less*
- Power*less*
- Hope*less*

THE GRACE COURSE | SESSION 3 | UNASHAMED!

▶Our old identity

Paul tells us that at one time we were (past tense) "by nature children of wrath" (Ephesians 2:3). ▶Jeremiah said our heart, the very core of our being, was "deceitful above all things, and desperately sick" (Jeremiah 17:9).

Our old identity

We were by nature children of wrath **Ephesians 2:3**

The heart is deceitful above all things, and desperately sick **Jeremiah 17:9**

We have all become like one who is unclean, and all our righteous deeds are like a polluted garment **Isaiah 64:6**

THE GRACE COURSE | SESSION 3 | UNASHAMED!

▶Isaiah rubs salt in the wound: "We have all become like one who is unclean, and all our righteous deeds are like a polluted garment" (Isaiah 64:6). A literal translation would be "all our righteous deeds are like a bloody menstrual cloth". The Law said that menstrual blood was unclean. The point is this: When you are unclean, no matter what righteous deeds you may do, they too are unclean.

So all of us had good cause to be ashamed of who we were. The Old Testament law contained sacrifices for sin to relieve guilt, which were fulfilled when Jesus became the ultimate sacrifice. There were also a whole set of rituals for cleansing. They never could — and were never intended to — remove our defilement, but pointed towards the sacrifice that would, that of Jesus.

The great exchange

▶2 Corinthians 5:21 reveals how: "For our sake he made him to **be** sin who knew no sin, so that in him we might **become** the righteousness of God."

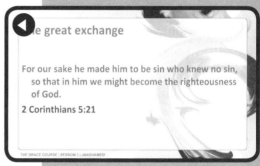

▶Jesus, God's Son, who knew no sin, actually became sin for our sake as He hung there on the cross. God took all of our shortcomings and failures and laid them on Christ. He did not die just to pay the penalty of your sin. He took on Himself your defiled, unclean nature and destroyed your inner contamination.

▶In exchange you became someone very different from who you were before. You became the righteousness of God. Your heart is no longer deceitful and beyond cure. That great prophecy of Ezekiel was fulfilled that we would have a new heart and a new spirit (Ezekiel 11:19).

We are no longer by nature objects of wrath. Peter tells us that now we actually share God's divine nature (2 Peter 1:4). Just think about that!

Our new identity

Rich Miller says: "I remember in the midst of the pain of the shame of my teenage years crying out to a God that I wasn't even sure existed, "I just want to be normal!" What I meant was that I wanted to not be so tall and skinny and awkward. I wanted the acne to go away. I wanted to have self-confidence and not be immediately rejected by everyone I met. God, as always, had a bigger, better plan. He didn't just want to make the old me look better; He wanted to make the old me into a completely new person."

Consider this:

> ▶ Therefore, if anyone is in Christ, he is a new creation. The old has passed away; behold, the new has come. (2 Corinthians 5:17)

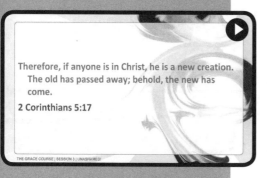

Two thousand years ago, you and I and all those who are in Christ died on the cross with Christ. Our old sin-loving, shameful self was killed. Dead. Gone. A biologist might translate 2 Corinthians 5:17, "If anyone is in Christ, he is a new species"!

Never before had such a creature existed... a human being given a brand new heart and a brand new start, with the Holy Spirit living inside them to give them grace and power over sin, and to walk with Christ in this fallen world!

Feelings of shame make us want to **draw back** from a holy, righteous God. But you don't have to run away any more. You don't have to hide. No matter what is in your past. In the Temple was a place called the Holy Of Holies, that only the High Priest was allowed to enter and then only briefly once a year. Because we have now become the righteousness of God, we can come into the Holy Of Holies at any time.

> ▶ Therefore, brothers, since we have confidence to enter the holy places by the blood of Jesus, by the new and living way that he opened for us through the curtain, that is, through his flesh, and since we have a great priest over the house of God, let us **draw near** with a true heart in full assurance of faith, with our hearts sprinkled clean from an evil conscience and our bodies washed with pure water. (Hebrews 10:19–22)

Because you have a totally new, clean identity in Christ, you are invited to draw near in full assurance and enter a deep relationship with God Himself in the Holy of Holies, because you have been cleansed and made holy in the deepest part of your being!

Don't be tempted to think that this invitation to draw near is conditional, that it depends on doing all the things you think a good Christian should do. That would be like living under the old system of continuous ritual cleansings and sacrifices. No further sacrifice is needed. And that's that!

The big question we all face is this: ▶Are you going to believe what God's Word says about you? Or are you going to believe what your past experiences tell you about yourself?

We saw earlier how Jesus healed an unclean leper. In Luke 17:11–19, He healed ten of them all at once. Again He didn't say "Be healed" and this time He didn't even say "Be cleansed." He simply said, "Go and show yourselves to the priests" (Luke 17:14). Luke tells us, "And as they went they were cleansed." There's something significant in His command to go and show themselves to someone else. For those who feel unclean and ashamed, opening themselves up and showing themselves to others is too painful to contemplate. It's the last thing they want to do. It feels safer to hide behind protective masks and walls than risk the pain of rejection.

▶Shame drives us into hiding from healthy relationships, the very thing we all need for life and growth. Shame makes us think that we don't belong; that nobody wants us; that nobody wants to be around us. That's how I felt until the Lord clearly showed me that I belong. I am as much a part of the family of God as anyone else!

▶Jesus says to us, "You are not contaminated any more. You are not unacceptable. You are clean. You are presentable. Take off the mask and take down the walls!"

A man became a Christian, and was so enthusiastic about his new relationship with Jesus. He read in his Bible the story of Jesus' baptism, in which a voice came from Heaven saying, "You are my beloved Son; with you I am well pleased" (Luke 3:22). He shared about this at a small group meeting in his church saying, "It's amazing. I am God's beloved son and He is well pleased with me." There was an embarrassed silence and he soon realized he had said the wrong thing.

But actually he hadn't. He had got hold of a key truth about his new identity. Of course, he is not **the** Son of God but he certainly is a son of God. Paul said:

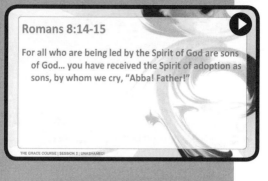

▶ For all who are being led by the Spirit of God are sons of God... you have received the Spirit of adoption as sons, by whom we cry, "Abba! Father!" (Romans 8:14–15)

[Rich Miller:] When we adopted our son, Lua, from Thailand in 1999 at the age of four, it was our choice to adopt that little boy. We didn't have to choose him, but we did. He was fatherless but I became his father. He had no family but he became part of ours... a Miller, with an older brother who loves him and sisters who adore him... usually! He had little hope for the future, but he is now being educated and will be taken care of for his whole life. You see, Lua is a special needs child and without guidance and supervision, he would be in deep trouble. He certainly had no inheritance, but now he is guaranteed by law all the rights and privileges of our other, biological kids. And he is now a citizen of a new country called America.

I hope you see the parallels with your new life, new family, new relationships, new hope, new future and new citizenship in the kingdom of God. How can we be ashamed when we have been chosen by God Himself to be part of the greatest family, the greatest kingdom, under the greatest King and greatest older Brother, the Lord Jesus Christ, that ever was or ever will be!

Oh, and there's one more thing new about Lua. We gave him a new name. His name is now Luke.

A new name

And you have been given a new name as well! Listen to Isaiah 62:2–4:

▶ The nations shall see your righteousness, and all the kings your glory,

And you shall be called by a new name that the mouth of the Lord will give.

You shall be a crown of beauty in the hand of the Lord, and a royal diadem in the hand of your God, you shall no more be termed Forsaken, and your land shall no more be termed Desolate,

But you shall be called My Delight Is in Her, and your land Married.

[Steve Goss:] I was having a quiet time one morning on holiday in Spain, and was reading a passage in Revelation that also talks about a new name. It says that those who overcome will be given a white stone with a new name on it (Revelation 2:17). I was struck by that and felt God saying, "What would you like your new name to be?" I immediately knew I'd like it to be "Free From Condemnation" — I've always struggled with condemning thoughts. That day we walked down to the local beach and our girls came running up to us with their hands full of smooth white quartz stones, saying, "Look at all these white stones. We could write our names on them." God was underlining the point. I still have my white stone with "Free From Condemnation" written on it. I can't wait to see what will be on the one I will actually be given.

We are going to read together some of the new names God's people have been given in the Bible. Every one of them describes you.

Before we do, let's just ask God to plant one of these new names deep in our heart:

Father, thank You that we have become completely new creations, a completely new species. Thank You that we have a new name. As we read through this list now, we ask that Your Holy Spirit will show us one special name that You want us to get hold of today. Amen.

Encourage each person to expect God to reveal to them a specific new name. It might even be one that is not on the list.

Let's read this together:

▶My new name is Beloved (Colossians 3:12)

My new name is Beautiful (Psalm 149:4, Song of Songs 4:1)

My new name is Chosen (Ephesians 1:4)

My new name is Precious (Isaiah 43:4)

My new name is Safe (1 John 5:18)

My new name is Loved (1 John 4:10)

▶My new name is Clean (John 15:3)

My new name is Presentable (Hebrews 10:22)

My new name is Protected (Psalm 91:14, John 17:15)

My new name is Welcomed (Ephesians 3:12)

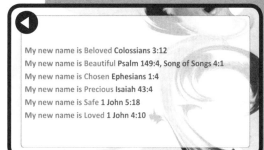

My new name is Beloved **Colossians 3:12**
My new name is Beautiful **Psalm 149:4, Song of Songs 4:1**
My new name is Chosen **Ephesians 1:4**
My new name is Precious **Isaiah 43:4**
My new name is Safe **1 John 5:18**
My new name is Loved **1 John 4:10**

THE GRACE COURSE | SESSION 3 | UNASHAMED!

My new name is Clean **John 15:3**
My new name is Presentable **Hebrews 10:22**
My new name is Protected **Psalm 91:14, John 17:15**
My new name is Welcomed **Ephesians 3:12**
My new name is Heir **Romans 8:17, Galatians 3:29**
My new name is Complete **Colossians 2:10**
My new name is Holy **Hebrews 10:10, Ephesians 1:4**

THE GRACE COURSE | SESSION 3 | UNASHAMED!

My new name is Forgiven **Psalm 103:3, Colossians 2:13**
My new name is Adopted **Ephesians 1:5**
My new name is Delight **Psalm 147:11**
My new name is Unashamed **Romans 10:11**
My new name is Known **Psalm 139:1**
My new name is Planned **Ephesians 1:11-12**

THE GRACE COURSE | SESSION 3 | UNASHAMED!

My new name is Gifted **2 Timothy 1:6, 1 Corinthians 12:11**
My new name is Enriched **2 Corinthians 8:9**
My new name is Provided For **1 Timothy 6:17**
My new name is Treasured **Deuteronomy 7:6**
My new name is Pure **1 Corinthians 6:11**
My new name is Established **Romans 16:25**
My new name is God's Work Of Art **Ephesians 2:10**

THE GRACE COURSE | SESSION 3 | UNASHAMED!

My new name is Helped **Hebrews 13:6**
My new name is Free From Condemnation **Romans 8:1**
My new name is God's Child **Romans 8:15-16**
My new name is Christ's Friend **John 15:15**
My new name is Christ's Precious Bride **Revelation 19:7, Song of Songs 7:10**

THE GRACE COURSE | SESSION 3 | UNASHAMED!

My new name is Heir (Romans 8:17, Galatians 3:29)

My new name is Complete (Colossians 2:10)

My new name is Holy (Hebrews 10:10, Ephesians 1:4)

▶My new name is Forgiven (Psalm 103:3, Colossians 2:13)

My new name is Adopted (Ephesians 1:5)

My new name is Delight (Psalm 147:11)

My new name is Unashamed (Romans 10:11)

My new name is Known (Psalm 139:1)

My new name is Planned (Ephesians 1:11–12)

▶My new name is Gifted (2 Timothy 1:6, 1 Corinthians 12:11)

My new name is Enriched (2 Corinthians 8:9)

My new name is Provided For (1 Timothy 6:17)

My new name is Treasured (Deuteronomy 7:6)

My new name is Pure (1 Corinthians 6:11)

My new name is Established (Romans 16:25)

My new name is God's Work Of Art (Ephesians 2:10)

▶My new name is Helped (Hebrews 13:6)

My new name is Free From Condemnation (Romans 8:1)

My new name is God's Child (Romans 8:15–16)

My new name is Christ's Friend (John 15:15)

My new name is Christ's Precious Bride (Revelation 19:7, Song of Songs 7:10).

▶That is who you have become. That is who you now are.

PAUSE FOR THOUGHT 2

OBJECTIVE:

TO HELP PEOPLE UNDERSTAND THE CRUCIAL IMPORTANCE OF KNOWING THEIR NEW IDENTITY IN CHRIST

▶QUESTIONS (ON PAGE 45 OF THE PARTICIPANT'S GUIDE):

WHICH ONE OF YOUR "NEW NAMES" PARTICULARLY STRIKES A CHORD WITH YOU?

WHAT COULD YOU DO TO MAKE THIS TRUTH REAL IN YOUR LIFE?

HOW MIGHT KNOWING THIS TRUTH IN YOUR HEART RATHER THAN JUST YOUR HEAD AFFECT HOW YOU RELATE TO GOD AND TO OTHERS?

▶Staying free of sin

We said earlier that one thing that breeds shame is when we get stuck in a particular sin.

Let's look finally at one of the implications of our new, fresh, clean, shame-free life — that we can keep it fresh, clean and shame-free and do not have to keep returning to the same old cycles of sin that keep us trapped in shame.

▶Your new identity is the key to knowing freedom from sin.

> We know that our old self was crucified with him in order that the body of sin might be brought to nothing, so that we would no longer be enslaved to sin. For one who has died has been set free from sin. (Romans 6:6–7)

How many here have died with Christ? [get people to raise their hands] How many have been set free from sin?

How do we stay free of sin?

THE GRACE COURSE | SESSION 3 | UNASHAMED!

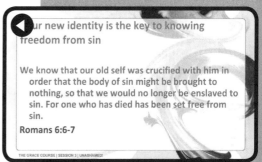

Your new identity is the key to knowing freedom from sin

We know that our old self was crucified with him in order that the body of sin might be brought to nothing, so that we would no longer be enslaved to sin. For one who has died has been set free from sin.

Romans 6:6-7

THE GRACE COURSE | SESSION 3 | UNASHAMED!

According to this passage, it had better be the same number of hands!

▶ "For one who has died has been set free from sin."

You may be thinking, "Well, I don't feel very free from sin. In fact I can't get out of it." The only appropriate response when you read a factual statement in the Bible is what.... ? To believe it! Your feelings and your past experience are not relevant. It's knowing the truth that sets you free.

In Romans 6, Paul goes on to say that, in the same way that death no longer has dominion over Christ, so neither does sin have dominion over you. That means we don't any longer have to dance to sin's tune.

[Jude Graham's testimony is this:] One day I was sitting at home when the Lord showed me the truth of Romans 6:6, that not only did Christ die on the cross, but somehow by faith I died with Him, and that the Jude-person who lives now was not the same person that existed before I became a Christian. This turned my life upside-down. He had gone right to the root of my problem. I had been believing I had to work hard to make myself BE better but He showed me that He had rubbed out the old on the cross and given me a brand new life! He became sin so that I might become righteous. God had destroyed my contamination and made me completely holy so I could live a holy life!

I remember as a boy watching a butterfly crawling along our driveway after a rain shower. Obviously its wings were wet and it had to let them dry before it could fly again. Looking back on that scene, what strikes me as strange is that this butterfly that was made to fly was crawling slowly along the ground, acting in fact exactly like a caterpillar. It once WAS a caterpillar, but by the marvellous transformation of metamorphosis it was changed into a totally different creature... a butterfly. And butterflies were meant to fly, not crawl.

Are you a butterfly that's still acting like a caterpillar? Many Christians are. Either they don't realize that they have been changed into new creatures in Christ, or they have allowed the stuff of this world and life to "wet their wings" so that they cannot fly.

You might say, "OK, I see the problem. What's the solution?" Paul goes on to tell us.

Realize you are now dead to sin

▶So you also should consider yourselves to be dead to the power of sin and alive to God through Christ Jesus. Do not let sin control the way you live; do not give in to sinful desires. Do not let any part of your body become an instrument of evil to serve sin. Instead, give yourselves completely to God, for you were dead, but now you have new life. So use your whole body as an instrument to do what is right for the glory of God. Sin is no longer your master, for you no longer live under the requirements of the law. Instead, you live under the freedom of God's grace. (Romans 6:11–14 NLT)

▶First we are to consider ourselves "dead to the power of sin." Why? Because we are! Being "dead to sin" doesn't mean you can't sin. You can and you do. Just ask your husband or wife or close friend! What it does mean is that you have a choice. You are no longer in a slave and master relationship with sin. Before you became a new person in Christ, when sin said, "Jump!" you had to say, "How high?" You had no choice but to give in to it. But no more. You are now in relationship with Christ who conquered sin and lives inside you, and He will give you His strength over sin any time you choose to draw on His power.

▶So, how do you stop sin from taking over? Paul says you make a choice not to surrender the parts of your body to it, but instead you give your body and all its parts to God... for doing right. Don't use your eyes to look at pornography. Surrender your hands to God so that you use them to help people, not hurt them. Surrender your sexual organs and your brain to God, so that your sexuality is fulfilled righteously. You get the idea. You can choose to use your body for good or for evil.

"Well, that's all very well," you may be thinking, "I tried saying no to sin but I don't seem to have that choice. I keep finding myself getting dragged back. I'm stuck and feel ashamed."

▶Suppose you were left alone in a room and had been told "under no circumstances must you open that door." But from behind the door you hear a pleasant voice telling you, "Come on, no-one is looking. It can't hurt!"

▶So you open the door. Behind the door is a big dog.

▶It proceeds to sink its teeth into your rear end and won't let go. The pleasant voice now brings accusation and condemnation. "You miserable failure. You're pathetic. You've blown it now." So what do you do?

Confess "O God I opened the door. Please forgive me!" Does He? Yes! In fact He's already forgiven you.

But is that an end of the matter? No. You've still got a dog hanging off your butt! Now there's one thing I forgot to mention. The dog is invisible. You can't see it and you don't know what it is. All you know is you did something wrong — you opened the door — and now you're in pain and you feel terrible. Who do you get angry with — the dog? No, you don't know it's there! You get angry with yourself or God.

Recognize the reality of the devil and resist him

Though we know the Bible talks about the devil and demons, most of us brought up in the West tend to ignore the reality of the spiritual world when it comes to living our daily lives and exercising our ministries. But the Bible tells us that when we sin, we give the devil a foothold — a point of influence in our lives.

It's all very well receiving forgiveness for your sin but you're still walking around with a foothold of the enemy, an invisible dog hanging off you! And that unresolved issue will short-circuit God's power to enable you to live righteously. It makes it difficult to resist further temptation, difficult to make the right choice, difficult to renew your mind. And the more you seem unable to get out of the cycle, the more the enemy accuses you and the more shame you feel. At this point so many give up and walk away.

[Steve Goss:] I remember being caught in a sin that I didn't seem to be able to get out of. I was watching the wrong sort of stuff on TV late at night. I'd watch something totally inappropriate, then say "Sorry Lord, please forgive me". I'd know I was forgiven but I'd still feel terrible. And then the next day or week I'd do it again.... And again. And end up feeling completely hopeless.

One day a preacher called Frank came to our church and described this situation I was trapped in down to a tee. Then he said "Do you want to know how to get out of that?" I really did. I sat bolt upright — then thought I'd better look cool in case someone lays hands on me or something.... But I really wanted to know how to get out of it. He said, "It's quite simple: just stop".

I thought "Thanks a lot — actually I've tried that several times and it doesn't work. In fact it was the very first thing I tried!" But he went on to show from Romans 6 that if the Bible says that the power of sin is broken in our lives as Christians, it is, whether it feels like it or not. I remember going home from church that day feeling really confused. I went upstairs, knelt down, and said something like, "Lord. It does say in Romans 6 that the power of sin is broken in my life. It really doesn't feel true. But I choose to believe it." I also recommitted myself to Him.

To my surprise, I walked away from that issue there and then and, although I've been tempted, I've never fallen for it again.

What we're saying is that there is more to stopping sin in mid-air than just an endless "sin-confess, sin-confess" cycle.

▶James 4:7 says, "Submit yourselves therefore to God. Resist the devil, and he will flee from you." When we confess, that's just the first part — the submitting. We need to finish what James says to do by actively resisting the devil, and taking back the foothold that we've given to the enemy that allows sin to reign in our body. We need to get rid of the dog and shut the door to other dogs!

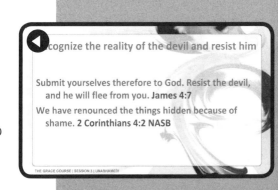

Most Christians have simply not been taught this. But it's actually quite straightforward. *The Steps To Freedom In Christ* is a great way to do this. It's a kind, gentle process that I use every year.

▶Paul says in 2 Corinthians 4:2 NASB, "we have renounced the things hidden because of shame". And that's exactly what we do in the Steps process under the guidance of the Holy Spirit. To renounce something is to declare to God and to the unseen spiritual world that your agreement with, allegiance to, and participation in that thing is over. It is the mouth speaking from a heart of repentance. To repent means to change your mind about your sin and turn away from the shameful practice. When you renounce the things in your life hidden because of shame, you are well on the road to freedom.

It's like stuff accumulated over the years in your home. You know — all those rooms and cupboards you are ashamed of and would never let a guest see because of the stuff that's there! We need to clean out the clutter and throw away the rubbish. Going through the Steps is like a total spring cleaning of your "house"... your body, which is the temple of God's Spirit.

Renew your mind

Bringing the things you have kept hidden because of shame out into the light is a freeing thing. If you are struggling, get some help from a gentle, gracious brother or sister in Christ. We are not meant to fight our battles against sin alone. So don't let the devil convince you to play the "I'm okay" game. When you share your shameful stuff with a brother or sister in Christ who has the Lord's compassion, and you don't find judgment but mercy, it's absolutely liberating!

Once you renounce that sinful, shameful practice and stop allowing sin to use your body for its evil purposes, you will find God's strength to do what's right. For you are not under law but under grace! Then you can go on to be transformed. How? ▶Paul says in Romans 12:2 that it is by the renewal of your mind. That means replacing the lies we've been believing with truth. There's a lie behind every sin you are caught in — it's promising you comfort or that you will feel better in some other way. But it doesn't deliver. It ends up making you feel worse and robbing you of your fruitfulness.

In the next session we'll look at a structured way of replacing lies with truth that we call Stronghold-Busting.

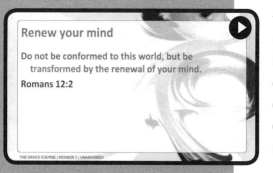

Renew your mind

Do not be conformed to this world, but be transformed by the renewal of your mind.
Romans 12:2

THE GRACE COURSE | SESSION 3 | UNASHAMED!

PAUSE FOR THOUGHT 3

OBJECTIVE:

TO UNDERSTAND THE RELATIONSHIP BETWEEN SHAME AND SIN AND HOW OUR NEW IDENTITY HAS FUNDAMENTALLY CHANGED OUR RELATIONSHIP WITH SIN.

▶**QUESTIONS (ON PAGE 48 OF THE PARTICIPANT'S GUIDE):**

WHAT EFFECT DOES IT HAVE ON US, AND THOSE WE ARE IN RELATIONSHIP WITH, WHEN WE TRY TO KEEP THINGS HIDDEN BECAUSE WE FEEL ASHAMED?

WHEN WE HAVE FALLEN INTO SIN, WHAT ARE THE STEPS WE CAN TAKE TO ENABLE US TO RECOVER FROM IT?

HOW WILL CONSIDERING YOURSELF "DEAD TO SIN" CHANGE THE WAY YOU RESPOND THE NEXT TIME YOU ARE TEMPTED TO SIN?

▶So, this is how God deals with us. He takes us from shame to grace. From humiliation to dignity. From rejection to acceptance. From isolation to belonging. From alienation to intimacy. In Christ.

So, what are some of the lies that this Session has helped you uncover? Let's pray:

Lord, again we ask You to show us areas where we are acting on assumptions that simply aren't true. Where are we making wrong choices because of faulty beliefs? Thank You. Amen.

So turn to your *Lies List* at the back of your Participant's Guide and consider what issues this session has brought up. Potential lies could be:

- that something in the past will always affect your identity

- that something that was done to you makes you inherently dirty when God says you are clean

- that you are somehow "less" than others

 You might consider dividing people into male and female groups for this Pause For Thought.

THE GRACE COURSE | SESSION 3 | UNASHAMED!

 Hand out the "My New Name" Biblical Truth postcard (see page 15) and encourage people to use it to remind themselves of the truths contained in the list.

- that you can't get out of a sin you have been caught in

Write down in the *Lies List* at the back of your Participant's Guide the ones God shows you, and work on finding what is actually true from God's Word before the next session.

There were two caterpillars talking when a butterfly flew past. Looking at it, one said to the other, "You'll never get me up in one of those things!" I said earlier that most Christians are butterflies behaving like caterpillars. Could today be the day that you take hold of the truth of who you have become and start to fly with God?

 WITNESS

How would you share your new name with a non-Christian friend and explain what it means to you?

 IN THE COMING WEEK

Look up the Bible references in the *My New Name* list. Tell one or more people who were not at the session about your new name.

If you are caught in a cycle of sin — confess, sin — confess where you keep returning to the same old sin, use the exercise on page 50 of the Participant's Guide (page 111 of this Leader's Guide).

My New Name

My new name is Beloved (Colossians 3:12)

My new name is Beautiful (Psalm 149:4, Song of Songs 4:1)

My new name is Chosen (Ephesians 1:4)

My new name is Precious (Isaiah 43:4)

My new name is Safe (1 John 5:18)

My new name is Loved (1 John 4:10)

My new name is Clean (John 15:3)

My new name is Presentable (Hebrews 10:22)

My new name is Protected (Psalm 91:14, John 17:15)

My new name is Welcomed (Ephesians 3:12)

My new name is Heir (Romans 8:17, Galatians 3:29)

My new name is Complete (Colossians 2:10)

My new name is Holy (Hebrews 10:10, Ephesians 1:4)

My new name is Forgiven (Psalm 103:3, Colossians 2:13)

My new name is Adopted (Ephesians 1:5)

My new name is Delight (Psalm 147:11)

My new name is Unashamed (Romans 10:11)

My new name is Known (Psalm 139:1)

My new name is Planned (Ephesians 1:11–12)

My new name is Gifted (2 Timothy 1:6, 1 Corinthians 12:11)

My new name is Enriched (2 Corinthians 8:9)

My new name is Provided For (1 Timothy 6:17)

My new name is Treasured (Deuteronomy 7:6)

My new name is Pure (1 Corinthians 6:11)

My new name is Established (Romans 16:25)

My new name is God's Work Of Art (Ephesians 2:10)

My new name is Helped (Hebrews 13:6)

My new name is Free From Condemnation (Romans 8:1)

My new name is God's Child (Romans 8:15–16)

My new name is Christ's Friend (John 15:15)

My new name is Christ's Precious Bride (Revelation 19:7, Song of Songs 7:10).

Breaking Sin — Confess Cycles

[This is a powerful exercise for people who are caught in a sin. Make sure that you draw people's attention to it at the end of the session. It is on page 50 of the Participant's Guide.]

Are you frustrated by returning again and again to the same sins?

We invite you to speak out loud the following declaration (based on Romans 6 and James 4). Instead of depending on your own strength and making rules for yourself to try to keep from sinning, you can enjoy living in the reality of your new identity, Christ in you the hope of glory! (Colossians 1:27) Speak it out every day as long as it takes.

I declare that I am now a new creation in Christ. I am dead to sin and alive to God. I confess my sins [specifically name any habitual sins] and turn away from them.

I specifically declare that the sin of [specifically name any habitual sins one by one] does not rule me any longer and I renounce its control of me. Jesus, who lives in me, is my loving Master and Ruler and all that I am now belongs to Him.

Thank You, Jesus, that You have made me a saint, a holy one, so I CAN glorify You in my body. Therefore I refuse to offer my body to be used to commit unrighteousness. Instead, I submit all that I am to my Heavenly Father who raised me to life with Christ. I now gladly offer the parts of my body: my heart; eyes; ears; mouth; tongue; hands; feet; sexual organs; mind; understanding; mental powers; emotions; imagination and reasoning to God, and I choose to use these parts of my body only for righteousness, completely relying on the power of His Holy Spirit within me to accomplish this.

So I submit myself completely to God and resist the devil who must flee from me now (see James 4:7).

Session 4:
COURAGEOUS!

Session 4: Courageous!

FOCUS VERSE:

Joshua 1:9: Be strong and courageous. Do not be frightened, and do not be dismayed, for the Lord your God is with you wherever you go.

OBJECTIVE:

To understand how to deal with unhealthy fears so that they do not control us.

FOCUS TRUTH:

We do not have to allow unhealthy fears to control us or set the agenda in our lives because God is all-powerful and everywhere-present and has given us the grace gifts of power, love and sound judgment.

Leader's Notes

Most people are not aware that they are a slave to unhealthy fears because they have simply learned to live with them, but we hope that this session will help them realize their presence and take the necessary steps to deal with them. "There is no fear in love, but perfect love casts out fear" (1 John 4:18). Understanding God's gracious love will resolve fear.

We do not want to teach people just the theory. We want them to experience how practically they can resolve unhealthy fears through grace. There are just two Pause For Thought times in this session and they are both very practical. In the first Pause For Thought, which is done as individuals rather than in a group, they will ask the Holy Spirit to help them identify unhealthy fears. In the second, which you can choose to do either as individuals or in a group, they will be encouraged to find the lie behind each fear, something that is not easy because the lie feels true to them. Be prepared to offer help and guidance and encourage them to persist. Identifying the lie is crucial to helping people go on to renew their mind.

The concept of Stronghold-Busting was mentioned briefly in the previous session but is explained more fully in this session. There will be further teaching on it during *The Steps To Experiencing God's Grace* ministry component between sessions 5 and 6. Stronghold-Busting is a structured approach to renewing the mind that is familiar to those who have used *The Freedom In Christ Discipleship Course*. We cannot emphasize strongly enough how life-changing this biblical process can be for those who are prepared to take it seriously.

At the end of the session are two further optional exercises for participants to work on at home to help them resolve fear and anxiety.

SMALL GROUP TIMINGS:

Welcome	6 minutes	0:06
Worship, prayer & declaration	8 minutes	0:14
Word part 1	15 minutes	0:29
Pause For Thought 1	20 minutes	0:49
Word part 2	25 minutes	1:14
Pause For Thought 2	25 minutes	1:39
Word part 3	21 minutes	2:00

 # WELCOME

What were some of the things you were afraid of when growing up?

[Listen for any common themes that may come out. You can then refer to them during the Word section later.]

 # WORSHIP

Suggested theme: Jesus and all in Him is mine! John 10:10, 16:14–15

John 10:10: "I came that they may have life and have it abundantly." Read out this list of titles given to Jesus in the Bible and invite people to praise Him along the lines of, "Dear Lord Jesus, thank You that You are _____ ."

Counsellor, Friend, Saviour, Master, Lamb of God, Redeemer, Bridegroom, Bread of life, Living water, Word of God, Gate, Shepherd, Way, Truth, Life, Teacher, King of kings, Light, Advocate, Vine, Bright Morning Star, Alpha and Omega, Lion of Judah

 # PRAYER & DECLARATION

My Father God, You are my Rock, my Shield, my Deliverer and my High Tower! How wonderful to know that I am in the palm of Your hand and no-one can snatch me away! In the strong name of Jesus my Lord. Amen.

I have not been given a spirit of fear so I turn away any spiritual attack of fear, anxiety or worry. I give them no permission to stop me hearing truth. I choose now to fix my eyes on Jesus and put my confidence in Him alone.

 **WORD**

Be strong and courageous

Sometimes in the Bible, people seem to hear God so clearly. It happened to Joshua.

When the whole generation of the Israelites who escaped from Egypt had died wandering around the wilderness, ▶God finally told Joshua to cross the Jordan and take the land that had been promised to them. It wasn't just empty land — ▶it was full of people who didn't want to move out. Some of them were very large and scary with a nasty array of weapons!

Paul tells us that God has planned some works in advance specifically for you to do (Ephesians 2:10). That's true, even if you feel you have been wandering aimlessly around in the wilderness for years.

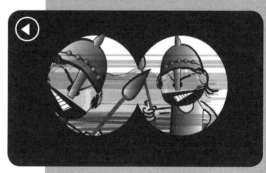

▶I don't know how you feel about that but we can get a pretty good idea about how Joshua was feeling by what God said next.

> "Just as I was with Moses, so I will be with you. I will not leave you or forsake you. Be strong and courageous." (Joshua 1:5–6a)

God then repeats Himself:

> "Only be strong and very courageous" and adds an instruction, "being careful to do according to all the law that Moses my servant commanded you. Do not turn from it to the right hand or to the left, that you may have good success wherever you go." (Joshua: 1: 7–8)

God then repeats Himself yet again:

> "Be strong and courageous. Do not be frightened, and do not be dismayed, for the Lord your God is with you wherever you go." (Joshua 1:9)

So three times in nine verses God tells him to be strong and courageous. Why? Precisely because He knows that Joshua was feeling quite the opposite, weak and frightened. And the basis that he could be strong and courageous? Not his own strength or abilities but simply the fact that God promised to be with him. That is grace, the undeserved favour of God giving us what we desperately need but cannot supply ourselves.

God didn't tell Joshua to make sure he was an expert on military strategy. Nor did He give him plans for the latest in weapons. The only thing God told Joshua to focus on was making sure that he took careful note of the Law given by God via Moses, and did what it said. If he did that, God promised that he would be successful in this crazy venture to take over the Promised Land with a rag-tag bunch of wilderness wanderers.

What does God say to us? The writer to the Hebrews tells us:

> He has said, "I will never leave you nor forsake you." So we can confidently say, "The Lord is my helper; I will not fear; what can man do to me?" (Hebrews 13:5–6).

We too are to keep our eyes on the truth that He will never leave us nor forsake us.

▶ Remember who you are: A child of God with the robe, the ring and the sandals. By His grace, we have everything we need to live a fruitful life. But fear is one of the major things that can hold us back. And if we are motivated by fear, we cannot be motivated by faith or love.

So God would say to us once, "Be strong and courageous...." Twice, "Only be strong and very courageous." And again, "Be strong and courageous."

But how do we put this into practice? In this session we're going to see how God gives us His grace so we can walk free from the fears that hinder us from living by faith in the love of God.

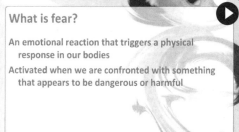

▶ What is fear?

At its core, fear is an emotional reaction that triggers a physical response in our bodies. It comes from the perception of impending danger or harm. ▶ It is activated when we are confronted with something that appears to be dangerous or harmful.

▶ In that situation, our brain quickly evaluates whether it is better to stay and fight or simply to run (what is often called the "fight or flight" response). It then sends a signal to our adrenal glands, which send hormones

around the body to enable it to react rapidly to protect itself from the perceived danger.

Rich Miller's Top 10 Fear List countdown as a child:

10.   Dangling my arm over the side of my bed at night and having the monster under my bed grab it

9.   Swimming in the ocean and being eaten by a great white shark

8.   Being sucked under an escalator

7.   Being kissed by my big-lipped aunt at Christmas

6.   Having my mother call me over with all the relatives around and asking to see how my acne was doing

5.   Having to go to the toilet and not being able to get my zipper down

▶4.   Falling into the toilet

3.   Being flushed down the toilet

2.   That my dog would die

1.   That my big brother WOULDN'T die!

▶If you think about it for a moment, you will see that fear is not necessarily a bad thing. We need to have a healthy fear of things that could harm us.

Healthy fear is fear that makes sense. Stuff like: You don't try and pet snarling, frothing-at-the-mouth dogs; you don't walk your dog in the middle of a road where there are fast cars; you don't put your hands on a hot stove, and that kind of thing.

Unhealthy fear

But then there is also unhealthy fear. That is fear that is not a reasonable response to what is happening, for example having a fear of all dogs, or the fear of driving a car anywhere, or the fear of being in the kitchen at all (a fear that most men seem to have!).

The focus in this session, of course, is on unhealthy fears. We may not even be aware much of the time of some of the unhealthy fears that operate in our lives. On the other hand, some fears can practically control us.

▶Unhealthy fears steal our peace and choke the joy out of living. They work like the coils of a boa constrictor or python. These snakes do not subdue their prey by venom, but by slow suffocation. The snake first bites its victim to gain a hold and then rapidly coils itself around its victim's torso. As the victim breathes out, the coils tighten so that its prey is unable to take as deep a breath as before. After several times of exhaling and the snake's tightening of coils, the victim suffocates, unable to breathe at all.

Fears can do that to us, reducing their victim's world into a smaller and smaller place. For example, someone who is afraid of heights takes an alternative route to work in order to avoid crossing a bridge. Or if that's not possible, he leaves that job and takes a new one closer to home. He won't go to certain other places because it would entail crossing a bridge, or he has an unwillingness to get into an elevator or sightsee in the mountains. And so it goes on. It becomes more and more restricting.

The more severe fears are known as phobias. They are usually the result of trauma, negative modelling from parents or other important adults, and lies they have believed from the evil one. A middle-aged woman was afraid of the dark, but she didn't know why. When she asked God about it, He reminded her that she and some of her friends had been stalked by a man while they were "trick-or-treating" one Halloween. They even had to call the police. She had been fearful ever since. She found her freedom through renouncing that fear and standing in the truth of God's protection over her.

Sometimes fears can become so suffocating that their victims develop agoraphobia (literally "fear of the marketplace"), where they become increasingly fearful of going anywhere because they think they might have a panic attack. Their world may eventually shrink down to just their own house or room.

▶Most of us don't have those kind of phobias. But that does not mean we are not affected by unhealthy fears. It's just that we have learned to cope with them. What do you see when you look at the land God wants you to take?

Maybe we have a fear of talking to people about Jesus. So we simply don't do it and have no expectation of doing it.

Maybe we have a fear of Satan and demons. So we walk away from situations where they may be involved.

Maybe we have a fear of not having money. So we hold on tightly to what we have and let making more money become a top priority in life.

Maybe we have a fear of failure. So we just keep on working as hard as possible, anxious about how well we are performing.

These fears may simply have become part of our lives, so that we think that's just how we are. But they keep us from being the people God created us to be. The great news is that every fear — no matter how severe — can be resolved in Christ, the One who came with grace and truth.

PAUSE FOR THOUGHT 1

OBJECTIVE:

THIS IS AN EXERCISE DURING WHICH PEOPLE ARE ENCOURAGED TO ALLOW THE HOLY SPIRIT TO HELP THEM REALIZE THE FEARS THEY ARE PRONE TO.

▶EXERCISE (ON PAGE 54 OF THE PARTICIPANT'S GUIDE):

FIRST LET'S PRAY THIS PRAYER OUT LOUD TOGETHER:

DEAR HEAVENLY FATHER,
I COME TO YOU AS YOUR CHILD AND I PUT MYSELF UNDER YOUR PROTECTIVE CARE. THANK YOU THAT YOU LOVE ME SO MUCH. I CONFESS THAT I HAVE BEEN FEARFUL AND ANXIOUS BECAUSE OF MY LACK OF TRUST AND UNBELIEF. I HAVE NOT ALWAYS LIVED BY FAITH IN YOU AND TOO OFTEN I HAVE RELIED ON MY OWN STRENGTH AND RESOURCES. I THANK YOU THAT I AM FORGIVEN IN CHRIST.

▶I CHOOSE TO BELIEVE THE TRUTH THAT YOU HAVE NOT GIVEN ME A SPIRIT OF FEAR, BUT OF POWER, LOVE AND SOUND JUDGMENT (2 TIMOTHY 1:7). THEREFORE I RENOUNCE ANY SPIRIT OF FEAR. I ASK YOU TO REVEAL TO MY MIND ALL THE FEARS THAT HAVE BEEN CONTROLLING ME. SHOW ME HOW I HAVE BECOME FEARFUL AND THE LIES I HAVE BELIEVED. I DESIRE TO LIVE A RESPONSIBLE LIFE IN THE POWER OF YOUR HOLY SPIRIT. SHOW ME HOW THESE FEARS HAVE KEPT ME FROM DOING THAT. I ASK THIS SO THAT I CAN CONFESS, RENOUNCE AND OVERCOME EVERY FEAR BY FAITH IN YOU. IN JESUS' NAME. AMEN.

NOW SPEND SOME TIME ON YOUR OWN WITH GOD AND, ON A SEPARATE SHEET, WRITE DOWN THE FEARS THAT YOU HAVE BEEN PRONE TO. THE FOLLOWING LIST MAY HELP YOU IDENTIFY SOME OF THEM BUT THERE WILL PROBABLY BE OTHERS TOO. YOU WILL HAVE THE OPPORTUNITY TO WORK FURTHER ON THE FEARS YOU HAVE IDENTIFIED BEFORE THE END OF THE SESSION. ▶

FEAR OF SATAN
FEAR OF DIVORCE
FEAR OF DEATH
FEAR OF NOT BEING LOVED BY GOD
FEAR OF NEVER BEING LOVED
FEAR OF NOT BEING ABLE TO LOVE OTHERS
FEAR OF MARRIAGE
FEAR OF REJECTION BY PEOPLE
FEAR OF NEVER GETTING MARRIED
FEAR OF NEVER HAVING CHILDREN
FEAR OF DISAPPROVAL
FEAR OF EMBARRASSMENT
FEAR OF FAILURE

FEAR OF FINANCIAL PROBLEMS
FEAR OF GOING CRAZY
FEAR OF BEING A HOPELESS CASE
FEAR OF THE DEATH OF A LOVED ONE
FEAR OF THE FUTURE
FEAR OF CONFRONTATION
FEAR OF BEING A VICTIM OF CRIME
FEAR OF HAVING COMMITTED THE
UNPARDONABLE SIN
FEAR OF SPECIFIC PEOPLE, ANIMALS, OR
OBJECTS
OTHER SPECIFIC FEARS THE LORD BRINGS TO
MIND

Power, love and sound judgment

There was a really loud thunderstorm one night as a little boy was getting ready for bed. "Mum, could you sleep in here with me tonight?" he asked hopefully, shaking with fear as a thunderclap rattled the house. "No, sweetheart," she replied, "I need to sleep with your Dad tonight." After thinking for a moment, the little boy replied, "The big sissy!"

▶ 2 Timothy 1:7 (HCSB) says:

"For God has not given us a spirit of fearfulness, but one of power, love and sound judgment."

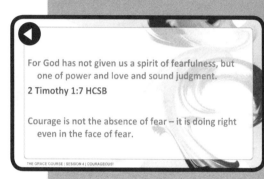

For God has not given us a spirit of fearfulness, but one of power and love and sound judgment.
2 Timothy 1:7 HCSB

Courage is not the absence of fear – it is doing right even in the face of fear.

THE GRACE COURSE | SESSION 4 | COURAGEOUS!

Those three gifts from God... gifts of His grace... are just what we need to deal a death blow to unhealthy fears in our lives. And note that this verse is in the past tense. God has already given us this spirit of power and love and sound judgment. If you are a Christian, this is not something you need to pray to receive but something you need to learn to use.

Fear robs us of power. It weakens us and immobilizes us — like a rabbit caught in the headlights of a car at night.

Fear also stops us being motivated by love. By definition, love is focused on others, but when fear grips you, all you can think about is your own safety, your own protection.

Fear steals away our sound judgment. It confuses us, distorts clear thinking and overwhelms us so that the only thing we can think about is the thing we're afraid of.

But God has not given us that kind of cowardly spirit. He has given us a courageous one. When we act out of fear, we are acting out of character.

▶ Courage by the way is not the absence of fear. It is not sinful to feel fear. It is human. Courage is doing what is right even in the face of fear. The problem comes when we allow that fear to control us and restrict us.

So let's briefly look at the power, love and sound judgment that God has graciously given us and how to use them.

▶ First, God has bestowed on us by His grace the gift of power.

THE GRACE COURSE | SESSION 4 | COURAGEOUS!

Power

Think about the power that raised Christ from the dead. Now that's power! The Bible assures us that this very same power lives in you through the Holy Spirit. (See Romans 8:11, Ephesians 1:18–21).

Remember your position. You are seated with Christ at the right hand of the Father far above all power and authority.

▶But this doesn't mean you have to take a deep breath and think, "Right, I'm going to be strong." It's not your strength that matters, it's the strength of God's Holy Spirit living within you. So why not... even right now... invite the Holy Spirit to take full control of your life and fill you? Let's pray:

Father, thank You for Your Holy Spirit who lives in us. I know there is no way I can live without Your power. I invite You to take complete control of me now. Please fill me to overflowing. Thank you. Amen.

Then it is no longer you by yourself trying to defeat fear, trying to be strong. It is Christ in you. And that makes all the difference in the world.

Love

The second gift that God's grace provides you with is love.

Take a look at what John had to say about this gift of love:

There is no fear in love; but perfect love casts out fear, because fear involves punishment, and the one who fears is not perfected in love.
1 John 4:18

▶There is no fear in love, but perfect love casts out fear. For fear has to do with punishment, and whoever fears has not been perfected in love (1 John 4:18).

If you still struggle with the fear that God will punish you or is constantly upset with you, it is practically impossible for you to trust His love. So you are thrown back onto your own resources to try to deal with your fears on your own. You have been stopped from experiencing God's grace.

Again, the answer is to remember who you are. You are a child of God! God loves YOU, and "There is therefore now no condemnation for those who are in Christ Jesus" (Romans 8:1). When you come to know and realize God's perfect love for you, the fear of His punishment is destroyed.

A church leader was being criticized by a portion of his congregation when his house was struck by lightning. The damage was so severe that he and his family had to move out. Well, you can imagine what the critical faction in the church was saying: "The lightning strike was punishment from God." He said, "I know that it's not punishment from God. All my punishment fell on Christ. He will never punish me. And in any case, I'm in a nice hotel being paid for by the insurance company and when we move back in, they will have redecorated the whole of the upper floor of our house. That's blessing!" God will never punish you if you're a Christian — did you know that? He may **discipline** you out of love but never **punish** you.

Fear of not being loved by God, losing the love of God, or never being loved by others causes us to become self-focused. And it stops us showing grace to others because we can't give away what we do not have ourselves.

Sound judgment

▶Which brings us to the third and final gift of God's grace... and that is sound judgment, sometimes translated as "a sound mind." We are all in a spiritual battle. It is essentially a battle between truth and lies and the battleground is our mind.

[Do you have a story from your own experience like this one from Rich Miller?]

ercising sound judgment

Sound judgment is about seeing things as they really are (how God says they are)

A fear is healthy when the thing we are afraid of is:
- present
- powerful

THE GRACE COURSE | SESSION 4 | COURAGEOUS!

When our son, Brian, was five years old, he developed a phobia of sugar. A dental hygienist had come to his school and talked about "sugar bugs", and so Brian was convinced that if he ate sugar he would get a cavity, and if he got a cavity he would die. Do you see the lie?

It wasn't until he renounced that lie and chose to trust God with his life that he had the chance to break that fear's control. We were all at an ice cream shop enjoying our ice cream... except Brian. I was there with Shirley, our two daughters, and him.

I was alone with Brian, praying so hard that Brian would take a step of faith and eat the ice cream. I told him, "Brian, there's only one way you're going to know that the thought in your head that you're going to die is a lie." "What's that?" he said. What's the answer? "Take a bite."

After a few agonizing moments, he took a bite. "Did you die?" I kidded him. "No..." "Then take another bite." So he did... and then another. Soon he was eating it just like a normal kid.

Then he turned to me and said, "Daddy, I just felt the fear inside of me break in two, just like a stick." Brian was set free from a spirit of fear, and he has not struggled with fear since. He is experiencing the power of the Holy Spirit, the love of God the Father, and the sound mind and judgment of Christ.

Sound judgement is just about seeing things as they really are. How God says they are.

For us to have a legitimate healthy fear of something, the thing that we are afraid of has to have two attributes. ▶It has to be 1) **present** and ▶2) **powerful**. In other words, it has to be nearby and has to have the capacity to hurt us.

Let me give you an example.

I am afraid of venomous snakes. Is that a healthy fear? Absolutely.

▶However, right now I'm not afraid of venomous snakes. Why not? Because there aren't any here. ▶But if you found one and threw it at me and it landed at my feet, hissing, I would hit a "10" on the fear scale and exit stage right... fast!

That snake would be both present **and** powerful. And so I'd be afraid — and I'd be right to be afraid. That is a healthy fear.

▶But what if someone threw a venomous snake at me but it was dead. Would I be afraid? Not once I was sure it was dead, because even though it would be present, it wouldn't be powerful. One of its attributes has been removed... its power. Likewise if I went to the reptile house of a zoo and behind a glass partition there was a spitting cobra. It could spit and strike all it wanted at the glass, but I wouldn't be afraid of it. Why? Because though it might be powerful, it would not be present. It would be completely blocked from getting near me.

The point is this: Neutralizing one of those attributes eliminates the fear. Just one.

How do you break the hold of an unhealthy fear over your mind? Remove one of those two attributes, either its presence or its power.

▶Every unhealthy fear comes from believing that the object of our fear is both present and powerful, when in fact it is not.

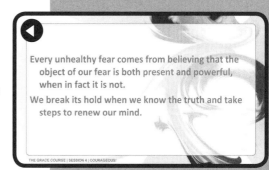

Jesus said that knowing the truth would set us free, and if you want to be set free from an unhealthy fear, ask God to show you the lie behind it. ▶Then you will be able to renounce the lie and take steps to renew your mind which, Paul says, will transform you (Romans 12:2).

Let's have a look at how this can work in practice. Most unhealthy fears are related either to the fear of death or to the fear of other people. If we resolve those two fears, we deal with a lot of other fears too. So let's see how!

The fear of death

▶The fear of death is apparently the second most common fear (the first being the fear of public speaking!).

Can you remove the presence of death? No, unless Jesus comes back first, every one of us is going to die. We could die at any time. So the possibility of death is always a present reality.

What about death's other attribute, its power?

▶The devil wants us to live in the fear of death, but Hebrews 2:14–15 says that Christ died, "that through death he might destroy the one who has the power of death, that is, the devil, and deliver all those who through fear of death were subject to lifelong slavery."

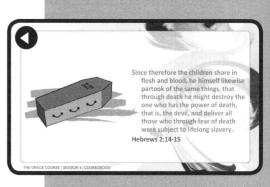

Death has been defeated and so has the fear of death. Fear keeps you in slavery but knowing the truth makes all the difference.

▶I love how Paul tells us the truth about death in 1 Corinthians 15:54–57:

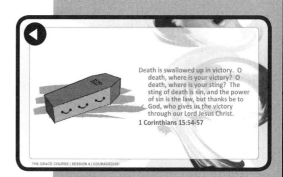

> Death is swallowed up in victory. O death, where is your victory? O death, where is your sting? The sting of death is sin, and the power of sin is the law. But thanks be to God, who gives us the victory through our Lord Jesus Christ.

Yes, death is going to happen — it is still present — but for us it is no longer powerful. It has lost its sting. Paul also makes another striking statement: "For to me to live is Christ, and to die is gain." (Philippians 1:21). If you are living for Christ, when you die it just gets better. Why? Because you get to be with Him, to experience all the joys of heaven.

However, if you believe the lie that says, for example, that no one can be certain that they have eternal life, death will still hold power over you. Behind every unhealthy fear is a lie.

By "lie", then, we mean anything that is at odds with what the Bible says. You deal with a lie by renouncing it and then making a conscious choice to believe the truth instead. When you do that, consistently and persistently, the fear disappears, maybe slowly at first but eventually — by the grace of God — to the point that you can say you are truly free from its control.

The fear of people

Now, let's look at the fear of other people for a moment — what's often called the "fear of man" (though there are some ladies I find pretty scary!). So many of us are afraid to speak up, afraid to share our faith, afraid to take a stand before other people. Proverbs 29:25 says, "The fear of man lays a snare, but whoever trusts in the Lord is safe."

▶ Let's say you've got a huge fear of your boss. He's an intimidating kind of person perhaps, but right now you are not afraid of him are you? Why not? He's not here. But when you go to work on Monday morning, there he is.

While you are having a cup of coffee with your colleagues, you are not afraid of him, are you? No, because he's over the other side of the building in his office. Powerful but not present. In fact, you may well want to get off your chest what you think about him. So you're venting off with your fellow employees, complaining about his latest terrible management decisions, and they suddenly start making little surreptitious signs and gestures desperately trying to warn you that the boss is approaching fast behind you. But you are well into your story and completely oblivious. Eventually you turn around and see him — standing there hands on hips with a tight smile on his face. He says, "Ahem, I'd like you to join me in my office." Now the fear is healthy...! Powerful AND present.

Or is it? You see, we're told not to fear people. So what can you do to stop the boss intimidating you even when he's present? Let's look at how a proper understanding of grace provides the cure.

You have to get rid of one of those attributes. He's a big guy so you can't do anything about the fact that he's present. So what about powerful?

Well, exactly what power does he have over you? What is the worst case scenario? "He might be able to fire me." True. How can you deal with that? Resign! Well, you don't actually have to write the letter — but be willing to if you have to.

You don't need to let anybody else have that kind of intimidating power over you. I am not giving you a licence to be rebellious to your employer. What I am saying is that if you are a good employee and your boss starts demanding that you do things that you know morally or ethically you can't do, then you must obey God rather than man. So the conversation could go, "I'm sorry. I can't lie for you." "I'll get somebody else who can." "That is your choice. I want to be the best possible employee I can, but I won't lie for you." Yes, he may fire you, but you can trust God to take care of you — and He will. Because there is a

Boss above your boss who is ultimately in charge... your heavenly Father.

So is the threat of being rejected by other people powerful and present? Obviously, God does not want us to remove ourselves from the presence of people. He wants us to be actively engaged with people, serving as salt and light in a dark and lost world. So, the possibility of someone not liking us and giving us the cold shoulder or worse is certainly ever present.

Is it powerful? Well that depends... On what? On you! By exercising the sound judgment that God has already given you; by resolving in your own mind today that, if push comes to shove, you will always obey God rather than people and take His opinion of you rather than theirs, you have in effect removed their power. They may be present but they are no longer powerful.

Jesus said, "If anyone comes to me and does not hate his own father and mother and wife and children and brothers and sisters, yes, and even his own life, he cannot be my disciple." (Luke 14:26). The New Living translation helpfully clarifies what He means. It says: "If you want to be my disciple, you must hate everyone else by comparison."

Jesus is saying that we need to come to the point where we resolve that He comes before other people. Even if those closest to us disapprove of what we're doing for Him, as long as we know that it's the right thing, we will not be afraid of them or their disapproval or rejection, but will choose to do the right thing.

In Psalm 56:11, David asks the question, "What can man do to me?" His answer to that question is "nothing". And he's not sitting at this point as king in the luxury of his palace surrounded by his armed guard. This psalm was written after he had been seized by his enemies, the Philistines. He had no idea what would happen to him. He was in a deep, deep hole. But he had resolved that, if he was doing what God wanted, the worst case scenario was OK. Overriding it God was in charge. God was good. The danger from other people was present, but ultimately it wasn't powerful.

PAUSE FOR THOUGHT 2

OBJECTIVE:

TO LEARN THE CONCEPT THAT THERE IS A LIE BEHIND EVERY UNHEALTHY FEAR AND TO START TO UNCOVER SOME OF THOSE LIES.

▶**QUESTIONS (ON PAGE 57 OF THE PARTICIPANT'S GUIDE):**

"BEHIND EVERY UNHEALTHY FEAR IS A LIE." LOOK AT THE FEARS BELOW — OR, BETTER STILL, WORK ON THE FEARS THAT YOU IDENTIFIED IN PAUSE FOR THOUGHT 1. IF SOMEONE IS PRONE TO THOSE FEARS, WHAT LIES MIGHT THEY BELIEVE? FOR EXAMPLE, A POSSIBLE LIE FOR (1) IS "SATAN IS MORE POWERFUL THAN I AM".

1. FEAR OF SATAN AND POWERS OF DARKNESS
2. FEAR OF THE FUTURE
3. FEAR OF REJECTION
4. FEAR OF FAILURE
5. FEAR OF CONFRONTATION
6. FEAR OF FINANCIAL PROBLEMS

WHAT TRUTHS FROM GOD'S WORD CAN YOU FIND FOR EACH LIE? FOR EXAMPLE, FOR (1) A GOOD VERSE WOULD BE JAMES 4:7: "SUBMIT... TO GOD. RESIST THE DEVIL, AND HE WILL FLEE FROM YOU."

Living in freedom from fear

▶All of us will have to do battle with unhealthy fears. That's just a fact of life. Being courageous simply means that we choose to act according to the truth rather than what our fears are telling us. So let's look at a plan of action to deal with them.

1. Deal with sin issues

First, it's crucial to realize that sin leaves us vulnerable to fear, so we need to resolve sin issues. We first come across fear in the Bible when Adam and Eve sinned in the Garden of Eden. Look what happened next:

▶After God called them and asked, "Where are you?" (Genesis 3:9), Adam responded:

"I heard the sound of you in the garden, and I was afraid, because I was naked, and I hid myself."
Genesis 3:10

THE GRACE COURSE | SESSION 4 | COURAGEOUS!

▶ "I heard the sound of you in the garden, and I was afraid, because I was naked, and I hid myself." (Genesis 3:10)

Sin produced shame, and shame caused them to feel fear for the first time in their lives.

Isn't it good to realize, though, that to make a mistake or even to sin doesn't make us bad people. It makes us human. And when we own up to our mistakes and sins, God forgives us, and others are given grace to forgive us, knowing that we are human just like they are. We saw in the last session that we don't need to keep returning to sin any more. We can walk in freedom from sin. And that's the first step to walking away from unhealthy fear.

So we would recommend that before everything else, you go through *The Steps To Freedom In Christ* to give God an opportunity to reveal to you every sin and then deal with every sin through confession and repentance.

I love what 1 John 1:9 says. "If we confess our sins, he is faithful and just to forgive us our sins AND to cleanse us from all unrighteousness." Do you see that? When we confess, God forgives us our sins. That's His antidote to guilt. But He also cleanses us. That's His antidote to shame.

Living in guilt and shame will produce fear in our lives. Understanding and living in God's grace, aware of His all-powerful presence is the antidote for guilt, shame **and** fear.

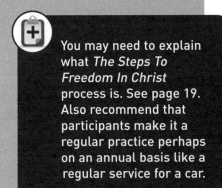

You may need to explain what *The Steps To Freedom In Christ* process is. See page 19. Also recommend that participants make it a regular practice perhaps on an annual basis like a regular service for a car.

2. Realize that God is always present AND always powerful

Secondly, recognize that there is just one fear that is always healthy. The fear of God. Why? ▶ Because God is everywhere present and all powerful.

At first, "the fear of God" sounds like we're supposed to be afraid of Him. Nothing could be further from the truth. ▶ Listen to Romans 8:14–15:

> For all who are led by the Spirit of God, are sons of God. For you did not receive the spirit of slavery to fall back into fear, but you have received the Spirit of adoption as sons, by whom we cry, "Abba! Father!"

Romans 8:14-15

For all who are led by the Spirit of God, are sons of God. For you did not receive the spirit of slavery to fall back into fear, but you have received the Spirit of adoption as sons, by whom we cry, "Abba! Father!"

THE GRACE COURSE | SESSION 4 | COURAGEOUS!

Does that sound like a cringing, suspicious, cowering mistrust of God? Not at all! In Christ we have not been given a spirit that enslaves us and makes us afraid. We are under God's grace. We are His sons and daughters, and the Holy Spirit moves us to cry out from our hearts, "Daddy!", like a young child running to hug their Dad when he walks in from work.

Rather than making us afraid, realizing just how holy and powerful God is should make us rejoice. Why? Because He's on our side! Even brave, courageous King David struggled with fear, but he found the way to keep that fear from overwhelming him. Listen to his words:

> ▶I will bless the Lord at all times; his praise shall continually be in my mouth. My soul will make its boast in the Lord; let the humble hear and be glad. O magnify the Lord with me, and let us exalt his name together! I sought the Lord, and he answered me and delivered me from all my fears. (Psalm 34:1–4)

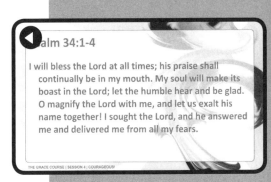

Fearing God starts when you recognize just who He is. And that's also the ultimate antidote to any unhealthy fear; to grasp by faith the truth that the all-knowing, everywhere-present, all-powerful, and absolutely-loving God of grace is right here with us and in us!

▶There is no better way to do that than to worship.

Think about the last time you were caught up in the joy of praising, adoring and worshiping God. Were you afraid? Of course not! You were so focused on Him and who He is that there was no room for fear... only faith!

Notice what David said, "I will bless the Lord at all times. His praise shall continually be in my mouth." Cultivating a lifestyle of praise and worship is essential to overcoming fear.

▶3. Work out the lie behind the unhealthy fear

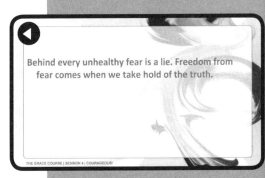

Behind every unhealthy fear is a lie. In order to root out the fear, we need to identify the lie. But this is not a purely psychological exercise, it is a spiritual exercise of seeking God for wisdom, and the gaining of that wisdom can be opposed by the enemy. Let's face it, whether we like it or not, we are all engaged in a spiritual battle with Satan, the one the Bible calls "the father of lies". He will try his best to keep us wallowing in the mire of his lies.

Maybe the mere mention of Satan's name makes the hair on the back of your neck stand up, so let's take that as an example of an unhealthy fear. If talking about Satan and demons makes you a little scared, what lie might you be believing? One possibility might be "Satan is more powerful than I am".

How can I say so confidently that that is a lie? Because of what is written clearly in God's Word. Ephesians 2:6 says that we are seated with Christ. Where is He? At the right hand of the Father in the heavenly realms far above all power and authority. And James 4:7 tells us that if we submit to God and resist the devil, he has to flee from us (not just depart in an orderly fashion!).

So you work out what is a lie by comparing what you believe to what God says in His Word is true. Recognize, however, that at first the lie will by definition feel true. So it can be good to get some help to do that.

▶ 4. Renew your mind

Then the final step is to renew your mind. In Romans 12:2 Paul says this will lead to transformation — that's a strong word. But imagine how different life would be if you weren't controlled by unhealthy fear. Could that be described as a transformation? For many of us, the answer is yes!

When a lie becomes deeply ingrained it becomes a "stronghold", a habitual way of thinking that is inconsistent with what God says in His word. It's like having a solid wall in your mind that prevents you from going the way God wants you to. But if you pound it enough with the demolition ball of God's Word, it will collapse. And you will be transformed.

How do you renew your mind? ▶ We have a strategy that we call "Stronghold-Busting". I'll talk about it a little more after we have been through *The Steps To Experiencing God's Grace*, but let me introduce the idea to you.

First of all, you need to work out what the lie is as we've just mentioned. It's helpful then to consider what effect believing the lie has had in your life. The lie that Satan is

THE GRACE COURSE | SESSION 4 | COURAGEOUS!

Stronghold-Busting

Work out the lie behind the fear (or other stronghold)

Find as many Bible verses as you can that state the truth and write them down

Write a prayer/declaration based on the formula:

    I renounce the lie that....

    I announce the truth that.....

Read the Bible verses and say the prayer/declaration out loud every day for 40 days

THE GRACE COURSE | SESSION 4 | COURAGEOUS!

stronger than you, for example, might lead you not to get involved in the spiritual battle of sharing your faith, perhaps, or to be paralysed in your walk with God, or to be constantly fearful. Realizing the negative effects should spur us on to tear the stronghold down.

Then, find as many Bible verses as you can that state the truth and write them down. A good concordance (or helpful pastor) will come in useful.

Write a prayer or declaration based on the formula:

> I renounce the lie that...
>
> I announce the truth that...

Finally, read the Bible verses and say the prayer/ declaration out loud every day for 40 days, all the time reminding yourself that God is truth and that if He has said it, it really is true for you. There is more information and an example of a couple of Stronghold-Busters in your workbook at the end of this session.

Why 40 days? Psychologists tell us that it takes around six weeks to form or break a habit. Once you have dealt with any footholds of the enemy — the dogs hanging off you where you have opened a door you shouldn't have — a mental stronghold is simply a habitual way of thinking. Can you break a habit? Of course — but it takes some effort over a period of time.

Do persevere until you have completed a total of 40 days, and bear in mind that throughout most of that time it will feel like a complete waste of time, because the lie feels like truth. I promise you that if you persevere you will tear the stronghold down.

A stronghold is anything that has a "strong hold" on you. And Stronghold-Busting is a great way of seeing them demolished.

God's Word or circumstances?

What will you choose to believe: God's Word or your circumstances?

Let's finish by looking at an incident (Mark 4:35–41) when the disciples learned that they did not have to be afraid despite terrifying circumstances. ▶Jesus had spent a full

day teaching, and when it got dark He got into a boat with His disciples and said, "Let us go over to the other side." So they took off across the treacherous Sea of Galilee. As often would happen on that lake, a ferocious storm with gale-force winds and high waves came crashing over them.

> But he was in the stern, asleep on the cushion. And they woke him and said to him, "Teacher, do you not care that we are perishing?" And he awoke and rebuked the wind and said to the sea, "Peace, be still!" And the wind ceased, and there was great calm. He said to them, "Why are you so afraid? Have you still no faith?" And they were filled with great fear and said to one another, "Who then is this, that even the wind and the sea obey him?" (Mark 4:38–41)

The disciples were experienced fishermen, yet even they were afraid they were going to drown. That must have been some whopper of a storm. Why did Jesus rebuke them for their lack of faith?

First, remember what Jesus said as they prepared to cross the lake: "Let us go over to the other side." When Jesus says you're going to do something, He means it. In effect this was a promise. So Jesus was basically saying to the disciples, "Don't you trust My words? Don't you know that I mean what I say?"

In Hebrews 13:5 God says unequivocally to you, "I will never leave you nor forsake you." Never are God's words of assurance put to the test more than when our

circumstances and feelings shout a message directly opposed to what God says is true. In the last session we asked this question: "Are you going to believe what God's Word says about you? Or are you going to believe what your past experiences tell you?" ▶ Let's ask ourselves a similar question in relation to fear: "Are you going to believe what God's Word says about you? Or are you going to believe what your circumstances tell you?"

Don't assume, by the way, that if your circumstances are difficult something is wrong. Provided the difficult circumstances we face are not a direct result of sin or something stupid we've done, they are probably there to help us grow. If you can get hold of that, you can actually get to the point — like Paul did — where you can rejoice in your difficulties, because you know they are helping you mature and bear fruit. One great piece of advice I received is, "Don't doubt in the darkness what God has shown you in the light." In other words, just because things are difficult now, don't assume that you heard wrongly from God. Trust what He said to you when things weren't so tough, and persevere through. The maturity that you will develop in the difficult times is probably what you will need in the place that He has called you to.

Fear is the opposite of faith — and faith is simply making a choice to believe what God Himself has told us is true.

▶ The rebuke from Jesus to the disciples was also a response to their question, "Teacher, do You not care that we are perishing?" What a slap in the face to Jesus. Now, we recognize that the disciples were scared witless and Jesus was asleep, but how could they even think that Jesus didn't care?

Jesus cares. He really cares — for you. He showed it by dying the most terrible death imaginable and He would have died for you if you had been the only person in the whole of history who needed Him to. God Himself is with you. God Himself cares for you.

No matter what the world throws at you, you have Jesus in your boat. So there's no need to be afraid. Go out there and do the things He has prepared for you to do. Take the land He wants you to take!

▶ "Be strong and courageous. Do not be frightened, and do not be dismayed, for the Lord your God is with you wherever you go." (Joshua 1:9)

By now you should be getting into the swing taking a few quiet minutes at the end of each session asking God to show you the lies you have believed. It is amazing how those lies can come to dominate our lives and control our thinking, feeling and acting... without our even realizing it! Let's pray together:

Thank You, Father, that You are the One who will never leave us or forsake us. Please show us now the lies we have believed, particularly those behind our fears. Thank you. Amen.

So turn to the *Lies List* on the last two pages of your Participant's Guide.

Remember that every controlling, unhealthy fear in our lives has at its root at least one lie that we have believed.

One very common lie that fuels our fear is: "If I say what I really believe, people will reject me and that will be too painful to endure. So it's safer to stay quiet."

Another is that God will not be there for us, that He will abandon us.

Some of the lies behind your fears may take a bit of unravelling. Be prepared to do some work on them in the coming days. But just think how different things could be if you were to get rid of those unhealthy fears! And that's absolutely possible.

I want to draw your attention to two additional exercises in your Participant's Guide at the end of the notes for this session for you to work through on your own. If you have become aware of unhealthy fears, we would very much recommend that you go through the *Steps To Overcoming Fear* process which starts on page 65 of your Participant's Guide. It's self-explanatory. Just work through it and allow the Holy Spirit to guide you. And if anxiety is an issue for you, there's a process called *Resolving Anxiety* (on pages 68–70 of your Participant's Guide), which helps you work out what is your responsibility and what is God's, so that you can do what is yours to do and then cast the rest onto Him. ▶

 **WITNESS**

How would you explain to someone who doesn't yet know Jesus the difference that He makes in enabling you to live free from controlling fears?

 IN THE COMING WEEK

If you have become aware that fear and anxiety are issues for you, go through two exercises, *Steps To Overcoming Fear* (on pages 65–67 of the Participant's Guide) and *Resolving Anxiety* (on pages 68–70 of the Participant's Guide). They were originally written by Dr. Neil T. Anderson as appendices to his *Steps To Freedom In Christ* and are used by permission. If you struggle a lot with fear and anxiety, you will benefit from having a mature Christian friend to help you as you go through them. If you have completed Pause For Thought 1 in this session, you have already made a good start on the first exercise.

Stronghold-Busting

This simple process is a straightforward way to renew your mind. This is how it works:

1. Work out the lie behind the fear (or other stronghold)

First of all, you need to work out what the lie is, as we did in Pause For Thought 2 in this session. Other people might be a great help at this point.

It's helpful then to consider what effect believing the lie has had in your life — this should spur you on to tear the stronghold down. The effect of believing the lie that Satan is stronger than you, for example, might be that you let the enemy deflect you from God's purposes for you.

2. Find as many Bible verses as you can that state the truth and write them down

A good concordance or helpful church leader might come in useful here.

3. Write a prayer or declaration based on the formula:

I renounce the lie that...

I announce the truth that...

You can see some examples of completed Stronghold-Busters on the next two pages to get the idea of what this might look like.

4. Read the Bible verses and say the prayer/declaration out loud every day for 40 days

Why 40 days? Psychologists tell us that it takes around six weeks to form or break a habit. Once you have dealt with any sin issues that give the enemy a foothold in your life, a mental stronghold is simply a habitual way of thinking. Can you break a habit? Yes — but it takes some effort over a period of time. Do persevere until you have completed a total of 40 days and bear in mind that throughout most of that time, it will feel like a complete waste of time because the lie feels like truth. If you persevere, you will tear the stronghold down.

Stronghold-Buster Example 1

Fear Of Disapproval

The lie: that I am not good enough or unacceptable.

Effects in my life: feeling intimidated; fearing people; compromising my convictions; changing my appearance; anxious about saying and doing the "right thing"

John 15:16

You did not choose me, but I chose you...

2 Corinthians 1:22

[He] has put his seal on us and given us his Spirit in our hearts as a guarantee.

Zephaniah 3:17

He will rejoice over you with gladness; he will quiet you by his love; he will exult over you with loud singing.

1 Samuel 16:7

Man looks on the outward appearance, but the Lord looks on the heart.

Psalm 118:6

The Lord is on my side; I will not fear. What can man do to me?

1 Thessalonians 2:4

We have been approved by God to be entrusted with the gospel, so we speak, not to please man, but to please God who tests our hearts.

Dear Father God,

I renounce the lie that I am not good enough or unacceptable. I announce the truth that You chose me and that I have received a new heart and therefore I have Your seal of approval. Even when others are not pleased with me, You take great delight in me and Your opinion matters much more. I now choose to please You rather than other people, and rely on Your promise to be with me wherever I go as I share the good news with others.

Amen.

Check off the days:

1	2	3	4	5	6	7	8	9	10	11	12
13	14	15	16	17	18	19	20	21	22	23	24
25	26	27	28	29	30	31	32	33	34	35	36
37	38	39	40								

Stronghold-Buster Example 2

Fear Of Failure

The lie: when I fail I am worth less than before.

Effects in my life: unwilling to attempt new challenges that are outside my comfort zone; being task-focused rather than people-focused; anger; competitiveness; striving for perfection

Isaiah 43:4

You are precious in my eyes and I love you.

Colossians 2:10

In [Christ] you have been made complete. (NASB)

Ephesians 2:10

We are his workmanship, created in Christ Jesus for good works, which God prepared beforehand.

Ephesians 3:20

[God] is able to do far more abundantly than all that we ask or think, according to the power at work within us.

Philippians 2:13

It is God who works in you, both to will and to work for his good pleasure.

Dear Heavenly Father,

I renounce the lie that when I fail I am worth less than before. I announce the truth that I have been handcrafted by You and am precious, honoured and loved by You regardless of the success or failure of what I do. I declare that I am already fully complete in Christ and that You are working in me for Your good pleasure and to do far more abundantly than all I could ask or think.

In Jesus' name. Amen.

Check off the days:

1	2	3	4	5	6	7	8	9	10	11	12
13	14	15	16	17	18	19	20	21	22	23	24
25	26	27	28	29	30	31	32	33	34	35	36
37	38	39	40								

Steps To Overcoming Fear

Analyze your fear under God's authority and guidance

Begin by praying the following prayer aloud:

Dear Heavenly Father,
I come to You as Your child and I put myself under Your protective care. Thank You that You love me so much. I confess that I have been fearful and anxious because of my unbelief and lack of trust. I have not always lived by faith in You and too often I have relied on my own strength and resources. I thank You that I am forgiven in Christ.

I choose to believe the truth that You have not given me a spirit of fear, but of power, love and sound judgment (2 Timothy 1:7). Therefore I renounce any spirit of fear. I ask You to reveal to my mind all the fears that have been controlling me. Show me how I have become fearful and the lies I have believed. I desire to live a responsible life in the power of Your Holy Spirit. Show me how these fears have kept me from doing that. I ask this so that I can confess, renounce and overcome every fear by faith in You. In Jesus' name. Amen.

The following list may help you recognize some of your fears. On a separate sheet, write down the ones that apply to you, as well as any others not on the list that the Spirit of God has revealed to you.

- ❑ Fear of Satan
- ❑ Fear of divorce
- ❑ Fear of death
- ❑ Fear of not being loved by God
- ❑ Fear of never being loved
- ❑ Fear of not being able to love others
- ❑ Fear of marriage
- ❑ Fear of rejection by people
- ❑ Fear of never getting married
- ❑ Fear of never having children
- ❑ Fear of disapproval
- ❑ Fear of embarrassment
- ❑ Fear of failure
- ❑ Fear of financial problems
- ❑ Fear of going crazy
- ❑ Fear of being a hopeless case
- ❑ Fear of the death of a loved one
- ❑ Fear of the future
- ❑ Fear of confrontation
- ❑ Fear of being a victim of crime
- ❑ Fear of speaking to people about Jesus
- ❑ Fear of having committed the unpardonable sin
- ❑ Fear of specific people, animals, or objects
- ❑ Other specific fears the Lord brings to mind

  _____

The root of any unhealthy fear is a belief that is not based in truth. These false beliefs need to be rooted out and replaced by the truth of God's Word. Take as much time in prayer as you need to discern these lies, because renouncing them and choosing the truth is a critical step towards gaining and maintaining your freedom in Christ. You have to know and choose to believe the truth in order for it to set you free. Write down the lies you have believed for every fear and the corresponding truth from the Word of God.

Ways you have been living under the control of fear

The next step is to determine how fear has prevented you from living a responsible life, compelled you to do live irresponsibly, or compromised your Christian witness. After you have gained the necessary insights into your fear, it is time to experience God's cleansing through confession and repentance (see 1 John 1:9, Proverbs 28:13). Confession is agreeing with God that what you did was sinful. Repentance is the choice to turn away from sin and to change your way of thinking. Express the following prayer for each of the controlling fears that you have analyzed above:

Dear Lord,
I confess and repent of the fear of _____. I have believed (state the lie). I renounce that lie and I choose to believe the truth (state the truth). I also confess any and all ways this fear has resulted in living irresponsibly, or compromising my witness for Christ (be specific).

I now choose to live by faith in You, Lord, believing Your promise that You will protect me and meet all my needs as I live by faith in You (Psalm 27:1; Matthew 6:33,34). In Jesus' trustworthy name. Amen.

After working through every fear the Lord has revealed to you (including their accompanying lies and sinful behaviour), then pray the following prayer:

Dear Heavenly Father,
I thank You that You are indeed trustworthy. I choose to believe You, even when my feelings and circumstances tell me to fear. You have told me not to fear, for You are with me; not to look about me anxiously, for You are my God. You will strengthen me, help me, and surely uphold me with Your righteous right hand. In Jesus' mighty name. Amen. (See Isaiah 41:10.)

Work out a plan of responsible behaviour

The next step is to face the fear and prayerfully work out a plan to overcome it. Somebody once said, "Do the thing you fear the most and the death of fear is certain." Fear is like a mirage in the desert. It seems so real until you move towards it, but then it disappears into thin air. But as long as we back away from fear, it will haunt us and grow in size, becoming like a giant.

Determine in advance what your response will be to any fear object

The fear of God is the one fear that can dispel all other fears, because God rules supreme over every other fear object, including Satan. Even though "your adversary the devil prowls around like a roaring lion, seeking someone to devour" (1 Peter 5:8), he has been defeated. "Having disarmed the powers and authorities, [Jesus] made a public spectacle of them, triumphing over them by the cross" (Colossians 2:15 NIV).

The presence of any fear object should prompt us to focus on God who is always present and all powerful. To worship God is to acknowledge and ascribe to Him His divine attributes. This keeps fresh in our minds the truth that our loving Heavenly Father is always with us and is more powerful than any enemy or circumstance.

Commit to carrying out the plan of action in the power of the Holy Spirit

Remember, you are never alone in the battle. "It is God who works in you to will and to act according to his good purpose" (Philippians 2:13 NIV).

Resolving Anxiety

Anxiety is different from fear in that it lacks an object or adequate cause. People are anxious because they are uncertain about a specific outcome or don't know what is going to happen in the future. It is normal to be concerned about things we value; not to do so would demonstrate a lack of care.

You can be temporarily anxious about an examination yet to be taken, attendance at a planned function, or the threat of an incoming storm. Such concern is normal and should ordinarily move you to responsible action. For some, the anxiety is more intense and prolonged. They struggle with a large number of worries and spend a lot of time and energy doing so. The intensity and frequency of the worrying are always out of proportion to the actual problem.

If persistent anxiety is a problem in your life, this exercise can help you to cast all your anxieties on Christ because He cares for you (see 1 Peter 5:7).

Pray

Prayer is the first step in casting all your anxiety on Christ. Remember Paul's word, "Do not be anxious about anything, but in everything by prayer and supplication with thanksgiving let your requests be made known to God" (Philippians 4:6). Ask God to guide you by expressing the following prayer:

Dear Heavenly Father,
I come to You as Your child purchased by the blood of the Lord Jesus Christ. I declare my dependence upon You, and I acknowledge my need of You. I know that apart from Christ I can do nothing. You know the thoughts and intentions of my heart and You know the situation I am in from the beginning to the end. I feel as though I am double-minded, and I need Your peace to guard my heart and my mind. I humble myself before You and choose to trust You to exalt me at the proper time in any way You choose. I place my trust in You to supply all my needs according to Your riches in glory and to guide me into all truth. I ask for Your divine guidance so that I may fulfil my calling to live a responsible life by faith in the power of Your Holy Spirit. "Search me, O God, and know my heart! Try me and know my thoughts! And see if there be any grievous way in me, and lead me in the way everlasting!" (Psalm 139:23–24). In Jesus' precious name. Amen.

Resolve any personal and spiritual conflicts

The purpose of *The Steps To Freedom In Christ* is to help you get radically right with God and eliminate any possible influences of the devil on your mind. Remember, "The Spirit clearly says that in later times some will abandon the faith and follow deceiving spirits and things taught by demons" (1 Timothy 4:1 NIV). You will be a double-minded person if you pay attention to a deceiving spirit. You need to have the presence of God so that "the peace of God, which surpasses all understanding, will guard your hearts and your minds in Christ Jesus" (Philippians 4:7).

State the problem

A problem well-stated is half-solved. In anxious states of mind, people typically can't see the forest for the trees. Put the problem in perspective: will it matter for eternity? Generally speaking, the process of worrying takes a greater toll on a person than the negative consequences of what they worried about. Many anxious people find tremendous relief by simply having their problem clarified and put into perspective.

Separate the facts from the assumptions

People may be fearful of the facts, but not anxious. We're anxious because we don't know what is going to happen tomorrow. Since we don't know, we make assumptions. A peculiar trait of the mind is its tendency to assume the worst. If the assumption is accepted as truth, it will drive the mind to its anxiety limits. If you make presumptions about tomorrow, you will suffer the negative consequences, or stress and anxiety. "Anxiety in a man's heart weighs him down" (Proverbs 12:25). Therefore, as best as possible, verify all assumptions.

Determine what you have the right or ability to control

You are responsible only for that which you have the right and ability to control. You are not responsible for that which you don't. Your sense of worth is tied only to that for which you are responsible. If you aren't living a responsible life, you should feel anxious! Don't try to cast your **responsibility** onto Christ — He will throw it back to you. But do cast your **anxiety** onto Him, because His integrity is at stake in meeting your needs if you are living a responsible and righteous life.

List what is your responsibility

You need to commit yourself to be a responsible person and fulfil your calling and obligations in life.

The rest is God's responsibility

Your only remaining responsibility is to continue to pray and focus on the truth according to Philippians 4:6-8. Any residual anxiety is probably due to your assuming responsibilities that God never intended you to have.

Session 5:
HUMBLE!

Session 5: Humble!

FOCUS VERSE:

Matthew 22:37–40: You shall love the Lord your God with all your heart and with all your soul and with all your mind. This is the great and first commandment. And a second is like it: You shall love your neighbour as yourself. On these two commandments depend all the Law and the Prophets.

OBJECTIVE:

To understand the importance God puts on humbling ourselves before others and what it means in practice.

FOCUS TRUTH:

When we understand our amazing position of security in God's love, we are free to humble ourselves before Him and others so that we can work together to reach the world for Christ.

Leader's Notes

In this session, we come to pride, the fourth and final false motivator that we will be looking at. Whereas participants have probably been able to identify with guilt, shame and fear issues in their lives, pride is much more difficult to recognize. If you are proud, you generally don't realize it.

When you consider Jesus' prayer in John 17 for those who came after His original disciples (that's us!), and see that the thing He chose to focus on is that we would be one "so that the world may believe that you have sent me" (John 17:21), you start to get a sense of why this whole area is such a spiritual battleground. Can you think of anything more important for the Church than being genuinely united?

Satan wants to divide us and keep us from experiencing the blessing that comes from unity. The ways he does this are subtle. Perhaps his most successful strategy has been to get us to focus exclusively on truth. Now this whole course is all about helping people get hold of the truth so that may sound a rather surprising thing for us to say. Of course, God's truth is of crucial importance. Yet, when we emphasize truth above grace, we end up just like the Pharisees and on the side of disunity rather than unity.

This is a difficult area. It can sound to some as if we are saying "anything goes" or "bad doctrine doesn't matter". We are not, of course, saying that at all. We absolutely 100% affirm the importance of believing God's Word. Yet if we have the best doctrine in the world but have no love, it's worth nothing at all.

SMALL GROUP TIMINGS:

Welcome	6 minutes	0:06
Worship, prayer & declaration	9 minutes	0:15
Word part 1	25 minutes	0:40
Pause For Thought 1	10 minutes	0:50
Word part 2	25 minutes	1:15
Pause For Thought 2	15 minutes	1:30
Word part 3	13 minutes	1:43
Pause For Thought 3	15 minutes	1:58
Word part 4	2 minutes	2:00

 # WELCOME

Who is the humblest person you have ever met?

 # WORSHIP

Suggested theme: We love because He first loved us — 1 John 4:19.

"Before a man can seek God, God must first have sought the man" (A.W. Tozer).

Ask people to look back at their lives and recognize the moments where God was pursuing them.

Encourage them to respond in love to God for all the ways He has sought to draw them into a deeper experience of His love for them.

 # PRAYER & DECLARATION

Dear Loving and Gracious Father, I can do nothing whatsoever of any real value without You. I offer myself to You now as a living sacrifice. Please lead me into all truth. I ask this in the humble name of Jesus Christ. Amen.

In Christ I am no longer under the Law but under grace. I choose no longer to follow "the Law" as my lord or "rules" as my ruler. I declare that Jesus Christ is my Lord and I command His enemies to leave my presence.

 **WORD**

Introduction

Do you get angry when God's truth is watered down? When those who are supposed to be God's people overlook the realities of the spiritual world, say there is no such thing as a real devil, and imply that miracles don't happen? Me too.

What me? A Pharisee?

If a group of ordinary people were formed in your area, who were radically committed to the whole of God's truth and to working out how to practically live out that truth in day-to-day life, would you be interested in joining them?

▶The Pharisees get a lot of bad press. We think of them as shallow hypocrites, but they were in fact exactly that group of ordinary people who were radically committed to truth. The religious establishment had become very liberal — many denied truths such as the resurrection and the reality of the spiritual world. The Pharisees, on the other hand, gave God's Word a very high place; they were completely committed to living pure and righteous lives untainted by evil; they wanted to handle tempting things like money and sex absolutely properly. They were the sincere, committed people of the day who really wanted to see God's Kingdom established and sin stamped out. And they were waiting for Messiah.

Then the most pivotal moment in all history came knocking on their door. Messiah had come! Here He was in their midst, even talking to them — but they completely missed Him! How could the Pharisees have messed up so badly?

The Pharisees' problem was that they had a grasp of truth, but they didn't have a clue about grace. The Pharisees knew a lot about the Law — God's Word — and they valued it highly. But they used it primarily to bolster their own egos, and as a weapon to keep others under their religious control. They are a classic example of the statement that Paul wrote, "Knowledge puffs up, but love builds up" (1 Corinthians 8:1).

In this session, we will look at the fourth hindrance to grace, pride. Pride is another false motivator that keeps us from being compelled by love. Pride robs us of experiencing God's grace.

If I'm honest, I know in my heart of hearts that, if I'd been there at that time, I'd probably have been a Pharisee.

During His time on earth, Jesus constantly clashed with the Pharisees. Let's take a look at a typical incident to try to understand the root of this issue.

The woman caught in adultery (John 8:3–11)

▶ The scribes and the Pharisees brought a woman who had been caught in adultery, and placing her in the midst they said to him, "Teacher, this woman has been caught in the act of adultery. Now in the Law Moses commanded us to stone such women. So what do you say?" (John 8:3–5)

The Pharisees had a good intellectual grasp of the truth. Moses did indeed command that adulterers should be put to death. Leviticus 20:10 says: "If a man commits adultery with the wife of his neighbour, both the adulterer and the adulteress shall surely be put to death." I've thought carefully about this and I'm having trouble working out how you can catch just one person in the act of adultery! So there's a big question as to why they singled out the woman and ignored the man, but nevertheless what they are saying is true. Their doctrine is correct.

Jesus bent down and wrote with his finger on the ground. And as they continued to ask him, he stood up and said to them, "Let him who is without sin among you be the first to throw a stone at her." And once more he bent down and wrote on the ground. But when they heard it, they went away one by one, beginning with the older ones, and Jesus was left alone with the woman standing before him. (John 8:6–9)

Jesus' amazing statement led to their having an uncharacteristic moment of clarity, and in their heart of hearts they all realized they had sinned too. It makes you wonder if the adulterer himself might even have been part of the crowd. They were in effect just like the woman. None of them had lived up to the righteous standards of the Law. They may not have committed this particular sin but all of them were guilty of some sin.

> ▶ Jesus stood up and said to her, "Woman, where are they? Has no one condemned you?" She said, "No one, Lord." And Jesus said, "Neither do I condemn you; go, and from now on sin no more." (John 8:10–11)

There was only one person there who had never sinned. There was only one person there who truly understood the truth of God's word, because He indeed was The Truth. He had every right to stone her to death. Yet He didn't speak a single word of condemnation.

The Pharisees thought that God's primary priority was that people's behaviour should be precisely right. Jesus, however, knew that the Father's desire was for His people to know His love and experience His pleasure in them, so that they would out of the overflow of His love, love others. Then His people would — out of that love — do what is right!

Religious people are into rules. God is into relationships.

Religious people put laws above love. God makes love the supreme goal.

Religious people are most concerned about being right. God is most concerned that we be real. Only then can we be right.

Religious people make their highest aim to know the Word of God. God wants us to make our highest aim to know the God of the Word.

John 1:17 NIV says, "For the law was given through Moses, grace and truth came through Jesus Christ."

To be fair to the Pharisees, God had given a lot of very specific rules for behaviour in the Old Testament, and it's easy to understand why they went down this particular blind alley. Now, the God of the Old Testament is exactly the same as the God of the New Testament. He has not changed and His eternal purposes have not changed.

Why did the God of grace give the Law?

▶So why did the God of grace give these rules which are collectively known as "the Law"?

In Galatians 3, Paul begins to answer this question. First he makes the point that the Law was not given until hundreds of years after God's original covenant with Abraham (Galatians 3:16–18). The series of promises that God makes to Abram in that original covenant are very interesting:

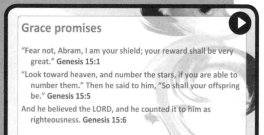

Grace promises

"Fear not, Abram, I am your shield; your reward shall be very great." **Genesis 15:1**

"Look toward heaven, and number the stars, if you are able to number them." Then he said to him, "So shall your offspring be." **Genesis 15:5**

And he believed the LORD, and he counted it to him as righteousness. **Genesis 15:6**

▶"Fear not, Abram, I am your shield; your reward shall be very great." (Genesis 15:1)

▶"Look toward heaven, and number the stars, if you are able to number them." Then he said to him, "So shall your offspring be." (Genesis 15:5)

There's no "If you do this, I will do that". God just makes unconditional promises — grace promises. Their outcome does not depend on what Abraham does but purely on God's grace.

▶"And he believed the Lord, and he counted it to him as righteousness." (Genesis 15:6)

Abraham does just one thing: Chooses to believe what God promises. It has always been the same. We enter into God's grace promises and blessing by faith and faith alone — not by anything we do.

...the law, which came 430 years afterwards, does not annul a covenant previously ratified by God, so as to make the promise void. For if the inheritance comes by the law, it no longer comes by promise; but God gave it to Abraham by a promise.
Galatians 3:17-18

▶Paul then fast forwards ahead a few centuries to the point where God met Moses on Mount Sinai and delivered to him the two tablets containing the Ten Commandments. And Paul reminds us that the giving of the Law 430 years after the promises to Abraham, did not change what God had said before.

When the Law came, it did not nullify the grace promises God had made. It's not as if the original plan was grace, and that God's plan somehow went badly wrong and had to be changed to Law.

▶Paul then asks the 64 million dollar question — one that you are probably asking yourself:

Why then the law? He then goes on to answer that question for us:

"It was added because of transgressions" (Galatians 3:19), that is, our rebellious sins against God.

What does that actually mean? ▶Let's turn now to Romans 3:19–20:

> "Now we know that whatever the law says it speaks to those who are under the law, so that every mouth may be stopped, and the whole world may be held accountable to God." (Romans 3:19)

The Law was given in fact to "stop every mouth"... basically to shut us all up and keep people from making excuses, such as "Oh, I didn't know that was wrong. How can God judge me for that?" and to make everybody — the whole world — accountable to God. Its main purpose was to bring the knowledge of right and wrong and to let us know that God was right and we were wrong. Paul continues:

> "For by works of the law no human being will be justified in his sight, since through the law comes knowledge of sin." (Romans 3:20)

---

hy did God give the Law?

To make us aware of our sinfulness
It was added because of transgressions **Galatians 3:19**

Now we know that whatever the law says it speaks to those who are under the law, so that every mouth may be stopped, and the whole world may be held accountable to God. For by works of the law no human being will be justified in his sight, since through the law comes knowledge of sin. **Romans 3:19-20**

THE GRACE COURSE | SESSION 5 | HUMBLE!

THE GRACE COURSE | SESSION 5 | HUMBLE!

▶The Law never was meant to provide a way to become acceptable to God through our own efforts. It was there so that we would become so aware of the awfulness of sin and its control over us, that we would realize the complete futility of trying hard to behave well in order to be acceptable.... In other words, it's there to show us our need of grace, our need of Christ. The Law itself was actually a means of grace!

The Pharisees didn't understand this. They thought that the point of the Law was to make you righteous in God's sight if you obeyed it.

They stretched it to the point of absurdity. For example, God had given a commandment that people were to rest on the Sabbath day. Trying to help people work out what that meant practically, the teachers of the Law had defined 39 types of activity that constituted work, including binding sheaves, threshing, kneading, shearing wool, writing two or more letters or erasing two or more letters, making a fire or extinguishing a fire.

Orthodox Jews today still have more or less the same traditions. The discovery of electricity caused a lot of debate for them — when you flick an electric switch to turn on a light, it causes tiny sparks. Does that constitute making a fire? Some teachers say it does; others say it doesn't. If your preferred authority says it does and you would prefer not to sit in darkness on the Sabbath, what can you do about that? Well, most decide to use electric time-switches so that they don't actually have to flick the switch themselves on the Sabbath, but the light still comes on. Very pragmatic!

Do you see how it has shifted from the real point of the commandment — to make sure that we have a time to rest and seek God in the midst of the busyness of life — to focusing on the mechanics of how a light switch is turned on!

Jesus delighted in frustrating the Pharisees' misuse of the Law. Since all work on the Sabbath was prohibited by the Pharisees (but doing good was not prohibited by God), Jesus loved to heal on the Sabbath. You might remember one Sabbath when a blind man was brought to Him. Jesus spat on the ground and made mud, put it on the man's eyes and healed him. Any idea why Jesus chose that method to heal? Because the Jews were happy for you to spit on a rock on the Sabbath, but not to spit on the dust... because spit juice + dust = mud, which was doing work, according to them. So Jesus had fun, healing the man and spitting in the eye, so to speak, of the Pharisees' ridiculous religious traditions!

How did Jesus fulfil the Law?

When Jesus came and refused to play their religious games, the Pharisees complained that He was breaking God's Law. They missed the point completely. Jesus said:

▶ "Do not think that I have come to abolish the Law or the Prophets; I have not come to abolish them but to fulfil them. For truly, I say to you, until heaven and earth pass away, not an iota, not a dot, will pass from the Law until all is accomplished." (Matthew 5:17–18)

Jesus put a very high value on the Law. He claimed to be its very fulfilment. How exactly did He do that?

▶ He became the perfect sacrifice and met all of the Law's righteous demands on our behalf.

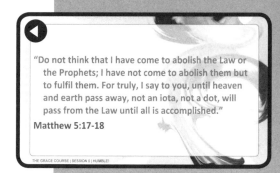

Romans 8:2–3 tells us that what the Law could not do for us, that is, make us perfect and sinless, God did through His perfect, sinless Son. Jesus condemned our sin, so that now **we** are **not** condemned, by paying the penalty of death for our sin through offering Himself on the cross for us.

▶ He helped us understand the true purpose of the Law

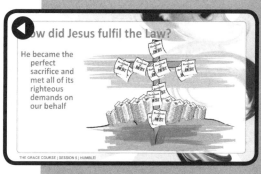

▶ Jesus goes on to make a statement that would have been absolutely shocking to those who were listening:

"I tell you, unless your righteousness exceeds that of the scribes and Pharisees, you will never enter the kingdom of heaven." (Matthew 5:20)

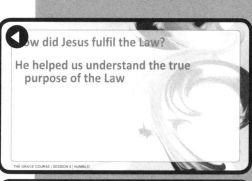

Imagine the people listening to this who are Jesus' followers. The scribes and the Pharisees were seen as the most righteous people of their day. But Jesus was saying that not even their standards were high enough to match God's standard of holiness. He then does perhaps an even

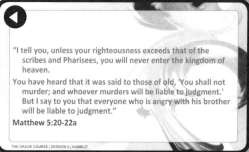

more astonishing thing. He takes the Law, which already seemed an impossible standard, and raises the bar even higher:

▶ "You have heard that it was said to those of old, 'You shall not murder; and whoever murders will be liable to judgment.' But I say to you that everyone who is angry with his brother will be liable to judgment." (Matthew 5:21–22a)

▶ "You have heard that it was said, 'You shall not commit adultery.' But I say to you that everyone who looks at a woman with lustful intent has already committed adultery with her in his heart." (Matthew 5:27–28)

And continues with a number of similar commands. Each time He sets the bar higher than the Law. Then at the end of that section He hammers the nail into the coffin:

▶ "You therefore must be perfect, as your heavenly Father is perfect." (Matthew 5:48)

▶ In a pole vault competition, the competitors keep jumping until the bar is too high for all of them. Even if there is just one person left, the bar keeps being raised. Ultimately he too will fail.

I guess there was at least a theoretical possibility that someone could fulfil all 613 parts of the Law. But Jesus raised the bar to such a height that it became impossible.

The true purpose of the Law was to show us that, without God's grace, we cannot be pleasing to God. It is meant to take us to the point where we throw ourselves on God's mercy in absolute desperation, realizing the extent of our need of Him. The Pharisees turned that around and used it to raise themselves up, to get respect from others, to convince themselves that they — and only they — were OK. And that's pride.

He enabled the Law to be written on our hearts

Jesus also fulfilled the Law by enabling it to be written on our hearts and on our minds.

Each time Jesus raised the bar, He moved it from a law that focussed on external behaviour to what is inside, the thoughts and intentions of our heart. That is what God is after... our hearts!

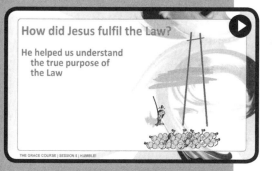

"You have heard that it was said, 'You shall not commit adultery.' But I say to you that everyone who looks at a woman with lustful intent has already committed adultery with her in his heart."
Matthew 5:27-28

"You therefore must be perfect, as your heavenly Father is perfect."
Matthew 5:48

THE GRACE COURSE | SESSION 5 | HUMBLE!

How did Jesus fulfil the Law?

He helped us understand the true purpose of the Law

THE GRACE COURSE | SESSION 5 | HUMBLE!

▶At one time, our hearts were "deceitful above all things" (Jeremiah 17:9). They are no longer. Many preachers would get a rousing chorus of "Amens" from their congregation by saying, "I'm just a wicked, dirty ol' sinner saved by grace. My heart and your heart is dirty and deceitful and desperately sick." Not true!

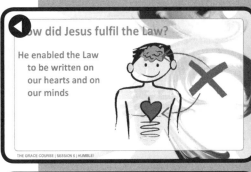

> ▶ "This is the covenant that I will make with them
> after those days, declares the Lord:
> I will put my laws on their hearts,
> and write them on their minds."
> (Hebrews 10:16)

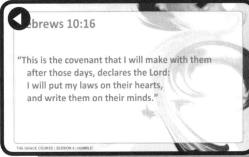

Now that we have become new creations in Christ, we have new hearts and our minds are being renewed by the truth. God's Law is no longer words on a tablet of stone. It's written inside us through the presence of the Spirit of God and the Word of Christ richly dwelling within us. How can our hearts be wicked when Ezekiel says God has given us a new heart and His Word is written there? Before Christ we could not obey because our hearts were dark. But now we can obey, not because we are being forced to, but because deep down we really want to, and because we have the power of the Holy Spirit within us to enable us to do so.

PAUSE FOR THOUGHT 1

OBJECTIVE:

TO HELP US UNDERSTAND OUR NATURAL TENDENCY TOWARDS PHARISAISM AND WHY WE DON'T HAVE TO GO IN THAT DIRECTION.

▶QUESTIONS (ON PAGE 76 OF THE PARTICIPANT'S GUIDE):

ARE THERE WAYS IN WHICH CHRISTIANS TODAY ARE TEMPTED TO THINK THAT THEY NEED TO OBEY CERTAIN "RULES"?

JESUS SAYS TO US, "BE PERFECT" (MATTHEW 5:48). HOW IS IT POSSIBLE TO KEEP THIS COMMAND?

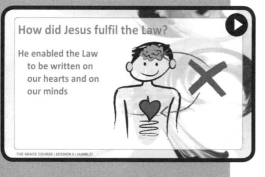

How did Jesus fulfil the Law?

He enabled the Law to be written on our hearts and on our minds

THE GRACE COURSE | SESSION 5 | HUMBLE!

It's not what we do but why we do it

▶When Jesus said, "Be perfect as your heavenly Father is perfect," how is it possible to keep this command?

Well, let's remind ourselves of some key truths that we've already looked at. When you came to Christ, what did you become?

Someone different than the person you used to be. You became a completely new creation. In fact an exchange took place. Jesus became sin and what did you become? The righteousness of God! You are righteous through and through. How perfect is that?

And on that basis, you are genuinely free to choose to do the right thing. You won't always do that — you will stumble from time to time. But that doesn't change the fact that you are the righteousness of God. So in Christ you fulfil this command!

Let's try to see how God's eternal purposes through the Law are worked out in us now that we are new creations.

▶We need to remember that it's not just about **what** we do but **why** we do it.

In Matthew 15, Pharisees and scribes criticized Jesus' disciples for not washing their hands when they ate. Sounds like my mother! There are good reasons for that, of course, to do with hygiene. But if you disregard this command, does it also affect your spiritual hygiene, the condition of your heart? Sorry to break the news to you, but "Cleanliness is next to godliness" is not in the Bible!

> ▶And he called the people to him and said to them, "Hear and understand: it is not what goes into the mouth that defiles a person, but what comes out of the mouth; this defiles a person…. For out of the heart come evil thoughts, murder, adultery, sexual immorality, theft, false witness, slander. These are what defile a person. But to eat with unwashed hands does not defile anyone."
> (Matthew 15:10–11, 19–20)

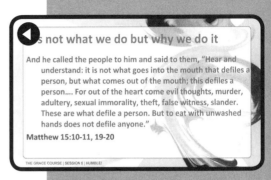

s not what we do but why we do it

And he called the people to him and said to them, "Hear and understand: it is not what goes into the mouth that defiles a person, but what comes out of the mouth; this defiles a person…. For out of the heart come evil thoughts, murder, adultery, sexual immorality, theft, false witness, slander. These are what defile a person. But to eat with unwashed hands does not defile anyone."

Matthew 15:10-11, 19-20

THE GRACE COURSE | SESSION 6 | HUMBLE!

▶Someone can look fantastic on the outside but inside where it matters it can be completely different. Jesus called the Pharisees "whitewashed tombs" — they looked great on the outside but inside they were a mess.

▶You might think that someone looks disreputable on the outside, but what really matters to God is what is going on inside.

We'd never be like the Pharisees would we? We would never think that it's what we do externally that matters more than what's inside, would we?

Actually every one of us has fallen into that trap! And our churches have historically been great at compounding the error.

When we first became Christians, probably no one actually put it like this, but many of us received the distinct impression that to be a "good" Christian we had to read our Bible every day, give a certain proportion of our income, go to church regularly and a load of other things. We often prefer it, in fact, if someone will give us a list of things to do, a list of dos and don'ts. Then if we do those things most of the time, we can feel good about ourselves. Doesn't that remind you of someone? Oh, yes the Pharisees!

Without love, no matter how good our actions or our beliefs may look, we're just making meaningless noise — like a "noisy gong or a clanging cymbal" (1 Corinthians 13:1). Let's look at an example: Is it good to give 10% of our income to the church? Yes. But how much better to get hold of the principle behind giving, rather than just follow a rule slavishly. Paul says:

▶The point is this: whoever sows sparingly will also reap sparingly, and whoever sows bountifully will also reap bountifully. Each one must give as he has decided in his heart, not reluctantly or under compulsion, for God loves a cheerful giver. (2 Corinthians 9:6–7)

God does not want us to give because we feel we are "under compulsion". But He does want us to understand that if we give generously financially, it will bring us a great harvest. He does not mean as some have thought that we will get more money back — giving to get more money back is a worldly principle, not a biblical one. Let's see how the passage continues:

▶And God is able to make all grace abound to you, so that having all sufficiency in all things at all times, you may abound in every good work. (2 Corinthians 9:8)

When we give generously in love, all grace will abound to us and we will abound in every good work. What comes back is much more valuable than money. It's a great increase in the fruit that we will bear for Him and the good works that we will do. If we understand this and experience it, it's quite likely that we will end up giving over and above the 10% — and we'll be doing it out of hearts of love rather than with the sense that this is some higher rate of income tax levied not by the government but by the church!

The essence of the Law

It's not a heavy burden

▶We also need to know that obeying from our new hearts is not to meant be a heavy burden. 1 John 5:3 NIV says, "This is love for God: to obey his commands. And his commands are not burdensome."

One Pharisee, a lawyer, came to Jesus with a question specifically to try to trap him: "Teacher, which is the greatest commandment in the Law?" (Matthew 22:36)

The point is this: whoever sows sparingly will also reap sparingly, and whoever sows bountifully will also reap bountifully. Each one must give as he has decided in his heart, not reluctantly or under compulsion, for God loves a cheerful giver.

And God is able to make all grace abound to you, so that having all sufficiency in all things at all times, you may abound in every good work.

2 Corinthians 9:6-8

THE GRACE COURSE | SESSION 5 | HUMBLE!

The essence of the Law

It's not a heavy burden

"You shall love the Lord your God with all your heart and with all your soul and with all your mind. This is the great and first commandment. And a second is like it: You shall love your neighbour as yourself. On these two commandments depend all the Law and the Prophets." Matthew 22:37-40

THE GRACE COURSE | SESSION 5 | HUMBLE!

▶ Jesus replied: "You shall love the Lord your God with all your heart and with all your soul and with all your mind. This is the great and first commandment. And a second is like it: You shall love your neighbour as yourself. On these two commandments depend **all** the Law and the Prophets." (Matthew 22:37–40)

The Pharisees had spent years trying to get the essence of the Law to make sure that they were living in exactly the right way, believing exactly the right things. They did it by expanding on what God had given, so they had vast numbers of "helpful" rules and regulations. ▶ But these had become a really heavy burden to ordinary people.

▶ Jesus, on the other hand, specifically called those who felt weary and heavy-laden and promised them rest. He invited them to take His light burden and His easy yoke. Instead of expanding the Law, Jesus reduced the whole thing to just two sentences.

▶ He summarized the Law in even fewer words in Matthew 7: "So whatever you wish that others would do to you, do also to them, for this is the Law and the Prophets." (Matthew 7:12)

▶ Paul took it one step further:

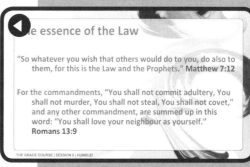

> For the commandments, "You shall not commit adultery, You shall not murder, You shall not steal, You shall not covet," and any other commandment, are summed up in this word: "You shall love your neighbour as yourself." (Romans 13:9)

If we perfectly fulfilled the Law, what would it look like? We'd be loving God and loving others. And that's the Law written on our hearts and the one that we can fulfil as we choose to live in the power of the Holy Spirit.

So how do we love God with all our heart, and with all our soul and with all our mind? The fundamental principle is "We love because He first loved us" (1 John 4:19). I hope that during these sessions, you've found yourself falling more and more in love with God. If so, that hasn't come by striving to follow a set of rules, it's just happened as you've realized how much you are loved by Him.

▶ An ongoing intimate relationship with the Father is your best defence against falling into the trap of the Pharisees, which is religiously performing to try and earn God's favour. Grace is a gift. It simply **cannot** be earned.

Loving others (Philippians 2:1–11)

The crucial importance of unity

Let's understand why God puts so much emphasis on loving others.

Just before Jesus went to the cross, He prayed specifically for those who would come after the original disciples — that's you and me. He could have chosen any number of things to pray for but He chose to focus on one single thing:

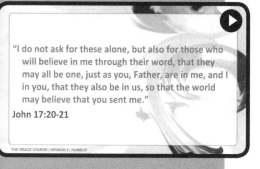

> ▶ "I do not ask for these alone, but also for those who will believe in me through their word, that they may all be one, just as you, Father, are in me, and I in you, that they also be in us, so that the world may believe that you sent me." (John 17:20–21)

How are we going to reach this world for Christ? In the only recorded prayer that Jesus prays specifically for you, He makes it crystal clear. Yes, we need our various outreach activities. But more fundamentally we need to love each other. Then the world will believe that God sent Jesus.

Psalm 133 says that where there is unity, God commands a blessing. It's clear that something happens spiritually where there is unity. If your outreach activities happen against a background of unity, you can expect them to be much more effective. In Philippians 2, Paul urges us to be united and tells us the key:

> ▶ "Do nothing from rivalry or conceit, but in humility count others more significant than yourselves. Let each of you look not only to his own interests, but also to the interests of others." (Philippians 2:3–4)

The key to unity is humility.

Humbling ourselves

What is true humility?

It's not being a doormat. Jesus was humble but certainly not a pushover. It's being the doorman... being secure in who you are so you can consider others more important than yourself.

Humility is really about where we place our confidence. Do we place it in Christ or do we place it somewhere else: Our own abilities; our theology, whether or not we always get everything just right? ▶Pride is putting confidence in something other than Christ. It's when we're deceived into thinking that we need to be lifted up, so we go about lifting ourselves up, puffing ourselves up.

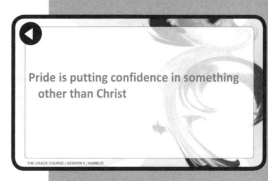

Pride is putting confidence in something other than Christ

[A story from Rich Miller:] In 1990 Shirley and I moved to Manila, Philippines, where we were sent to lead a city-wide ministry to high school students. That summer several hundred short-term missionaries came over to help launch that ministry. By the time that short-term project was over, we had boxes containing over 52,000 cards with the names and addresses of Filipino students who wanted more information about Christ. And we had to send follow-up material to them... doing all the work by hand!

I went from ministry director to ministry dictator, driving everyone crazy and myself into exhaustion. I had promised the ministry that we'd take a half day of prayer a week, but that went out the window fast. Shirley would remind me of my promise. "WE DON'T HAVE TIME TO PRAY!" I'd say. During that time, I heard a Christian song about God's mercy. I mocked the song, "Lord have mercy! Lord have mercy! Lord have mercy!" What a cheesy song!

Soon after that I had to go into the hospital with severe diarrhoea and dehydration. While I was in there I got pneumonia in both lungs. Unknown to the doctors, I also developed asthma. They gave me some antibiotics and sent me home with a nebulizer to help me breathe. One night about two in the morning, I could hardly breathe. I nebulized until I was blue in the face. No help. Lying there, gasping on the floor, I found myself crying out to God... saying... you guessed it... "Lord have mercy!" Thank the Lord He did! I needed to humble myself before God and others, but since I didn't, God took care of that for me!

▶When pride controls you, you're constantly trying to pull yourself upwards.

Where are you right now, what is your position? You are already seated in Christ at the right hand of the Father! You can't get any higher than that!

When we act out of pride it shows that we don't know who we are. You can't be truly humble unless you have grasped the amazing truth of who you now are in Christ, and you know that the only reason you can operate in any kind of ministry is because of the work of Christ on that cross, and the power of Christ in you. When you do know that, you can, in fact, be the most confident person in the world, yet still be walking in humility.

▶So, humility could be defined as "confidence properly placed in Christ".

Paul continues:

▶"Have this mind among yourselves, which is yours in Christ Jesus, who, though he was in the form of God, did not count equality with God a thing to be grasped, but emptied himself, by taking the form of a servant, being born in the likeness of men. And being found in human form, he humbled himself by becoming obedient to the point of death, even death on a cross." (Philippians 2:5–8)

▶Humility is about lowering ourselves — the direction is downwards. It's about making ourselves bondslaves even though we don't have to — just because we love to serve the One who loves us and who chose to humble Himself.

It's difficult to get our minds around how far God lowered Himself. First, God Himself became a man. But then the One who is perfectly holy became sin. The Prince of Life died at the hands of the very ones He had created. God is asking us to lower ourselves in the same way, to have the same mind, the same attitude, as Jesus had.

As we choose to look at things with the mind of Christ rather than our own flawed thinking, we know that we can't do anything good in our own strength. We know that we aren't better than others. We know that we don't need to bolster our own egos by criticizing others.

So we'll constantly be looking for ways of going lower. We'll be secure enough to own up to our own shortcomings in relationships with others. We'll be happy to humble ourselves before those whom God has put in leadership over us, even when we are tempted to think that we know better.

When others hurt us or attack us, we will forgive and keep forgiving, rather than lash out. That's humility, and God's grace always flows downward like water... to the place of humility.

Humility is confidence properly placed in Christ

THE GRACE COURSE | SESSION 5 | HUMBLE!

Have this mind among yourselves, which is yours in Christ Jesus, who, though he was in the form of God, did not count equality with God a thing to be grasped, but emptied himself, by taking the form of a servant, being born in the likeness of men. And being found in human form, he humbled himself by becoming obedient to the point of death, even death on a cross.
Philippians 2:5-8

THE GRACE COURSE | SESSION 5 | HUMBLE!

HUMILITY

THE GRACE COURSE | SESSION 5 | HUMBLE!

PAUSE FOR THOUGHT 2

OBJECTIVE:

TO ALLOW THE HOLY SPIRIT TO REVEAL TO US WAYS IN WHICH WE HAVE BEEN PROUD AND TO RENOUNCE THOSE WRONG ATTITUDES.

▶EXERCISE (ON PAGE 79 OF THE PARTICIPANT'S GUIDE):

ON YOUR OWN BEFORE GOD, SAY THE FOLLOWING PRAYER:

DEAR LORD,
I CONFESS THAT I HAVE BELIEVED THAT MY WAYS AND MY PREFERENCES ARE BETTER THAN THOSE OF OTHER PEOPLE. I ASK YOU TO REVEAL TO ME NOW THE WAYS IN WHICH THIS SIN OF PRIDE HAS BEEN AN ISSUE IN MY LIFE SO THAT I MIGHT TURN AWAY FROM IT. IN JESUS' NAME. AMEN.

▶WRITE DOWN AREAS OF YOUR LIFE WHERE YOU NOW REALIZE THAT YOU HAVE BEEN PROUD. CONSIDER, FOR EXAMPLE, YOUR ATTITUDE TOWARDS:

- FAMILY MEMBERS
- CHURCH LEADERS
- CHRISTIANS FROM OTHER PARTS OF THE CHURCH
- WORK COLLEAGUES

CONSIDER TOO IF YOU HAVE BEEN PROUD OF:
- YOUR UNDERSTANDING OF CHRISTIAN DOCTRINE
- YOUR WORLDLY ACHIEVEMENTS
- THE THINGS YOU HAVE DONE FOR GOD

FOR EACH AREA THAT THE HOLY SPIRIT HAS BROUGHT TO MIND, PRAY THIS PRAYER:

▶LORD JESUS,
I CONFESS AND RENOUNCE THAT I WAS PROUD BY/TOWARDS _____ (SAY WHAT YOU DID AND TO WHOM). I NOW CHOOSE TO HAVE THE SAME ATTITUDE YOU HAD. I HUMBLE MYSELF BEFORE YOU AND BEFORE OTHER PEOPLE. I DECLARE THE TRUTH THAT I AM IN NO WAY BETTER THAN THEY ARE AND I CHOOSE FROM NOW ON TO CONSIDER THEM MORE SIGNIFICANT THAN MYSELF. THANK YOU THAT, BECAUSE I KNOW I AM YOUR CHILD, I NO LONGER HAVE TO LIFT MYSELF UP BUT CAN RELY ON YOU TO LIFT ME UP IN DUE COURSE.
IN YOUR NAME. AMEN.

▶[A story from Steve Goss:] A few years ago, I was going through a period of intense conflict in ministry with someone else. By the way, conflict is not a bad thing, it's inevitable that it will happen. It's how you handle it that matters. Everything within me wanted to prove that I was right, that I knew best. I wanted to get people onto my side. And God was patiently telling me that what really mattered was my character and whether I handled the conflict in a godly way. I went through a few nights where I hardly slept because my nose blocked up and I couldn't seem to unblock it. In the end I decided I'd go to the doctor and see if I could get something for it. I was signed up with a new doctor that I hadn't visited before so, before he looked at my nose, he decided to give me a basic check-up. He measured all my dimensions and tapped them into his computer. Then he said, "Hmm, let's see if we can get your arms a bit shorter — stretch them out again..." So he measured my arms again and said, "No, they're still too long." I said, "They've been fine all my life. Is that a problem?" He explained that having overly long arms is one of the pointers to a condition called Marfan's syndrome, which causes muscles to become very flexible. It causes double-jointedness and is a problem because ultimately the heart muscles become so flexible that they don't really function, and it can be fatal. So he said, "Right, I'll book you an appointment at the hospital for a heart check-up." He tapped away at his computer and handed me the appointment form. I said, "But what about my nose?" "Oh it will clear up in a few days".

So I found myself having my heart checked up. They laid me down in front of a big screen and did an ultrasound. The sound of my heart was played through loud speakers — it was wheezing and squeaking and sounded terrible. Then there was a massive picture of my heart on the screen in front of me. But as I lay there watching my heart on a huge screen and listening to it, I felt God say, "In the middle of this conflict situation, all I'm looking at is your heart." There was no medical issue with my heart. I needed to make sure there was no spiritual issue either by choosing to go on humbling myself before God and before other people.

Look what happened to Jesus as a result of His humbling Himself:

▶ Therefore God has highly exalted him and bestowed on him the name that is above every name, so that at the name of Jesus every knee should bow, in heaven and on earth and under the earth, and every tongue confess that Jesus Christ is Lord, to the glory of God the Father. (Philippians 2:9–11)

And as we make ourselves lower and lower, as we choose to come underneath others, we will find that we will supernaturally experience more of God's grace and that He will lift us up.

James 4:10 has a significant promise: "Humble yourselves before the Lord, and he will exalt you." How much better to be lifted up by God's everlasting arms, than to depend on anything that we could do to make our lives significant!

Therefore God has highly exalted him and bestowed on him the name that is above every name, so that at the name of Jesus every knee should bow, in heaven and on earth and under the earth, and every tongue confess that Jesus Christ is Lord, to the glory of God the Father.

Philippians 2:9-11

THE GRACE COURSE | SESSION 5 | HUMBLE!

▶ Focus on the essential

It is so easy for us to become the elder brother. [Steve Goss says:] When I became a Christian as a teenager, I was really hungry for the truth. I bought a whole load of Christian books and devoured them. I still have some of them and looking through, you can see places where I have written the initials "DU" in the margin. Do you know what that meant? Actually, as I look at them now, I can see that it was written next to things I didn't understand so you might think that DU stood for "Don't understand". In fact it didn't. It stood for "Doctrinally unsound"! Even as a teenager who had been a Christian a matter of months, I somehow had absorbed the concept that I needed to measure what others were saying against a definite set of doctrinal criteria and test them for error, and I felt qualified to stamp anything I didn't understand as "DU"!

Growing up as a Christian, I somehow absorbed the view that I needed to be very careful around Christians that I didn't know or who were from a different background; the unspoken implication being that only WE believed the "right" things.

How arrogant is that! Instead of coming to others with grace, we put up barriers of truth that they have to jump. Division has become almost part of our DNA.

A ship weighed anchor at a remote island. Upon arriving at the shore, the crew were met by a shipwreck survivor. He said, "I'm so glad you're here! I've been alone on this island for over ten years!"

They asked, "If you're all alone on the island why are there three huts?"

The survivor said, "Oh. Well, I live in one, and go to church in another."

"What about the third hut?" they asked.

"That's where I used to go to church."

Which are the parts of the Church that you were taught to be suspicious of? Maybe you even got the impression that if people attend a particular branch of the Church, or believe or practise certain things, they can't possibly be Christians.

Have you ever checked out for yourself what you were told about them, with a spirit of counting others better than yourselves?

What is it that makes you a Christian?

▶If you declare with your mouth, "Jesus is Lord," and believe in your heart that God raised him from the dead, you will be saved. For it is with your heart that you believe and are justified, and it is with your mouth that you profess your faith and are saved. (Romans 10:9–10 NIV)

▶That's it! It's like this car. It's probably not your idea of the ideal family vehicle. But it has what it needs to take you from A to B — just! Yes, there are bits missing, but at the end of the day it does the job. The Pharisees kept wanting to add to the Law, but it can be summed up by saying, "Love God, love your neighbour". That's it! In the same way we can be tempted to add to what it means to be a Christian, when actually it's really straightforward.

Is it important to have good theology? Of course! But sometimes we can almost end up feeling like we're saved by good theology. In John 5:39–40, Jesus says to the Pharisees, "You search the Scriptures because you think that in them you have eternal life; and it is they that bear witness about me, yet you refuse to come to me that you may have life." It's entirely possible to have such a focus on the truth of the written Word of God that we miss the One who is the Truth, the Living Word of God.

Is anyone honestly going to say that you and your particular church have a 100% correct theology? ▶At the end of the age, there isn't one of us that won't look back at our present beliefs, slap our forehead and go "Duh!"

Recognize that none of us has a complete understanding

Theology is just our human attempt to understand God's truth. In the last 10 years my theology has changed. What hasn't changed is truth. I don't know about you, I don't want to be committed to a particular theology. But I am absolutely committed to truth.

What do you think Jesus cares about more: What people believe in their head about the bread and the wine or whether they love others from the heart?; What people believe about just one verse in the New Testament that mentions a thousand year period or whether they are ready to forgive as God has forgiven them?

In the wake of the outbreak of the Charismatic Movement, there were sharply differing views on the exercise of spiritual gifts. Some churches said that you could not be sure you were a Christian unless there was evidence that you had spoken in tongues. Others said that if you spoke in tongues it was evidence that you weren't a Christian! What does the Bible say? "Do all speak with tongues?" (1 Corinthians 12:30) asks Paul, a rhetorical question to which the clear answer is "No". A few paragraphs later he says, "Earnestly desire the spiritual gifts." (1 Corinthians 14:1) which clearly includes tongues. Then in 1 Corinthians 14:39, he says, "Earnestly desire to prophesy, and do not forbid speaking in tongues." I've looked that up in the original Greek — "do not forbid speaking in tongues." Do you know what it actually means? "Do not forbid speaking in tongues!"

But above all that he makes clear in 1 Corinthians 13 — slap bang in the middle of two chapters about spiritual gifts — that the main thing is love. No matter how much speaking in tongues you do or don't do, no matter how "right" the position you hold on the matter, if you don't have love you gain precisely nothing.

So am I saying that you should condone things that may happen within some parts of the Church that are blatantly not in line with the Bible? No, absolutely not. When Jesus was face to face with the woman caught in adultery, He explicitly said that He did not condemn her, but neither did He condone her wrong behaviour. He didn't pretend that the sin wasn't an issue. He said clearly, "Go and from now on sin no more." However, His heart was not to condemn her but to motivate her to righteous living. And however counter-intuitive it seems, it's grace that does that.

▶If you make doctrine the main thing, even if you're right, you're wrong. If you are secure in knowing who you are in Christ, you don't have to be proved right; you don't have to indulge in arguments. You can just keep lowering yourself before others and loving them.

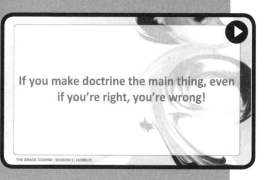

If you make doctrine the main thing, even if you're right, you're wrong!

Come with both grace and truth

But what about truth? Again, please don't hear us saying that truth is not important. It's crucially important. ▶ John 1:14 and 17 tell us that Jesus came "full of grace and truth". We need both grace and truth. The question is which do we lead with?

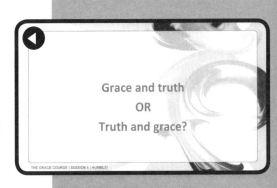

For the Pharisees, truth was the important thing. And, left to our own devices, we too instinctively come first with truth: "You should be doing this." True. "Christians shouldn't do that." True. "You should behave like this." Good true advice. Jesus on the other hand always held truth in balance with grace. And He led with grace.

Historically, the Western Church has not done this well. Like the Pharisees we have tended to emphasize truth above grace, with the result that churches have split and split again, and often there is a huge level of mutual mistrust between different parts of the Church. There is no mutual humility — in fact they probably don't even talk to each other. Yet these are all children of God.

The key to unity is humility. Disunity comes from pride.

People often say that they live in a particularly dark area. Sometimes they want to know if they should confront the evil spirits that are opposing the Church there. It's just possible that I might be able to reveal to them the name of the most significant spirit that is likely to be opposing the Church in their area. Do you want to know what it is? If there's significant disunity borne out of pride, it will be the Holy Spirit!

▶What! James 4:6 makes this very clear. "God opposes the proud, but gives grace to the humble."

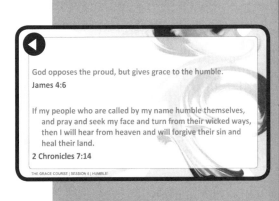

If we want the Church to grow and reach the people out there, it's easy to blame our lack of progress on the enemy. But he's defeated. The real issue is likely to be closer to home. Why is the enemy being given so much leeway? Think instead about the need for us to make ourselves right with God. ▶He says,

> "If my people who are called by my name humble themselves, and pray and seek my face and turn from their wicked ways, then I will hear from heaven and will forgive their sin and heal their land." (2 Chronicles 7:14)

We can all make a start by resolving to humble ourselves before God and before others. If we do, God's grace will meet us in that place.

Let's pray:

Father, would You please reveal to us the ways we are walking in pride, and the lies that are behind that. Thank You. Amen.

PAUSE FOR THOUGHT 3

OBJECTIVE:

TO CONSIDER WHAT IT MEANS IN PRACTICE TO BE ONE WITH OUR BROTHERS AND SISTERS IN CHRIST.

▶QUESTIONS (ON PAGE 81 OF THE PARTICIPANT'S GUIDE):

WHEN YOU COME ACROSS SOMEONE WHO "CONFESSES WITH THEIR MOUTH THAT JESUS IS LORD AND BELIEVES IN THEIR HEART THAT GOD RAISED HIM FROM THE DEAD" (SEE ROMANS 10:9–10), YET ON OTHER MATTERS BELIEVES DIFFERENT THINGS TO YOU, HOW SHOULD YOU APPROACH THEM? IF THEY ARE TRYING HARD TO CONVINCE YOU THAT THEIR OPINION IS THE RIGHT ONE, WHAT SHOULD YOUR ATTITUDE BE THEN?

WHAT MIGHT IT LOOK LIKE IN PRACTICE FOR YOU AND YOUR CHURCH TO HUMBLE YOURSELVES BEFORE OTHER CHRISTIANS IN YOUR AREA? HOW MIGHT YOU PLAY A PART IN THAT?

THE GRACE COURSE | SESSION 5 | HUMBLE!

▶Take a few minutes, as you turn to the *Lies List* section at the back of your Participant's Guide, to listen to Him as He reveals any lies that have fuelled your pride. Have you felt the need to build yourself up by comparing yourself to others? Have you felt the need to overemphasize doctrine and "right" theology?

Don't believe any thoughts like, "I don't need to do this. This is a waste of time!" Those are lies too. You may need to write them down as expressions of pride!

WITNESS

Ask God to give you an opportunity to show love to someone this week in such a way that only He will see it.

 # IN THE COMING WEEK

Say the Declaration of Humility and Unity (on the following page and on page 82 of the Participant's Guide) every day to commit yourself to answering Jesus' prayer in John 17:20–23.

Declaration of Humility and Unity

Lord Jesus,

I join You in Your prayer to the Father that Your children would be one — because, like You, I want the world to believe that the Father sent You. You have said in Your Word that where there is unity, You command a blessing of life and I want to see that blessing come in full force.

Just as You — the great King of Kings — humbled Yourself by taking the form of a slave, even to the point of choosing to die a humiliating and agonising death on a cross, I choose to give up my ridiculous pretensions of being in any way righteous or right in my own strength and I humble myself before You. It's all about You and Your Kingdom, Lord, and not about me.

I choose also to humble myself before my brothers and sisters in Christ and to come to them not just with truth but with grace — just as You come to me. I choose to consider them more important than myself and to put their interests above my own. I recognize that without genuine love, anything I do is no more than a noisy gong or clanging cymbal. Even if my Christian doctrine and tradition are 100 per cent right, without love they are worth precisely nothing.

Lord, I am eager to maintain the unity of the Spirit in the bond of peace. I therefore ask You to fill me afresh with the Holy Spirit and to lead me in love. I choose to be a peacemaker not a nitpicker. I choose relationship above rules. I choose love above law. I choose to be real rather than right.

Please show me how practically I can serve and bless those You have called to different parts of Your Church.

I pray this in the name of the humble Jesus, the One who has now been lifted up to the very highest place and has the name that is above every other name.

Amen.

(Based on Psalm 133, John 1:14–17, John 17:20–23, 1 Corinthians 13, Ephesians 4:1–7, Philippians 2:1–11)

THE STEPS TO EXPERIENCING GOD'S GRACE

The Steps To Experiencing God's Grace

FOCUS VERSE:

James 4:7: Submit yourselves therefore to God. Resist the devil, and he will flee from you.

OBJECTIVE:

To lead participants through a process of repentance so that they can resolve their personal and spiritual conflicts by submitting to God and resisting the devil, and thereby experience a deeper understanding of God's grace in their lives.

FOCUS TRUTH:

Christ has set us free (Galatians 5:1), but we will not experience that freedom without genuine repentance.

Confession (admitting that we did wrong) is the first step to repentance, but as we saw in Session 3, is not enough on its own.

We must submit to God and resist the devil. We must also make a choice about what we believe and how we are living, and decide to change. If we want to grow in Christ we must choose to renounce the lies we have believed and any sin in our lives, and announce our choice to believe that what God says is true and start to live accordingly.

Leader's Notes

The notes for this session are different from others in the course because for the most part they are intended primarily for the leader of the session rather than being a script. The session does, however, end with a 10-minute talk on renewing the mind and there is a script for that. We recommend that you read through the notes and instructions for the session thoroughly before leading it and also view *The Steps To Experiencing God's Grace* session on the DVD if possible.

There are two ways to lead this session. You can either use *The Steps To Experiencing God's Grace* session on *The Grace Course* DVD Set (available separately — see page 15) or lead it yourself using the PowerPoint presentation on the CD that accompanies this Leader's Guide and the notes that follow. The PowerPoint presentation features the prayers and declarations that your group will say out loud together. Each participant will need their own copy of *The Steps To Experiencing God's Grace* which is in their Participant's Guide starting on page 93. You will also need a copy as the process itself is not printed in this Leader's Guide. Page numbers in the notes that follow refer to the Participant's Guide.

We recommend that everyone who does *The Grace Course* goes through *The Steps To Freedom In Christ* before going through *The Steps To Experiencing God's Grace* if possible.

The process is straightforward: the participants ask the Holy Spirit to show them areas in their lives where they need to repent, and then choose to do so. We would encourage you to go through the process yourself before leading others through. Being able to share your own experiences of going through the process with your group gives them the assurance that they are not being asked to do something you haven't first done yourself.

A suggested timetable for an away day retreat is on page 193.

Introduction

Seeing people go through *The Steps To Experiencing God's Grace* is exciting! It's a gentle, kind, undramatic process but it can make an enormous difference to their lives. There is no need to feel nervous about leading the process. You are simply facilitating an encounter between those seeking freedom and Jesus who is the Wonderful Counsellor.

The Steps To Experiencing God's Grace has the following benefits:

- The method is transferable because it doesn't require experts — it can be conducted by any reasonably mature Christian who is walking in freedom.

- It produces lasting results because the "freedom-seekers" are the ones making the decisions and assuming personal responsibility, rather than a pastor or counsellor doing it for them.

- It doesn't bypass the person's mind.

- The focus is on Christ and repentance. The real issue isn't Satan, it is God and our walk with Him. The six steps cover six issues that are critical between ourselves and God.

The Steps To Experiencing God's Grace doesn't set anyone free! Who sets them free is Christ. What sets them free is their response to Him in repentance and faith.

Approaches To Taking People Through The Steps

Participants should be given an opportunity to go through *The Steps To Experiencing God's Grace* between Sessions 5 and 6. There are two different ways you can approach this and you need to decide well in advance of starting the course which will suit your situation:

1. An Individual Grace Steps Appointment

This is the ideal. In this scenario each individual is led through the process by an "encourager", with a prayer partner in attendance, in a session that typically lasts three or four hours. It can be incredibly upbuilding when people in a church or small group are willing to confess their sins to one another and pray for each other (see James 5:16). Encouragers and prayer partners do not generally need any special skills other than a reasonable maturity in Christ and an understanding of the biblical principles of freedom, but will benefit from having attended a Freedom In Christ *Helping Others Find Freedom In Christ* course (see page 24) or having read *Discipleship Counseling* by Neil Anderson (Regal Books, 2003). They will also benefit from joining the Freedom Fellowship run by Freedom In Christ Ministries (see page 24).

2. As A Group On An Away Day Retreat

Taking your group away for a day (or even a weekend) to go through the Steps works well. It allows everyone to go through the Steps at the same time whilst ensuring that people have enough time to do business with any issues that the Holy Spirit brings to their mind. It is best to book a location away from your church and to include times of worship. You will need leaders to make themselves available to participants who may need help at various times. Whether you have been through the *Freedom In Christ Discipleship Course* already or not it can be helpful to include Session 9 ("Forgiving From The Heart") from that course in the away day retreat directly before your group goes through Step 4 "Forgiveness".

Even if you are using the away day retreat approach, you will need to make some provision for personal appointments. We recommend that those leading the course have personal appointments, for example, and you will probably find that people with deeper issues will not be able to get everything done on the away day retreat or will struggle and will need a personal appointment. Simply see how they get on and arrange a personal appointment afterwards if needed.

Taking An Individual Through *The Steps to Experiencing God's Grace*

1. Preparation

The person going through the process (the "freedom-seeker") should have completed a Confidential Personal Inventory before the appointment. You can find this in the appendix of *Discipleship Counseling* by Neil Anderson or in the material available to members of the Freedom Fellowship (see page 24). You have permission to copy the inventory or adapt it for your own use. Bear in mind, however, that many people will not disclose certain confidential information in writing so there may well be more to come out. The Confidential Personal Inventory provides important information concerning their physical, mental, emotional and spiritual life. However, its primary function is to help the freedom seeker prepare for their appointment.

Encourage them to prepare for the Steps appointment by completing the *Lies List* at the back of their Participant's Guide (in particular filling in the "truth" column) as they go through the teaching sessions each week and the Holy Spirit reveals things to them.

Choose a comfortable room and allow for several hours. Have a box of tissues available, and some water. Take occasional breaks. We strongly recommend that you get the freedom-seeker to complete a Statement of Understanding which confirms for legal reasons their understanding that the encourager is not functioning as a trained counsellor — a version is available in the Freedom Fellowship material (see page 24).

2. Lead Them Through *The Steps To Experiencing God's Grace*

The primary focus of the Steps for the freedom-seeker is their own relationship with God. The process is different from most counselling approaches, because the one who is praying is the one who needs the help, and they are praying to the only One who can help them.

It is recommended that as well as the leader ("the encourager") and the freedom-seeker, a prayer partner is also present.

Explain to the freedom-seeker what they are doing and why they are doing it. Try to go through all six steps in one session. They may not need every step but you want to be thorough for their sake. Have them read every prayer and affirmation aloud. Ask them to share with you any mental opposition or physical discomfort. When they do, thank them for sharing it with you. Once it is acknowledged, simply go on. In most cases there is very little opposition.

Forgiveness (Step 4) is usually the most critical step. Every person has at least one person and usually several people to forgive. Unforgiveness affords the biggest door into the Church for Satan. If we can't help a person forgive from the heart, we can't help them be free from their past.

When they pray and ask God whom they need to forgive, rest assured that God does reveal names to their mind. If they say, "Well there is no one," then respond by saying, "Would you just share the names that are coming to your mind right now?" Usually, several names will surface, and they should record them on a sheet of paper. It is not uncommon for freedom-seekers to have names come to mind that surprise them. And it is not uncommon for them to recall forgotten painful memories while in the process of forgiving.

Explain what forgiveness is and how to do it. There is a brief summary in the Participant's Guide on pages 113–114. Once they have completed their list of names ask if they would be willing to forgive those people for their own sake. Forgiving others is primarily an issue between them and their Heavenly Father. Reconciliation may or may not follow.

When they have finished the whole process, ask the freedom-seeker to sit comfortably and close their eyes. Then ask, "What do you hear in your mind? Is it quiet?" After a pause they usually respond with a relieved smile and say, "Nothing. It's finally quiet in my mind."

3. Keep Pointing Them Towards Truth

Getting free in Christ is one thing; staying free is another. Paul says in Galatians 5:1, "It was for freedom that Christ set you free; therefore keep standing firm and do not be subject again to a yoke of slavery."

Renewing of the mind is the key issue here. Run them through the teaching on renewing the mind outlined on pages 189–192 of this Leader's Guide. Talk to them about the key things that have been raised during the appointment to help them uncover lies.

Most people caught in a spiritual conflict have a distorted concept of God and themselves, and it will help you if you can determine what those false beliefs are. Defeated Christians often have a distorted concept of the two kingdoms. They think they are caught between two equal but opposite powers. Bad old Satan is on one side, good old God is on the other, and poor old me is caught in the middle. That of course is not true, and they are defeated if that is what they believe. The truth is; God is omnipresent, omnipotent and omniscient. Satan is a defeated foe and we are alive in Christ, and seated with Him at the right hand of the Father, the ultimate seat of power and authority in the universe.

The freedom-seeker will derive enormous benefit if you can keep encouraging them to: identify lies; list Bible verses that say what is really true; develop Stronghold-Busters and persevere through them (one at a time) for 40 days.

Taking A Group Through *The Steps to Experiencing God's Grace* On An Away Day Retreat

You will find a suggested timetable for an away day retreat on page 193 to assist in planning. You will find it very helpful to watch the session on the *Grace Course* DVD (available separately) beforehand.

It is recommended that you hold the away day retreat in pleasant surroundings, away from your church if possible. Aim to provide lunch or make sure that people bring packed lunches — it is recommended that you maintain a quiet atmosphere over lunchtime and suggest that people remain on the premises.

The room you use should be large enough for participants to have some degree of privacy. It is helpful if people can spread out. Have some quiet music playing in the background so that people can pray out loud without feeling that others are listening. Instrumental music works best as it is less distracting.

Each participant will need their Participant's Guide which contains *The Steps To Experiencing God's Grace* and a pencil. A notebook is also helpful.

Most use the Steps session on the *Grace Course* DVD to guide people through the process because it does most of the work for you and stops automatically in the right place. You will obviously need a TV monitor or projector that everyone can see, and a DVD player. Alternatively you can use the presentation on the CD in this Leader's Guide which has slides for all the prayers and declarations that are said together. You will need a computer and a TV monitor or projector to show this.

People will at times benefit from individual attention during those steps that they find difficult. Plan to have a reasonable number of people whose role is to walk around and help those who are struggling (one for every ten people would be a good starting point). These should be mature Christians who have been through the Steps themselves.

Start with prayer, and then explain how the session will work. The group will be praying several prayers together out loud. Then they will spend some time alone with God. Nobody will be embarrassed or asked to share anything with the group or another person. It is solely an encounter with God.

Explain to the group that some will get in touch with real pain, and tears are understandable and acceptable. Some people will have very little to deal with on some steps, whereas others may have a lot. You can suggest that those who do not have much on a particular step spend time praying for those who do: that the Holy Spirit will reveal everything that needs to be revealed; and that Satan's attempts to interfere in the process will be ineffective. If people have too much to deal with in the time available, reassure them that this is not a one-off opportunity and that they will be able to catch up in due course, ideally by having their own personal appointment.

Start each step with a brief explanation of what it is about, get everyone to say the opening prayers together and then allow them time alone with the Lord to deal with the issues the Holy Spirit shows them. When the prayer and final instructions for the step have finished, the DVD pauses automatically. Wait until everybody has finished that step or that part of the step and is ready to continue before moving on (then press "Play" if you are using the DVD).

The following notes are to guide you, especially if you are leading without the DVD. They are written from the point of view of a group leader speaking to their group, and are meant to prompt you as you introduce each part of the process. They link to the slide presentation (images from the presentation are not shown — it will be obvious to you when to move the presentation on). You will find useful additional explanatory information in the Participant's Guide itself.

Explain the steps and then have the group pray together and out loud the prayer that begins each step. Then allow them to have time alone with God.

Notes For The Group Leader

[For each step these notes contain an introduction and then a bullet-pointed list of things that need to be done.]

Introduction

The process is based on James 4:7: "Submit... to God, resist the devil, and he will flee from you." You will be asking the Holy Spirit to show you any footholds that the enemy has in your life through past sin. As He shows you, you will simply repent and renounce them in order to take away the enemy's right to influence you.

Having submitted to God, at the end of the process you will command the enemy to leave your presence. Because you have dealt with the issues that the Holy Spirit has revealed to you, the enemy will have no option but to flee from you.

This is a kind and gentle process. You are in control and the outcome is in your hands. It's just between you and God. If you deal with everything the Holy Spirit shows you, at the end of the process you will be free in Christ and much more able to experience His grace.

Be aware, however, that the enemy will try to deceive you by giving you thoughts such as "This is not working", "I can't do this", or even "I've got to get out of here". If that happens to you, simply work out where the thought is coming from and tell the enemy to leave your presence. Ask for help if you need it.

On some steps you might have a lot to deal with; on others, not very much. It will be different for each person depending on their background. If you find that you have time left over, please spend that time praying for those who have a lot on that particular step: ask the Holy Spirit to keep revealing truth and ask God to prevent the enemy from interfering in the process. If on the other hand you find that you do not have enough time to complete a particular step, you can always come back to it later, either at home or in an individual appointment. This is not a one-off process; you can come back to it at any time should you discover something else that needs to be dealt with.

Opening prayer and declaration

Before beginning these Steps you may find it helpful to look at the introduction on pages 94 and 95 in the Participant's Guide. To get started, as a group say out loud together the opening prayer on page 95 followed by the opening declaration on page 96. The prayer is to God. The declaration is to all in the spiritual world... God, angels, demons... that happen to be tuning in. [This prayer and all other prayers to be spoken out loud will be shown on the relevant slides if you are using the PowerPoint presentation on the CD.]

Step 1 — Renouncing Lies and Choosing Truth

This step gives the opportunity to proclaim some very powerful truths about our relationship with God the Father, God the Son and God the Holy Spirit by declaring out loud the wonderful affirmations of what is true about each one of us now that we are God's precious children. We will also renounce lies we have been believing.

As each one speaks these truths out, they may become aware that there are some which are more difficult to believe as being true about them, right here, right now. They will add these to their *Lies List* at the back of their Participant's Guide.

They may already have filled in quite a few lies as they have gone through the first five sessions of *The Grace Course*.

*   Read the opening prayer on page 96 out loud together.

*   Declare the affirmations of truth out loud together (pages 97 and 98).

*   Ask each one to take some time on their own to go carefully through the affirmations again and mark any truths they are struggling to take hold of. Ask them to write each of these truths in the "Truth" column of their *Lies List* on pages 127–128. Have them ask the Holy Spirit to reveal the corresponding lie, i.e. the thing that feels more true to them at this moment than God's truth, and write it in the "Lies" column.

*   The table on pages 98 and 99 can then be worked through and the *Lies List* completed in the same way.

*   When they have completed their *Lies List*, they can then pray the prayer on page 100 on their own for each lie and truth they have recorded.

*   Allow them time to do this and to speak it out from their hearts. As some come to grips with how these lies have controlled their lives, it may be very emotional. Reassure them again that it's OK to allow the emotions and feelings to surface, expressing and releasing them to the Lord in prayer.

Step 2 — False Expectations

The first part of Step 2 gives the opportunity for each participant to ask the Holy Spirit to open their eyes to the ways they have allowed false and unhealthy standards, rules and expectations of others to control them. These are dealt with by using the appropriate prayer. The second part deals with how participants may have picked up false beliefs about who God is and how they may have come to view Him as a hard taskmaster who is rarely pleased, seldom smiling and never satisfied with what they do. They then have the opportunity to renounce the lies and by contrast announce the truths about their heavenly Father.

The final part is to take time to process these wonderful truths about Father God by making a commitment to choose to believe God's truth, no matter what their perceptions of Him have been in the past.

*   Pray out loud together the opening prayer on page 101.

*   Ask each person to spend some time with God considering the areas listed on pages 101 and 102. When the Holy Spirit reveals it, ask them to write down any specific expectations they have felt it necessary to live up to under each heading. They may want to record these false expectations on a separate piece of paper, so that when they are finished they can tear it up to symbolize that they choose from now on to trust in Jesus alone to make them right with God.

- Ask them to use the prayer on page 102 to renounce each false expectation they have marked off or written down.

- When everyone has finished the prayer, go on to read out loud together the "My Father God" truths on page 103 and 104, renouncing the lie then affirming the truth about His character. Work left to right, through the truths, beginning each time with "I renounce…" and then "I joyfully accept…".

- Now ask them to look back over the list they have just read and mark any truths that are difficult for them to receive. They can then use the prayer at the bottom of page 104 to confess and repent of the lies that they have believed about Father God. They should also write these lies on the *Lies List*.

Step 3 — Confessing Sin

Confession means literally "to say the same thing" or "to come into agreement with". So when we confess our sins to God we are saying that He is right in His assessment that what we have done is wrong. We agree with Him. We admit that He is right and we were wrong. And we also come into agreement that our sins are already forgiven in Christ.

1 John 1:9 is such a fantastic verse and gives us such a tremendous promise: "If we confess our sins, he is faithful and just to forgive us our sins and to cleanse us from all unrighteousness."

We can come to God humbly and freely to acknowledge our wrongdoing because God is gracious and merciful, slow to anger and great in lovingkindness. "There is therefore now no condemnation for those who are in Christ Jesus" (Romans 8:1).

The reality of life is that when we believe lies, we eventually end up sinning.

In this step, there are seven areas of sin to consider that are fairly common for people struggling to live in the grace of God. There is also a section specifically dealing with issues of pride.

Once we have confessed our sin and taken hold of the truth of who we now are in Christ we conclude with declaring the truth of our new names in Christ.

- Start by praying out loud together the prayer on page 105. Now ask participants to work through the list on pages 106–108, marking those that the Holy Spirit is showing them. They can add any not on the list that may come to mind.

- Each one can now use the prayer at the top of page 109 to make their confession to God by naming all the sins they have listed.

- We now look at the area of pride. Pray the prayer at the bottom of page 109 out loud together. Look at the prompt list on pages 109 and 110 and ask them to write down the areas where they realize that they have had a proud attitude. Each one can now pray the prayer on page 110, including all areas where pride may have been blocking their relationship with God.

- At this point in the step, invite the Holy Spirit to reinforce the truth of their new identity in Christ by speaking a new name into their hearts. Read out loud together the prayer on pages 110–111. Give them some time alone with God to read and declare the list of new names, expecting Him to reveal a new name He wants to give! They may find that He will give them one that isn't included on the list but will be deeply significant.

- Finish this step by having participants use the prayer on page 112 on their own to declare their new name or names.

Step 4 — Forgiveness

[We would encourage you to show Session 9 — "Forgiving From The Heart" — from the *Freedom In Christ Discipleship Course* before you take them through this step].

Step 4 is all about forgiveness. It may be the most liberating step for many as they allow God to show them the people that have hurt them, pressurized them to conform, abused them physically, verbally, emotionally or sexually, or in some other way tried to control them. For some people, the most difficult person to forgive is themselves. Many have believed the lie that they deserve to be punished for what they have done, so they beat themselves up instead of receiving God's forgiveness in Christ, who was punished for us.

- Say together the opening prayer on page 114 and ask people to spend time simply writing a list of people that the Holy Spirit brings to mind — at this point they don't need to worry about why the people need forgiving; they should simply make a list of names that come to mind. There is a prompt list on page 115 to help them.

- Emphasize briefly:

    This is between you and God, not you and the person who hurt you.

    It is for your sake that you forgive.

- When they have their list, ask them to pray the forgiveness prayer on page 116 for each person. Suggest that they keep a list of the words they have used after "which made me feel". Repeated words are likely to reveal strongholds which they can work on later, for example "dirty", "unloved", "worthless". Allow people to work through their list of names. If the time allotted is not long enough, emphasize that they can finish the step at home, or they may want to request that they have their own individual appointment.

- After they have forgiven each person on their list, ask them to pray the blessing at the bottom of page 116 over each name, including themselves.

Step 5 — Freedom From Fear

There are two exercises that participants will be working through in this step. The first will involve identifying three things: unhealthy controlling fears; the lie or lies that fuel that fear; and the antidote to those, which is the truth. What each one should come to see in going through this exercise is that every unhealthy, controlling fear has at least one lie behind it. Usually it will have something to do with an inadequate grasp of who God is or who we are in Christ. Whatever the lie may be, putting your finger on it and being able to state it clearly will expose the fear for what it is... a fraud! If we can come up with a truth from God's Word to counteract that lie, we will be well on our way to becoming free from the fear.

The second exercise in this step focuses specifically on the fear of people.

- Pray out loud together the prayer on page 117.

- Get them to look at the prompt list on page 118. This may help them recognize some of the unhealthy fears that have been hindering their walk of faith. They can mark the ones that apply to them as well as writing down any others not on the list that the Holy Spirit reveals.

- Turn to page 119 and ask them to list the fears they have marked in the first column. They can use a separate piece of paper if needed. Give them time now to discern the lies that have allowed that fear to control them and write them in the second column. Also during this time, encourage them to go on to complete the table by writing the corresponding truths in the third column.

- Now they can use the prayer at the bottom of page 119 to pray separately for each of the fears that they have listed in the table, stating also the lies and the truth where possible and all the ways these fears may have influenced their behaviour.

- In part two of this step they will invite the Holy Spirit to show them how one specific area of fear may have been controlling them; the fear of people. Proverbs 29:25 says "The fear of man lays a snare but whoever trusts in the Lord is safe." Fearing man ultimately leads to pleasing people – and that indeed is bondage.

- Pray out loud together the prayer on page 120. Then ask them to mark any areas the Holy Spirit is showing them from the list on pages 120 and 121.

- Each person can now use the prayer on page 121 to work through all the ways in which the fear of people has been controlling them.

- To finish this step join together as a group to read the prayer on page 122 out loud.

Step 6 — Surrendering To God

It is a difficult thing to put ourselves unreservedly into the hands of another, even if it is God! As we come to the final step this is our opportunity to weigh up all the areas which we may have withheld from God, and choose to surrender them. There is a list of the different areas of our lives to help us think through this decision. Many of these are blessings which God delights to give us, as an expression of His Fatherly love to His children. We stay in freedom as we continue to recognize them as gifts and not as entitlements.

It's good to take time on this step. These are weighty decisions to relinquish control of every area of life! People should do it one by one and should in no way feel compelled — this must be a personal choice, of our own free will.

- Pray out loud together the prayer on page 123.

- Ask participants to look through the prompt list on page 124 and put a mark beside any rights they have felt were theirs to hold onto but now choose to surrender to God.

- On their own each person can now pray the prayer at the top of page 125 listing all the rights that they are choosing to surrender to God.

- To finish read out loud together the declarations on pages 125 and 126.

- And finally, at the end of *The Steps to Experiencing God's Grace*, pray as a group the concluding declaration and prayer at the bottom of page 126.

Concluding Remarks

At this point you may want to say something like:

Close your eyes and be quiet for a minute [pause].

In your mind is it quiet? Is there a sense of peace?

You might feel on cloud nine right now — or you might just feel tired! Remember that the point of this process was not to get a good feeling but to claim your freedom in Christ. If you have honestly dealt with everything the Holy Spirit has shown you today, then you have claimed your freedom. Now you need to concentrate on walking in it.

The Lord may well show you more areas you need to deal with in the next few days, weeks, months and years — but you now know what to do. Wherever you are, it's easy simply to renounce wrong things and move on.

In the meantime be prepared to put some effort into maintaining the freedom you have gained.

[Now have a break before moving on to talk about "Renewing your mind" using the DVD or the notes on the following pages.]

RENEW YOUR MIND

THE GRACE COURSE | THE STEPS TO EXPERIENCING GOD'S GRACE

James 1:22-25 NIV

Do not merely listen to the word and so deceive yourselves. Do what it says. Anyone who listens to the word but does not do what it says is like someone who looks at his face in a mirror and, after looking at himself, goes away and immediately forgets what he looks like. But whoever looks intently into the perfect law that gives freedom, and continues in it – not forgetting what they have heard, but doing it – they will be blessed in what they do.

THE GRACE COURSE | THE STEPS TO EXPERIENCING GOD'S GRACE

Renew your mind

▶ Do not merely listen to the word and so deceive yourselves. Do what it says. Anyone who listens to the word but does not do what it says is like someone who looks at his face in a mirror and, after looking at himself, goes away and immediately forgets what he looks like. But whoever looks intently into the perfect law that gives freedom, and continues in it – not forgetting what they have heard, but doing it – they will be blessed in what they do.

(James 1:22–25 NIV)

James says it would be ridiculous for someone to look intently into a mirror and then to go away and forget what they look like. Mind you, some of us might prefer to forget!

But actually it is very easy to look at God's Word and to agree with it mentally but then to carry on our lives without it having any effect on us. How many Christian books have you read or conferences attended where you've thought, "That's fantastic. It will revolutionize me." but the effect has lasted just a couple of days or weeks?

But, says James, if we look intently into the perfect law that gives freedom, and if we continue to do that and don't forget what we have heard, we will be blessed.

Now, you've invested quite a lot of time in *The Grace Course*. Your time is precious. We hope that you have done business with God and that you have taken hold of some wonderful truths. The question now as we approach the final session, is, is it going to make any lasting difference in your life or was it just a nice course that you went on for a few weeks? Are you going to take seriously your responsibility to burrow deep into God's Word or are you going to go away, get on with other things and eventually forget what you've learned?

All of us have a different family background, different past experiences and differing worldviews. We have all unconsciously developed a set of beliefs, default behaviour if you like. We may not really be aware of them but they are there. And many of them do not agree with God's Word. I have come to realize that, for me, the ongoing process of maturing as a Christian is all about uncovering my faulty beliefs and replacing them with what is really true. So that I can go on to make good choices and decisions that are based on a solid foundation.

We have put a lot of emphasis on truth and lies. Why? Because Jesus said that it's knowing the truth that sets you free. But He doesn't mean just a head knowledge where we look at the Word and don't apply it. Before you can be said really to **know** the truth, you need to have taken hold of it in your heart. But that journey from head to heart can seem a very long one.

Perhaps the main issue is that there is a battle going on for our minds. A battle between the Spirit of Truth and the Father of Lies. In the *Steps To Experiencing God's Grace* you have had the opportunity to root out the footholds of the enemy, particularly in the areas of guilt, shame, fear and pride. You have removed those invisible dogs hanging off you and closed the door to other dogs by submitting to God through confession and repentance and resisting the enemy so that he has had to flee from you (James 4:7).

Once you have dealt with any footholds of the enemy, a mental stronghold is simply a habitual way of thinking. Can you break a habit? Of course — but it takes some effort over a period of time. As I mentioned before, it takes about 6 weeks or 40 days to form or to break a habit.

So right now you should be in a really good place to take hold of the truth in your heart not just your head. But the process of renewing your mind through which you will be transformed will take time.

I hope that God has revealed to you a number of the faulty beliefs that you developed over the years. Take a look at your *Lies List*.

Let's look again briefly at the process we mentioned in the fourth session which we call ▶Stronghold-Busting. This is a very practical and effective way of renewing your mind. You can see it outlined on pages 62-64 of your Participant's Guide (at the end of Session 4) including a couple of examples. Both of those examples are to do with fears but, of course, a stronghold is anything that has a strong hold on you — it could be a habitual sin, or a deeply-held belief that you are, for example, unlovable or dirty.

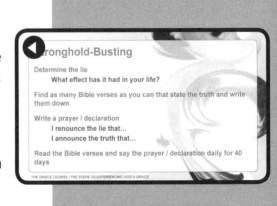

▶First of all, you need to work out what the lie is. Get it as concisely as possible. Ignore your feelings as you do this. Just focus on God's Word. Get someone to help you if you're struggling to work it out. The problem is that, by definition, the lies behind strongholds feel really true to you.

▶When you've got that, think about the effect that believing the lie has had in your life. Realizing the negative effects should spur you on to tear the stronghold down.

▶Then, find as many Bible verses as you can that state the truth and write them down. A good concordance (or helpful pastor) will come in useful.

▶Write a prayer or declaration based on the formula:

I renounce the lie that I am (for example) dirty...

I announce the truth that (for example) I have been washed clean by the blood of Jesus, that I am pure and holy, that I can draw near to God in full assurance...

▶Finally, read the Bible verses and say the prayer/declaration out loud every day for 40 days, all the time reminding yourself that God is truth and that if He has said it, it really is true for you.

If some of you started Stronghold-Busters at the end of Session 4, you are probably part way through the 40-day period. You'll know that as you get up every morning and read out your verses and your declaration, it can feel like a complete waste of time. It will feel like that right up to the point that the stronghold breaks. Whatever you do, don't stop now!

Ed Silvoso tells of how a pastor friend of his watched a concrete wall being demolished. It withstood 10, then 15, then 30, then 35 blows with no visible sign of being weakened. That's how it can feel as you work through a Stronghold-Buster day after day. However, each day you renounce the lie and commit yourself to truth is making a difference. A wall might appear not to have been weakened right up to, say, ▶37 swings of a demolition ball. However, sooner or later, (say on the ▶38th swing) a few small cracks will appear. ▶On the next these cracks will get bigger until, finally, ▶the wall completely collapses. Even though only the final three swings appear to have had an effect, without the previous 37, the wall would not have fallen.

So do persevere until you have completed a total of 40 days and bear in mind that throughout most of that time, it will feel like a complete waste of time because the lie feels like truth. I promise you that if you persevere you will tear the stronghold down.

> Whoever looks intently into the perfect law that gives freedom, and **continues** in it – not forgetting what they have heard, but doing it – they will be blessed in what they do. (James 1:25 NIV)

Don't do more than one Stronghold-Buster at a time. The process of renewing your mind is a long-distance race not a sprint. What is the most significant lie that you have become aware of during the course? Start with that one. When you have seen that torn down, do another one. And so on.

People who really get hold of this, can do 6, 7 or 8 Stronghold-Busters a year and they are totally transformed by getting hold of the truth of God's Word in their hearts not just their heads.

Take a look at your *Lies List*. Just imagine how different your life could be if those things weren't affecting you any more. Go for it! ▶

Suggested Timetable For An Away Day Retreat

This is a suggested timetable for taking a group through *The Steps To Experiencing God's Grace* on an away day retreat.

9.45	Welcome and worship
10.10	Introduction/prayer/declaration (15 minutes)
10.25	Step 1: Renouncing lies and choosing truth (40 minutes)
11.05	Step 2: False expectations (35 minutes)
11.40	Break (20 minutes)
12.00	Step 3: Confessing sin (50 minutes)
12.50	Lunch Break
13.50	Step 4: Forgiveness (40 minutes)*
14.30	Step 5: Freedom from fear (50 minutes)
15.20	Step 6: Surrendering to God (30 minutes)
15.50	Break (20 minutes)
16.10	Renewing your mind talk (15 minutes)
16.25	Worship and finish

* Including the teaching on forgiveness from *The Freedom In Christ Discipleship Course* (Session 9) directly before Step 4 will be of great benefit to participants if you are able to do that. It lasts about 40 minutes (do not use the Pause For Thought questions). You could shorten the lunch break by 15 minutes so that the whole day is only 25 minutes longer than shown above.

Session 6:
FRUITFUL!

Session 6: Fruitful!

FOCUS VERSE:

John 15:5: I am the vine; you are the branches. Whoever abides in me and I in him, he it is that bears much fruit, for apart from me you can do nothing.

OBJECTIVE:

To help people move their focus from "doing ministry" to "remaining in the vine" which, paradoxically, will make their ministry much more effective.

FOCUS TRUTH:

If we want to be fruitful, our focus needs to be not on bearing fruit but on staying close to Jesus.

Leader's Notes

This final session should hammer the final nail into the coffin for any idea that this course is about "cheap grace". It brings home the uncomfortable truth that the gateway to fruitfulness is brokenness.

Some will struggle to understand that God could bring into our lives events that are painful and hard. It's important to help them see that, if God does that, it is for our ultimate good and for the good of His purposes.

It's also important not to let people think that every bad thing that happens is from God. We must not ignore the effects of sin and the fact that we have an enemy, Satan.

Much of this session is based on personal stories. By definition, everyone in fruitful ministry has been through some breaking experiences so do try to use your own stories where possible. Alternatively, if you are teaching this yourself, you may find it helpful to show the portions from the DVD presentation which feature these personal stories.

As the course comes to an end, do emphasize the importance of ongoing renewing of the mind and recommend Stronghold-Busting to those who have not yet tried it. You will see that the "In The Coming Weeks" section is all about this.

SMALL GROUP TIMINGS:

Welcome	5 minutes	0:05
Worship, prayer & declaration	7 minutes	0:12
Word part 1	21 minutes	0:33
Pause For Thought 1	8 minutes	0:41
Word part 2	24 minutes	1:05
Pause For Thought 2	18 minutes	1:23
Word part 3	18 minutes	1:41
Pause For Thought 3	15 minutes	1:56
Word part 4	4 minutes	2:00

 # WELCOME

If you were writing a book about your life, what would you like the next chapter to be entitled?

 # WORSHIP

Suggested theme: The Kingdom of God. 1 Chronicles 29:10–13, Revelation 19:6–9.

You could have someone read out 1 Chronicles 29:10–13 and someone else Revelation 19:6–9.

Then invite people to praise God that His glorious Kingdom will one day come in all its fullness and that we will be present at the wedding feast of the Lamb.

 # PRAYER & DECLARATION

Our Father, Your Kingdom come! Your will be done! I repent of striving in my own strength to bring about Your Kingdom purposes. Please teach me to depend upon the power of Your Life within me. I choose to make knowing You my highest goal. Amen.

I am a branch of the true vine, Jesus, a channel of His life. I choose to remain in Him so that I can bear much fruit.

 **WORD**

Introduction

There was a global conference of experts on different religions who were discussing whether the Christian faith had anything unique about it. The debate went on for some time without finding something that they could agree on. Then C. S. Lewis came into the room and asked what was going on. On hearing that they were discussing what Christianity's unique distinctive was, Lewis responded, "Oh, that's easy. It's grace."

We hope that you are coming to a deeper appreciation of grace and the things that stop us operating in grace. Hopefully you are seeing God begin to root out guilt, shame, fear and pride so that you will simply be motivated by love. As that happens, the key question becomes, how can my life really count for eternity? How can I bear much fruit?

How can we bear fruit?

In this session we'll be looking at how walking in God's grace is the key to living a fruitful life and we'll see that, like just about everything else to do with grace, it works precisely the opposite to how we'd naturally expect it to.

[Steve Goss says:] I met a guy at a conference who really wanted his life to be fruitful. He said he felt God wanted him to start a Christian ministry. He had been looking at how Freedom In Christ Ministries had grown so quickly in the UK and said, "How did you do it?"

I said, "I don't really know. It just kind of happened. If God wants you to do something similar, He will do it — just stay close to Him and co-operate with Him."

That clearly didn't satisfy him because after the conference he sent me an e-mail asking me again to tell him step by step how to create a ministry like FIC.

I honestly did think hard about how I could help him. Clearly I could have said some practical things like "Get a board of godly people together" or "Put a basic strategy together". But I really sensed that here was a guy who felt

that his value would come from "doing ministry" and was trying in his own strength to make it happen.

So I sent him a mail back saying much the same as I'd said when we met, adding that it's when we persevere through difficulties that God really seems to prepare us for future ministry.

I never heard from him again!

▶That man's question is the same question many of us ask God or think about ourselves as we seek to be fruitful disciples: How can we bear fruit and keep on bearing fruit? It's important to know how the rest of our lives can count for something for eternity.

Earlier is this course we looked at Paul's warning in 1 Corinthians 3:11–15, that believers can either build on the foundation Jesus has laid with wood, hay and straw that will be burned up and count for nothing, or with gold, silver and precious stones that will last for eternity. We've seen that it may not be obvious just by looking at someone outwardly what they are building with, because it is a matter of our heart, our motivation.

▶Imagine you got an invitation from Jesus Himself to have a coffee with Him at your local coffee shop at 10 am tomorrow. How would you feel in anticipation of that meeting? Excited? Scared? Curious? Nervous? And when you sat down at the table across from Him, what do you imagine the first words out of Jesus' mouth might be? How you answer those questions depends a lot on your view of Jesus.

Rich Miller says, "I know for much of my Christian life I felt like I was letting God down. Like my parents' favourite expression to me growing up, I could easily imagine the Lord Jesus taking a sip of coffee, looking me straight in the eye and, as he set His cup down, slowly shaking His head and saying something like, "Shape up or ship out! When will you finally learn to get it right? When will you get your act together?""

I hope you have realized as we have progressed through *The Grace Course* that that is not what Jesus would say to you at all. Now I know that it is risky to put words into Jesus' mouth, but here is what I can easily imagine Jesus saying to you, based on Scripture: "Grace to you and peace from God our Father." That was what Paul wrote to the saints in Ephesus.

And you will find words like this at the beginning of almost all of Paul's letters, but they are not just the first century equivalent of "Hi! How are you?" They are not just a greeting; they are a blessing. Will you receive that blessing of grace and peace now? Grace to YOU and peace. God's undeserved favour and blessing, and delight and welcome. And His shalom — fullness, wholeness, completeness, peace. It's when we walk in grace and peace that we find the path of true fruitfulness.

Our responsibility is to "remain in the vine"

▶So how can we bear fruit for Jesus? Some of His most important words, coming near the end of His earthly life, shed light on this:

> "I am the true vine, and my Father is the vine dresser. Every branch in me that does not bear fruit he takes away, and every branch that does bear fruit he prunes, that it may bear more fruit. Already you are clean because of the word that I have spoken to you. Abide in me, and I in you. As the branch cannot bear fruit of itself, unless it abides in the vine, neither can you, unless you abide in me. I am the vine; you are the branches. Whoever abides in me and I in him, he it is that bears much fruit, for apart from me you can do nothing."
> (John 15:1–5)

I am the true vine, and my Father is the vine dresser. Every branch in me that does not bear fruit he takes away, and every branch that does bear fruit he prunes, that it may bear more fruit. Already you are clean because of the word that I have spoken to you. Abide in me, and I in you. As the branch cannot bear fruit of itself, unless it abides in the vine, neither can you, unless you abide in me. I am the vine; you are the branches. Whoever abides in me and I in him, he it is that bears much fruit, for apart from me you can do nothing."

John 15:1-5

If you ever venture into a vineyard, I can assure you that there is one thing you will never hear. You will never hear the sound of branches grunting and groaning, straining to get grapes to pop out on them. And there is something I will guarantee you will not see. You will not see branches disconnected from the vine with healthy fruit growing on them.

Two laws of the vineyard

▶ Branches don't bear fruit because they try really hard. And neither do we.

Branches that are not attached to the vine do not and cannot bear fruit. These are two inviolable laws of the vineyard.

What is the branch's one responsibility? Our natural reaction would be to say, "To bear fruit!" No. It is to abide in, stay close to, remain with, and be at home in the vine. The gardener knows that if he makes sure the plant is healthy, with the branches firmly connected to the vine, it will bear fruit.

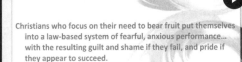

Christians who focus on their need to bear fruit put themselves into a law-based system of fearful, anxious performance... with the resulting guilt and shame if they fail, and pride if they appear to succeed.

But Christians who focus on simply abiding in Jesus enter into a life of "grace-rest" where, paradoxically, they bear much fruit.

▶ Here's a key principle: Christians who focus on their need to bear fruit put themselves into a law-based system of fearful, anxious performance... with the resulting guilt and shame if they fail, and pride if they think they succeed.

▶ But Christians who focus simply on abiding in Jesus enter into a life of "grace-rest" where, paradoxically, they bear much fruit.

There is a progression I believe we need to go through in our understanding of who Jesus is. First He is our Saviour and always will be our Saviour. But it is not enough to know Jesus as Saviour, though that is the essential starting place for all of us. Second, He is our Lord, our Master, and we need to come to the place of surrendering to Him as Lord. But it is not enough to know Him as Lord, though He is Lord and will always be Lord. We need to a third understanding of Jesus, that He is our very Life (Colossians 3:3).

▶ Then we simply need to stay connected to Him.

Jesus Himself modelled this for us. He is the Son of God. Everything that has been created was created through Him. Yet when He chose to give up all the glory of Heaven and came to this earth, He took on an attitude that is amazing and even shocking:

> "Truly, truly, I say to you, the Son can do nothing of his own accord, but only what he sees the Father doing." (John 5:19)

In verse 30 of the same chapter, He added "I can do nothing on my own."

Even though He was God, numerous times Jesus made it clear that He was not living life or ministering out of His "God-ness". He lived life in full dependence upon the Father, in the energy and power of the Holy Spirit. He was actually modelling how God wants His fully alive people — that's us! — to live: Knowing that we can do absolutely nothing apart from Him.

Have you heard that Martin Luther once wrote that he had so much to do one day that he had to get up three hours earlier than usual to pray? How did that make you feel? Guilty probably! Did any of you try to emulate him? I did. I lasted about 40 minutes! How many of us feel we should be praying more? Probably all of us.

Let's see how Jesus approached prayer. It was a lifestyle for Him. He too was usually up early, walking the mountains and talking to His Father. This is not a formal, dutiful prayer life. I imagine there were long times of silence as you often get between people who know each other well — a comfortable silence. It's an intimate love relationship existing between the Father and Son. Sons rest in the assurance that they already have the love and acceptance of their Father, and don't have to work to earn it. Their work is motivated by love for their Father.

God probably isn't asking you to get up three hours earlier to pray right now. But He would be so delighted if you came to Him just because you want to — with no agenda — even for 10 minutes. As you do that more and more, you will probably get hold of the truth, like Jesus did and Luther did, that without God you can do nothing whatsoever of any lasting value.

And you may well end up getting up early to pray — not out of guilt or the need to fulfil a duty, but out of a real understanding of truth and because you just love spending time with God. You will not be focussing on the fruit — how many hours of prayer you can do — but on the One who is the True Vine. And paradoxically you will bear fruit!

Rest in Him

Jesus made an offer, specifically to people who felt overwhelmed by the demands of trying to live up to a certain set of expectations. And it was this:

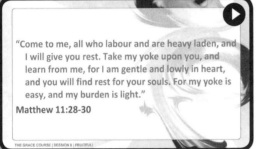

> ▶ "Come to me, all who labour and are heavy laden, and I will give you rest. Take my yoke upon you, and learn from me, for I am gentle and lowly in heart, and you will find rest for your souls. For my yoke is easy, and my burden is light." (Matthew 11:28–30)

What an amazing statement of grace! Can you imagine any other god from any other religion making that kind of offer? God doesn't want us to wear ourselves out and live with religious burdens on our shoulders. He wants us to find rest from that sort of life. He genuinely offers us a yoke that is easy and a burden that is light. As we've seen, as Christians there is nothing that God forces us to do. Absolutely nothing.

▶Yet the picture Jesus gives us when He offers us rest is that of two oxen ploughing a field. That looks more like hard work than rest doesn't it?

I don't want you to get the impression that the Christian life is supposed to be something where you just float along singing lovely songs and hearing God's voice all the time.

The rest we're talking about here does not mean lying around doing nothing. It's an internal rest in the midst of working with Jesus in His harvest field, that is based on faith and dependence upon God. Our focus is not on bearing fruit but on remaining in the Vine, cultivating our trust relationship with Jesus. There's a sense that we rest from our works so that God's works get done.

▶ Did you notice what Jesus said right at the end of the John 15 passage we looked at? He didn't say, "Apart from Me you can get along pretty well." Nor did He say, "Apart from Me you can't do very much." He said, "Apart from Me you can do **nothing**."

Now, you can get out of bed, eat breakfast, brush your teeth, get dressed, go to work, make a living, raise a family, grow old, retire and die without Jesus. Millions do that every day. So what did Jesus mean when He said, "Apart from Me you can do nothing"? Simply that you can do nothing of eternal value unless you depend completely on Him, unless it is from a position of resting in His ability.

Principles of rest

Rest then work

God has always wanted His people to understand that rest is key. Look at creation: God worked for six days and then rested on the seventh day. But what about Adam? Just the opposite. He was created on day six, so the first full day of Adam's life was the seventh day when God rested. Everything was already done. Everything he needed was on hand. There was nothing whatsoever to worry about.

So he rested first and then God put him to work taking care of the animals and the garden. And that's the principle God wants us to work to. We rest, then we work. It's not meant to be that we work hard and then rest to recover. It's the other way around. Out of rest comes fruitful ministry.

▶ If you want to bear fruit that will remain... if you want to have an impact on this planet that lasts into eternity... if you want to come into alignment with God's kingdom purposes for your life, your family and your world... then it has to start with resting in the true Vine, Jesus Christ, who is our very Life.

PAUSE FOR THOUGHT 1

OBJECTIVE:

TO START TO EXPLORE THE CONCEPT OF COMPLETE DEPENDENCE ON THE FATHER.

▶QUESTIONS (ON PAGE 86 OF THE PARTICIPANT'S GUIDE):

IN WHAT WAYS DID JESUS' LIFE ON EARTH DEMONSTRATE HIS COMPLETE DEPENDENCE UPON HIS FATHER?

IN WHAT WAYS MIGHT OUR LIVES LOOK DIFFERENT IF WE DEPENDED COMPLETELY ON GOD?

Don't try to control events

▶How can we tell if we are relying on our own strength to bear fruit?

▶We saw in the last session that pride boils down to putting our confidence in something other than Jesus, so that's a sign that we're working in our own strength. There's a related issue too, control.

▶The guy who was desperately trying to start a ministry was trying to control events. He had probably heard accurately from God that He wanted him to start a ministry, but his role was then primarily to remain in the vine and let God make it happen, not to try and bring it about himself.

[Rich Miller:] I was appointed to take over as president of Freedom In Christ Ministries in the U.S. in the spring of 2006. When I received that news, if I had not been outside of a church in Iowa, I would have been curled up in the foetal position somewhere! The ministry was in a very rough spot at that time. Later that summer and into the fall I experienced periods of rapid heartbeat. When it happened, I'd rush to the doctor or the emergency room (as the doctor instructed me to do), but it would always correct itself before I got there!

Finally, my heart went ballistic... 195 beats per minute for 3 ½ hours. The ambulance came to get me and they tried every chemical on the planet to slow it down. I was diagnosed with ventricular tachycardia (a potentially dangerous condition) and they finally had to cardiovert me to get my heart back to normal rhythm.

The doctors decided to implant a defibrillator/pacemaker into my chest. While I was waiting for the operation the ministry pressures mounted, and I was frustrated because I was not available to do anything about them. It was out of my control and I didn't like that. I remember yelling at God, "I DON'T HAVE TIME FOR THIS!" The Lord knew better.

As I lay on my bed frustrated and angry, stewing over the eight major crises in our ministry, the Lord clearly spoke to me, "Why don't you give them to Me?" Wow! What a radical concept. I imagined that I had eight tennis balls resting on my chest, representing the eight crises. I took one and tossed it up to the Lord. "I'll take that!" He said. Then I tossed another and another until they were all in His hands. Nothing had changed circumstantially, but I had changed. And within 13 months of that moment of brokenness and surrender, the Lord had resolved every one of those eight crises!

Don't try to control people

▶Sometimes we can also try to control people. The Pharisees were zealous for God, and were trying to win favour with Him by imposing their strict interpretations of the law on everyone, even to the extent that some of them were sneaking around trying to catch people in the act of adultery and then bringing them out to be punished. The elder brother reminded his father of all the good works he was slaving away at, but he was effectively trying to control the father by using his good works to try to make the father bless him.

Those who realize that apart from God they can do nothing do not need to try to control either events or people. They rest in the knowledge that their Father God can be trusted to take care of those people and events that are outside of the realm of their control. They know that He really does work all things together for their good (Romans 8:28).

Pride and control are in effect saying to God — "I'm the one that can make it happen. And I'll do it my way, in my time and in my strength." They are a "declaration of independence." They keep us from experiencing the fullness of God's provision and blessings.

Entering into the grace-rest life

▶So how do you enter the grace-rest life?

I remember during a time of deep heart searching and longing for the Lord... when as much as I can ever recall I wanted Him and all He had for me. I recall praying, hoping that my prayer would open the gateway to a new and fresh spiritual dimension. I prayed, "Lord, I repent of everything in my life that displeases You. I reject everything that doesn't look like You or reflect Your glory and goodness." I lifted my head, sincerely expecting to have entered into a new echelon of spirituality. And I can remember the impression on my heart from my heavenly Father being loud and clear, "My son, it is not that easy."

God's right of course. It isn't easy. We have a natural inclination not to abide in the vine and rely completely on Jesus, but to rely instead on our own strength and abilities. As long as we think we still have one more brainy idea, one more trick up our sleeve, one more talent or giftedness to fall back on, one more area of experience or expertise to depend on, that is what we will tend to put our trust in. But that is not the way of rest nor of fruitfulness.

Still and quieten your soul

▶ Let's look at an example of someone who had been through it. King David wrote a lovely psalm with just three verses, Psalm 131 (NIV):

> My heart is not proud, O Lord, my eyes are not haughty; I do not concern myself with great matters or things too wonderful for me. But I have stilled and quietened my soul; like a weaned child with its mother, like a weaned child is my soul within me. O Israel, put your hope in the Lord both now and for evermore.

This is King David writing. Who's he kidding that he doesn't concern himself with great matters? He has to deal with life and death decisions every day! What does he mean then? It's not that he doesn't do these things. He just recognizes that if he thought he could do them in his own strength, it would be pride.

▶ He says that the antidote to pride is that he has stilled and quietened his soul. David recognizes that deep inside there's a part of him — the very human part of him that we would call "flesh" — that cries out constantly like a child still on breast milk. Our flesh is always crying out — from fear or shame or guilt, or because it craves to fulfil the urges that come with the subtle voice of temptation: Or because we want to control people or events. There's a restlessness.

So how did David learn to still and quieten his soul? He was anointed to be king when he was still a young man. But it was years before it actually happened, and he found himself thrown into a nightmare scenario, where he spent years in the wilderness in fear of his life as King Saul tried to track him down. He learned that God is real and can be trusted to keep His word. He learned that God is good and has plans to give him a hope and a future and that He will bring about those plans in His time when we are ready.

Like David we need to learn to still and quiet our soul, to come to the point of complete dependence on God. When we feel guilty, we need to lay our sin at the foot of the cross and walk away. When we feel ashamed, we need to recognize that we are new people with a new name. When the fleshly urges come, we need to know that they only produce bondage, and we can choose not to give in to them. When fear comes, we need to remember that only God has the right to be feared, and He is for us. When we are tempted to pride, to know that we can do absolutely nothing apart from Him. It's about choosing truth over lies.

The gateway of brokenness

So, how does God help us deal with the pride and control that He so hates, and get us to a point of grace-filled rest? I wish I had good news for you! Well, actually it really is good news. It just isn't easy news.

▶His cure is to bring us to a point of brokenness, in order to teach us how absolutely dependent we are on Him, that apart from Him we really can do nothing at all that is of any eternal value. Being completely dependent on someone else is a nightmare scenario for most of us — think about growing old and infirm for example — yet Jesus wants us to learn to be dependent on Him, and in His grace He works on us as gently as He can. But it can still be very painful.

There is a process of cutting and hacking away at fleshly self-centeredness and self-reliance that all of God's people... no exceptions... must go through in order to enter God's rest. Jesus called it "pruning". Hebrews 12 calls it "discipline". And the writer of that letter tells us to be diligent to enter into God's rest. It's not easy. And it is not fun. In fact, it is downright painful, which is why it requires diligence or endurance... hanging in there. But it is the gateway into the grace-rest life. And believe me, it is more than worth it.

Let's take a closer look at Hebrews 12:

> ▶"My son, do not regard lightly the discipline of the Lord, nor faint when you are reproved by him; For those whom the Lord loves He disciplines, and He scourges everyone whom He receives... All discipline for the moment seems not to be joyful, but sorrowful; yet to those who have been trained by it, afterwards it yields the peaceful fruit of righteousness." (Hebrews 12:5–6,11 NASB)

My son, do not regard lightly the discipline of the Lord, nor faint when you are reproved by him; for those whom the Lord loves he disciplines, and he scourges every son whom he receives... All discipline for the moment seems not to be joyful, but sorrowful; yet to those who have been trained by it, afterwards it yields the peaceful fruit of righteousness.
Hebrews 12:5,6,11 NASB

Ouch. I don't think I like that word "scourges". Scourging was what they did to Jesus with the terrible cat-o-nine-tails whip prior to His crucifixion. Could the measures God uses on us be that strong? Yes. The strongholds of self-sufficiency, self-reliance, self-satisfaction, and... well ... selfishness run very deep; they require strong measures to remove them. God's cure is to discipline us in love, to bring us to the point of brokenness. He wants us to see — and we **need** to see — how utterly futile our own efforts are, and how absolutely dependent upon Him we really are. We need to learn... not just in our head, but in our heart... that apart from Jesus we really can't do anything of eternal value. We need to discover Jesus as our Life.

This may be surprising to you, but the writer to the Hebrews makes clear that even Jesus had to learn obedience through difficulties: "Although he was a son, he learned obedience through what he suffered" (Hebrews 5:8). There is no shortcut but, when we understand that difficult situations are actually helping us grow and bear fruit, we can learn to embrace them and endure them even though we won't enjoy them.

Let me share with you some of what God has done to help me deal with pride. [You may have examples of your own to share here instead of this story from Steve Goss:]

I was on the leadership team of a small church, and a lady on the team was really struggling because she felt that she had heard from God something that was very difficult to share. This is what I wrote in my journal at the time:

> Last night at the leaders' meeting, Sandra came. Turns out she has had a very specific word from God that has caused her real agony and upset since Sunday. The main point was that God is grieving over our church because we are hard-hearted.

> She then had very specific things for each of us. Mine was having a "holier than thou" attitude, not being vulnerable, making people think they cannot be as holy as me — apparently this is causing discouragement to Christians and putting non-Christians off.

I remember being quite shocked and mumbling something like, "Thank you for that Sandra. I can't quite see that myself but will certainly go and pray about it." I then looked around the room at the other leaders, certain, I think, that they would back me up and reassure me that that's not what I was like at all. But they all studiously avoided meeting my gaze! No one felt the need to jump in and correct or even modify slightly what Sandra had said!

Let me read a little more from my journal:

> Zoë and I talked this evening and concluded that basically we have been brought up to believe that we can "handle" things — and indeed in one sense we can. As capable people, we tend to rely on our own resources. As a result, we hardly ever ask for help because we don't think we need any; we don't let people get close because we don't think we have any needs; I am ready to offer advice and "wisdom" but don't seem to need any myself...
>
> I don't think we yet realize what an offence this attitude is to God. Tonight we repented and prayed that God would smash the strongholds of pride, independence and self-sufficiency in us.

I remember that led to a period where I just became increasingly aware and increasingly horrified of how proud I had been. I spent hours in prayer just saying sorry to God. Often I would just end up lying flat out on the floor before Him.

Let me read you one last entry from my journal for that period:

> I have realized that my relationship with Jesus is very weak and that much of my Christianity has been about making me feel good — building myself up in the eyes of others etc.
>
> I feel totally weak and helpless and happy and excited.

▶ It's strange but when you get to that point of realizing your weakness and helplessness and throw yourself onto God's mercy, it somehow feels like the place you were always meant to be. It feels like you've come home. Like the younger brother when he returned and fell into his father's arms.

And you know what? Every time there is a breaking of our stubborn self-sufficiency, it's like a door to a room in the house of our life that had been closed and locked and bolted against the love of God, suddenly swings open and His presence floods in.

Pride, however, literally does come before a fall: Because God opposes the proud (James 4:6). So God in His love for us intentionally and relentlessly unleashes events in our lives that overwhelm us, that take us out of our comfort zone and into realms where we find ourselves beyond our ability to cope. Why? Because we never get to experience the power of God in our lives unless we are brought to "an end of ourselves." We don't know Jesus is all we need until Jesus is all we've got.

Whatever breaking instrument God uses in our lives, loss of reputation, misunderstanding, injustice, health issues, job stress, family conflicts or financial difficulties, it will be tailor-made to get down to the issues of pride and control in our lives. God's goal is to strip away those things that we have made to be substitutes for God. God in His persistent love for us always sets out to woo us back to Himself. He wants to rescue us from all attachments that would draw us away from Himself, and restore the intimacy of our relationship with Him.

The apostle Paul had been given amazing insights into the truth of God that could easily have made him proud. Yet he found a depth of the grace-rest life that few have attained. He tells us how:

> ▶ Because of the surpassing greatness of the revelations…to keep me from exalting myself, there was given me a thorn in the flesh, a messenger of Satan to torment me… Concerning this I implored the Lord three times that it might leave me. And He has said to me, "My grace is sufficient for you, for power is perfected in weakness." Most gladly, therefore, I will rather boast about my weaknesses, so that the power of Christ may dwell in me. Therefore I am well content with weaknesses, with insults, with distresses, with persecutions, with difficulties, for Christ's sake; for when I am weak, then I am strong.
> (2 Corinthians 12:7–10 NASB)

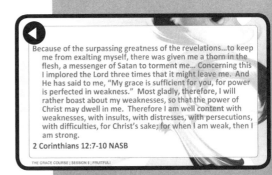

Because of the surpassing greatness of the revelations…to keep me from exalting myself, there was given me a thorn in the flesh, a messenger of Satan to torment me… Concerning this I implored the Lord three times that it might leave me. And He has said to me, "My grace is sufficient for you, for power is perfected in weakness." Most gladly, therefore, I will rather boast about my weaknesses, so that the power of Christ may dwell in me. Therefore I am well content with weaknesses, with insults, with distresses, with persecutions, with difficulties, for Christ's sake; for when I am weak, then I am strong.
2 Corinthians 12:7-10 NASB

THE GRACE COURSE | SESSION 6 | FRUITFUL!

So… if you want to be proud of anything, be proud of your weaknesses!

PAUSE FOR THOUGHT 2

OBJECTIVE:

TO REALIZE THAT THE GATEWAY TO FRUITFULNESS REALLY IS BROKENNESS.

▶QUESTIONS (ON PAGE 89 OF THE PARTICIPANT'S GUIDE):

IF YOU ARE WILLING, SHARE WITH THE GROUP BRIEFLY ABOUT A TIME THAT YOU EXPERIENCED BROKENNESS. DID IT LATER PRODUCE ANY FRUIT IN YOUR CHARACTER OR IN YOUR LIFE?

HOW DO YOU FEEL ABOUT THE POSSIBILITY THAT GOD MIGHT TAKE YOU THROUGH HARD TIMES?

HOW DO YOU THINK PAUL COULD BE "CONTENT WITH WEAKNESSES, WITH INSULTS, HARDSHIPS, PERSECUTIONS, AND CALAMITIES" (2 CORINTHIANS 12:10)? DID HE REALLY MEAN IT?

This questionable joke even has its own PowerPoint slides! If you don't use the joke, you'll need to skip over them.

▶A man had a dream in which he was looking back at his life with Jesus and seeing it as footprints in the sand. Most of the time there were two sets of footprints as he and Jesus walked together. But in the times when he went through great difficulties there was just one set of footprints. That prompted him to say, "Lord, why did you leave me on my own in the hard times?"

"My son," said the Lord, "I didn't desert you. ▶I thought it might cheer you up if we both hopped for a while!"

Rising up like eagles

▶Eagles are huge birds. They can have a wing span of 9 feet and can weigh over 25 pounds. That's about the same as a medium-sized dog such as a cocker spaniel (the weight, not the wing span!). If you've ever seen an eagle you know that they fly to a great height — imagine the energy needed to get a bird that big so high. Huge... Or is it?

▶I'm sure you know how eagles get to that height. They simply jump off a high place, find some rising warm air and circle in it. They have a mechanism that means they can simply lock their wings in place so there is practically no energy required to get them to those amazing heights. It's all done by the warm air.

> ▶Even youths shall faint and be weary,
> and young men shall fall exhausted;
> but they who wait for the Lord shall renew their strength;
> they shall mount up with wings like eagles;
> they shall run and not be weary;
> they shall walk and not faint. (Isaiah 40:30–31)

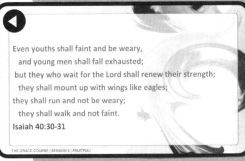

Part of resting is waiting for God, looking for the warm air if you like. The idea behind the Hebrew word translated here as "wait" is something like "to gather together", much as strands in a rope are bound together to make something much stronger. There's a sense that as we wait on God we are bound together with Him.

▶What a great picture of how God wants us to be with Him. As we lock our wings and rest in Him, He renews our strength and we rise up.

One very simple practical way in which we can wait for God, rather than rush ahead in our own understanding, is to build some space into our decision-making process to allow God to have the lead. Do you have a decision to make? If you can, why not try delaying it for a few days — maybe a week — to invite God to put His plan in place, if it should contradict yours?

[Again, you may have a "breaking" story of your own to replace this one from Steve Goss:]

Let me share with you another breaking experience from my own life, this time more recent. I am wired to "do". I love having loads of things to do and can quite easily run on pure adrenaline. At those times I am likely to charge ahead in my own strength, with the result that I often get stressed and overloaded. Yet if I don't have enough to do my soul shouts out, and I feel aimless and unsettled. This is not a good way to live and really gets in the way of entering God's rest. God has been gently teaching me about all this and blessed me with a really difficult period, the most difficult period of my life so far. It lasted two years or so.

Zoë, my wife, collapsed in the middle of the night with no warning. I thought she had died at one point. She couldn't get up. I called an ambulance that took her to hospital. We then embarked on a variety of different tests to try to work out what had happened and what might be wrong with her — I now know she has a brain because I've seen a picture of it! One by one every obvious thing was ruled out, which was a relief. But she didn't regain her usual strength and at various points when she did a little too much, she would relapse. She was very tired. She felt ill. She had a headache. Each time she relapsed, she got worse until she was at a point where she couldn't really leave the house. Once every two or three days she could perhaps shuffle the 50 yards or so to the postbox, and that was it. Finally she got a diagnosis of Chronic Fatigue Syndrome. Not a great comfort — it's an extremely debilitating illness and the doctors have very little success with it.

I was having to keep the home and the family going. It became quite stressful but in a way I thrived on all the doing... But I had to ease off on my ministry commitments. I accepted hardly any speaking engagements. I cut back a lot on my time in the office. Guess what? I found God was able to keep everything going and even develop the ministry without me.

During this period one of our intercessors tentatively sent me a word that she felt God wanted to say to me:

> Am I not your hope? If there were no ministry, would I not still be your hope? Your joy? If everything was stripped away, would I be enough? This is a hard question for My beloved. So many believe they need to be My slaves in order to please Me, when it is their hearts I brood over.

▶It is indeed a hard question! If everything were stripped away, would Jesus be enough?

Shortly after that, and during this two-year period of Zoë's illness, I went out to Portugal to meet Samuel Paulo, a pastor who was interested in getting FIC started there. I could see he was an incredibly busy man, involved in running a busy church, co-ordinating evangelicals across Portugal, and leading projects to feed the poor locally and help children in Africa. On the way back to the airport at the end of the trip, I said to him, "Please don't start FIC because you feel you have to, only if you feel called to." He said, "Don't worry, I won't" and told me his story.

He told me how he had once been so driven to keep doing things that his marriage and ministry were at the point of meltdown. He finally got alone with God and felt Jesus saying, "If you didn't have any of this ministry would I be enough?"

At which point the hairs on the back of my neck stood up! He was honest enough to tell me that his answer was, "Not really, Lord, no." And I knew straightaway that my honest answer was exactly the same.

▶He worked through it to the point where now he can say, "Yes, Jesus, You are enough". He is still an incredibly busy guy with lots going on, but internally he is now at rest. He is doing only what the Father is telling him to do, and I'm so glad the Father did — a couple of years later — tell him to start FIC in Portugal. He is seeing great fruit in a really difficult place.

I can do all things through him who strengthens me. Philippians 4:13

Zoë was ill for two years but made a complete recovery. Both of us in that time learned a deeper level of dependence on God. The proof of the pudding is in the eating, of course, and I know I would find it really hard if the ministry were taken away from me, but the bottom line is, yes, Jesus, You are enough.

> Through many dangers, toils and snares
> I have already come;
> 'Tis grace has brought me safe thus far;
> And grace will lead me home.

The sky's the limit!

I love the fact that God's hand has so clearly been on what has happened with FIC. I know that I could never have done it. Having seen all that, I know there's no point my trying to make things happen. I also know that the sky is the limit regarding future fruitfulness, because it doesn't depend on me but on God Almighty Himself. There's a wonderful corresponding truth:

▶ I can do all things through him who strengthens me. (Philippians 4:13)

▶ So, what is the fruit that God wants to see in your life? We tend to think in terms of outward ministry, the things we do. And indeed there are works that God has prepared just for you to do since before you were born. You don't know what they all are yet.

No matter how impossibly big they may seem to be to you, if God is behind them they are all completely possible.

Yet God is much more interested in what you are inwardly than what you do outwardly. He looks at the heart. The fruit of the Spirit is not external ministry, it's love, joy, peace, patience, kindness, goodness, gentleness, faithfulness and self-control. All of those are **character** attributes. The beauty of how God works is that as you develop those character attributes inside, they will flow over into the things we do outside.

In Matthew 16:21, we see a crucial moment in Jesus' ministry where God reveals to Simon Peter exactly who Jesus is.

From that time Jesus began to show His disciples that He must go to Jerusalem and suffer many things from the elders and chief priests and scribes, and be killed, and on the third day be raised.

Peter then actually tries to control Jesus and tells Him He's got it wrong. Think about that — you've just had it revealed to you that this is God Himself and you tell Him He's made a mistake! How arrogant can you get?

Jesus rebukes him severely and continues with His train of thought. He has just told them that He will die. With that image of His own future death on the cross in His mind, He says:

> ▶ "If anyone would come after me, let him deny himself and take up his cross and follow me. For whoever would save his life will lose it, but whoever loses his life for my sake will find it." (Matthew 16:24–25)

I invite you right now to make a radical commitment to God.

Father, I lay down absolutely everything at Your feet — my health, my past, my present, my future, my money and property, my family, my ministry. I reaffirm that I am willingly making myself Your bondslave. I surrender to Jesus as Lord, that's the Boss, of my life and I recognize that You are my Life. Amen.

This kind of surrender cannot be forced, but must be an absolutely free decision you make because you want to.

▶ Thankfully you don't have to do this in your own strength, but you can come to Him in complete weakness and trepidation and collapse into His arms, letting Him know you are completely dependent on Him. That's the place you're meant to be anyway. He'll always be there. He'll never leave you. He'll never take you beyond what you can bear in Him but will fill your life with good gifts that will amaze you.

What a great God!

But it's crucial that you take the responsibility to do the things that God says you are to do. He won't do those for you. So only you can forgive. Only you can renew your mind with the truth in God's Word — and an ongoing strategy of Stronghold-Busting will help you do that.

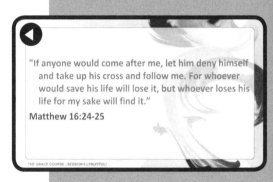

"If anyone would come after me, let him deny himself and take up his cross and follow me. For whoever would save his life will lose it, but whoever loses his life for my sake will find it."

Matthew 16:24-25

THE GRACE COURSE | SESSION 6 | FRUITFUL!

THE GRACE COURSE | SESSION 6 | FRUITFUL!

PAUSE FOR THOUGHT 3

OBJECTIVE:

TO GIVE PARTICIPANTS THE OPPORTUNITY TO SHARE HOW THEY HAVE BEEN IMPACTED BY DOING *THE GRACE COURSE*.

▶**QUESTIONS (ON PAGE 91 OF THE PARTICIPANT'S GUIDE):**

AS WE COME TO THE END OF THE COURSE, SHARE WITH THE GROUP WHAT YOU HAVE LEARNED ABOUT GOD'S GRACE AND WHAT IMPACT IT HAS MADE ON YOU.

THE GRACE COURSE | SESSION 6 | FRUITFUL!

▶ Conclusion

Dietrich Bonhoeffer coined the phrase "cheap grace" to describe someone who wants to enjoy all the benefits of the kingdom of God without any true heart discipleship of taking up our cross and following Christ. By now, we hope you realize that living in grace does not lead to laziness or being "soft on sin". If someone has that mentality they are not experiencing the true grace of God.

True grace is not timid or lukewarm or soft or complacent. True grace is robust, virile, liberating and strengthening.

Let's remind ourselves of what God's grace means to us every day of our lives.

▶He paid an unimaginable price so that your true guilt could be paid in full, to leave you completely innocent. By His grace the verdict on you has been declared: Not guilty!

THE GRACE COURSE | SESSION 6 | FRUITFUL!

▶An amazing exchange has taken place. Jesus became sin on your behalf and in return you became the righteousness of God. You are holy through and through. In fact you're a whole new creation with some brand new names. Shame is gone!

▶You have no need to have any unhealthy fears any more. By His grace, you are safe and secure in the hands of the Almighty God and He loves you.

▶At any time you can come and cast yourself on His mercy. Knowing that you can do nothing in your own strength but that He can do everything is a good place to be.

But remember that because of His grace, you don't have to grovel into His presence. You don't have to turn your eyes to the floor even.

▶Here you stand, a son or daughter of the Living God, dressed in your rich robe, your ring of authority and your sandals.

And God Himself is looking at you. To see what you've done wrong? No! He looks at you for one reason only; because He finds you so wonderful. He looks with eyes of pure love.

And you say, "God, what do You want me to do for You?" And His response might be, "There are things for you to do. But what I really want is **you**."

God's grace has saved you. You have received your introduction into His grace through faith. You are now to grow in the grace and knowledge of our Lord and Saviour Jesus Christ. It is by God's grace you stand. By the grace of God you are who you are, and I am who I am. God's word of blessing to you today is "Grace and peace."

Does it sound like grace is important to God? Clearly it is. In fact, the very last words of God to us in His Word provide a fitting conclusion to *The Grace Course*:

> The grace of the Lord Jesus be with God's people. Amen. (Revelation 22:21)

Amen!

 **WITNESS**

Many people are genuinely hindered from becoming a Christian because they believe they could never live up to God's standards afterwards. How would you respond to them?

 **IN THE COMING WEEKS**

Most of us have had the experience of coming back from a Christian conference or course feeling that it was going to be life-changing, only to realize a few weeks down the line that in fact nothing much had changed after all. If you want to be transformed by the truth you have heard on this course, there's only one way — by the renewing of your mind (Romans 12:2). So, in the coming weeks, revisit your *Lies List*. Spend time finding the corresponding truths. Write Stronghold-Busters for the key areas where you realize that your thinking is not in line with what God says is true. Work on them one at a time and persevere through each one for 40 days.

Freedom In Christ Ministries Around The World

Freedom In Christ Ministries is a resource ministry that exists to serve the Church. Our role is to equip church leaders around the world with tools and resources to help them make **disciples** (not just converts) and set their people, marriages and ministries free in Christ. We are trusting God to raise up people to take our discipleship approach to every country where He wants it established. For the latest details of where we operate and for contact details, see our international website at **www.FICMinternational.org**.

National Offices: Canada, India, Switzerland, UK, USA

Countries With FICM Representatives: Argentina, Australia, France, Liberia, Malaysia, Mexico, Nepal, New Zealand, Portugal, South Africa, Spain, Sri Lanka, Thailand, Venezuela

Countries In Initial Stages: Albania, Côte d'Ivoire, Croatia, Democratic Republic Of Congo, Ethiopia, Hungary, Iran, Italy, Latvia, The Netherlands, Romania, South Korea, Trinidad & Tobago

For further information: **www.FICMinternational.org**

FRUSTRATED THAT FAR TOO MANY CHRISTIANS STRUGGLE TO TAKE HOLD OF BASIC BIBLICAL TRUTH AND LIVE IT OUT IN DAILY LIFE?

Take a look at *the best selling, award-winning Freedom In Christ Discipleship Course.*

- Explains what Jesus has done in a way that Christians can integrate into their daily life
- Helps believers understand and overcome in the battle against the world, the flesh and the devil
- Helps believers grasp the authority they now have to resolve personal and spiritual conflicts
- Equips Christians to take personal responsibility for living in the freedom gained so that they mature and bear fruit

The Freedom In Christ Discipleship Course is a straightforward and effective way for any church to implement discipleship that really works. With clear, concise teaching – each of the 13 sessions focuses on just a few key points – it is excellent for new Christians and mature Christians alike. Either present it yourself or use video presentations by Steve Goss, available on DVD with the addition of some superb video testimonies to illustrate the key points.

The course has been used by over 150,000 people in around 3,000 churches. It's flexible enough to be used in a variety of different formats. Most use it as a small group resource, often after Christian basics courses such as Alpha.

PLUS! Training DVDs to equip your team and a series of additional optional resources for participants including the *Discipleship Series* of books by Steve Goss (see pages 24–25).

Make **disciples**, not just **converts**!

More information at www.ficm.org.uk

FOR YOUNG PEOPLE

FREEDOM IN CHRIST

> "EVERY YOUNG DISCIPLE IS LOOKING TO ENGAGE WITH JESUS IN A WAY THAT WILL CHANGE LIVES. THIS INNOVATIVE, EXCITING COURSE WILL HELP YOUNG PEOPLE DISCOVER THE TRUTH OF WHO THEY ARE IN CHRIST AND BE SET FREE TO BE ALL THAT GOD HAS MADE THEM AS A RESULT."

Mike Pilavachi, Founder & Director of Soul Survivor

- The aim of *Freedom in Christ for Young People* is to set young people firmly on the way to becoming fruitful disciples, sold out for God and making a radical difference. Watch them change as they connect with the truth about who they are in Christ, become free from pressures that hold them back and learn to renew their thinking.

- The course was produced in partnership with Youth For Christ and provides relevant, interactive, multi-media-based material tailored to meet the needs of 11–18 year-olds. It is split into two age ranges, 11–14 and 15–18. Much work has been done to address the different needs of each age range.

- Each session is packed full of age-appropriate games, activities, discussion starters, film clip suggestions and talk slots. At the heart of each session are segments of contemporary video on DVD. Presented by Nathan Iles and Kate John from Youth For Christ, the video material was shot entirely on location around and is punchy, entertaining and very well received by participants.

www.ficm.org   www.ficm.org.uk